THE **COMPLETE GUIDE** TO
EVEN MORE
VEGAN FOOD
SUBSTITUTIONS

© 2015 Fair Winds Press
Text © 2015 Joni Marie Newman and Celine Steen

First published in the USA in 2015 by
Fair Winds Press, a member of
Quarto Publishing Group USA Inc.
100 Cummings Center
Suite 406-L
Beverly, MA 01915-6101
www.fairwindspress.com
Visit www.QuarrySPOON.com and help us celebrate food and culture one spoonful at a time!

19 18 17 16 15 1 2 3 4 5
ISBN: 978-1-59233-681-4

Digital edition published in 2015
eISBN: 978-1-62788-283-5

Library of Congress Cataloging-in-Publication Data

Newman, Joni-Marie
  The complete guide to even more vegan food substitutions : the latest and greatest
methods for veganizing anything using more natural, plant-based ingredients /
Joni Marie Newman and Celine Steen.
     pages cm
  ISBN 978-1-59233-681-4 (paperback)
  1. Meat substitutes. 2. Vegan cooking. I. Steen, Celine. II. Title.
  TX838.N486 2015
  641.5'636--dc23

                                                                    2014047821

Book and cover design by Carol Holtz | holtzdesign.com
Book layout by Megan Jones | meganjonesdesign.com
Photography by Celine Steen | www.celinesteen.com
Illustrations by Mattie Wells | mattiewells.com

Printed and bound in China

The information in this book is for educational purposes only. It is not intended to replace
the advice of a physician or medical practitioner. Please see your health care provider before
beginning any new health program.

THE COMPLETE GUIDE TO
EVEN MORE
VEGAN FOOD
SUBSTITUTIONS

The Latest and Greatest Methods
for Veganizing Anything Using
More Natural, Plant-Based Ingredients

Joni Marie Newman and Celine Steen

Fair Winds Press
100 Cummings Center, Suite 406L
Beverly, MA 01915

fairwindspress.com • quarryspoon.com

CONTENTS

INTRODUCTION
Vegan Substitutions Are Always in Style

YOU MIGHT FIND YOURSELF WONDERING WHY a popular book with the word *complete* in its very title might need a companion volume. We happen to think it's quite a clever question.

Here's the method to our madness: *The Complete Guide to Vegan Food Substitutions* came out in 2010, already 5 years ago at the time of this publishing. During that time, it has become even easier to be vegan! Can you believe it? New and improved plant-based products have been popping up left and right. The artisan vegan cheese movement has exploded, and just about every kind of nut- and seed-based milk is available on store shelves. Even Bill Gates himself jumped on the bandwagon and backed Ethan Brown, founder of Beyond Meat, to help him develop the perfect plant-based chicken. He has also supported Josh Tetrick, of Hampton Creek foods, in his effort to create a perfect substitute for eggs. All of these products are better for our health, better for the environment, and, of course, better for the animals. Oh, and did we mention they taste great, too?

Although vegan convenience foods are, well, convenient, something else has happened in the past five years as well. Both the vegan world and our cooking styles have undergone a shift. We have moved toward using less processed, more natural, mostly homemade, truly wholesome ingredients in our recipes for animal-friendly substitutions.

The Complete Guide to Even More Vegan Food Substitutions recognizes this lifestyle and health shift. We aim to empower readers (you!) with the tools and techniques needed to substitute for dairy, eggs, meat, and seafood using more homemade, natural, and vegetable-centric ingredients, as well as providing options to work with less soy and oil. But first, let us introduce a few ingredients that might be new to you before jumping into the crux of the vegan-food-substituting matter.

< *Sunflower Artichoke Salad, page 198*

Glossary

We always try to use ingredients that are easy to find. If you cannot locate some of the following ingredients at your local grocery store, international foods store, or natural food store, don't forget about the wonderful world wide web and its frequent free shipping offers.

Agar: Also known as *kanten*, this all-vegetable gelatin is derived from red algae. It can be used in sweet or savory applications as it is colorless and odorless. Because it is available in various forms (flakes, powders, sticks, and rods), we will give its measure in weight. Choose agar that is free of additives, such as the Now Foods brand.

Black salt (a.k.a. *kala namak*): Not to be confused with black lava salt, this sulfur-y salt adds an eggy flavor to all sorts of foods. Don't let the name fool you: It's actually rose pink in color. And a little goes a long way, so don't overdo it.

Chia seeds: These tiny, little seeds are rich in omega fatty acids, and they contain 3 g of protein and 5 g of fiber per tablespoon (10 g). When stirred into liquids, in ground or whole form, they form a mucilage (a goopy mixture) that works well as a binder, making the seeds ideal to use as an egg replacer. Both white and black chia seeds are available in most markets. We will specify which kind is best for the recipes in which they're used.

Chickpea flour: Also known as gram flour, garbanzo bean flour, and besan, this flour is made from ground chickpeas. We use it frequently and have to warn you that while the cooked results are outstanding, you should not have a taste of uncooked chickpea flour. It can be bitter and (thankfully) not at all indicative of the final recipe results. Note that garbanzo fava bean flour (a blend of chickpea and fava bean flours) can be used in place of chickpea flour.

Evaporated cane juice: We use the organic kind of this unrefined granulated sugar. It isn't processed with bone char and is therefore guaranteed to be vegan. If you know your regular granulated sugar isn't processed with bone char, you can use it instead. We favor the Wholesome Sweeteners brand, because it's also fair trade.

Harissa paste: This spicy North African paste is made from a blend of hot peppers (such as guajillo and chipotle chiles) and other spices (such as coriander and caraway). You can find it in the ethnic aisle of well-stocked grocery stores.

Jackfruit: When it is ripe, this starchy fruit has a very mild flavor similar to a cross between a pineapple and a banana. When young and green, it takes on the flavors of whatever you cook with it. As it cooks, jackfruit breaks down into a stringy, almost meaty texture, which makes it a perfect medium for dishes simulating pulled pork or shredded chicken. It's almost impossible to find fresh jackfruit, and when you do it is almost always well ripened and too sweet for most applications in this book. While we usually choose fresh or frozen fruits and vegetables over canned, this is the exception. We stick to canned jackfruit packed in brine or water (*not* syrup) for savory recipes.

Maca powder: This dried root is packed full of nutritional benefits. Maca is rich in vitamins B, C, and E, and it provides plenty of calcium, zinc, iron, magnesium, phosphorus, and amino acids. In addition, it boasts a malted, buttery, nutty flavor. A little goes a long way, so don't be too heavy-handed, and follow our guidelines when adding it to recipes.

Miso: This fermented soybean paste has many uses, and comes in several flavors. The kind we use the most is mellow white miso (also known as shiro miso), preferably organic. It makes a very versatile and simple broth, and when added to sauces, stews, and even cheese sauces, it imparts a great depth of flavor and sharpness. Miso can be found in most Asian grocery stores and sometimes in the refrigerated section of your local health food store.

Neutral-flavored oils: We often choose neutral-flavored oils, unless otherwise specified, because they don't overwhelm the other flavors of the dishes in which they're used. Our favorite neutral-flavored oils include: corn oil, grapeseed oil, light olive oil, peanut oil, safflower oil, and more. Choose organic oils, if possible. (Also see "Oil-free or low-oil cooking.")

Nuts: Nuts such as almonds, cashews, and walnuts are frequently used in vegan baking and cooking for the healthy fats, great flavor, and creaminess they add to many dishes once soaked and blended. Working with nuts makes it a breeze to cut back on the use of soy and added extracted oils, which is something that was occasionally requested by readers since the first volume of *The Complete Guide to Vegan Food Substitutions* came out. Alas, we're aware that using nuts means the food budget goes a bit higher than when just using good ol' tofu. That's why it's important to look for better deals by shopping around and buying in bulk whenever possible. If the nuts you purchase are stored properly in the refrigerator or freezer to prevent them from going rancid, they will last for about 6 months.

Nutritional yeast: This flaky yellow yeast is usually grown on molasses. It has a nutty, rich, almost cheesy taste that adds flavor and a nutritional boost to your foods (Hello, B vitamins!). Do seek out formulas labeled "vegetarian support." Nutritional yeast can be found in the vitamin and supplement section of most health food stores. It comes in various sizes of flakes, which makes its weight vary. We get ours in bulk, and the flakes look quite fine. If you can only find large flakes, pulse them in a food processor before measuring for the most accurate results.

Oil-free or low-oil cooking: We've attempted to use as little added extracted oils as possible, or to offer alternatives where we could. If you do wish to cook without added oil, you can simply replace it in sautéing applications with the same amount of prepared vegan vegetable broth, adding extra as needed to prevent the food from sticking to the pan. While we've had great success reducing the amount of oil in cooking applications, it is a little trickier in our baked goods. When experimenting, keep in mind that the outcome may be different.

Smoked salt: Smoked salt is a type of finishing salt that is exactly what it sounds like: smoked salt. Available in a variety of flavors from hickory to maple, it can be purchased at gourmet stores, well-stocked supermarkets, and online. This salt will impart a salty smokiness wherever you add it.

Sriracha: Sriracha is a hot chili sauce from Thailand. The original is made by Huy Fong Foods and it can be found in most grocery stores. Many versions have popped up since, so make sure to double-check ingredients as some brands contain fish paste.

Tahini: Tahini is a sesame seed paste most commonly used to prepare hummus (page 222), but is also used in dressings (pages 31 and 230), and even meat alternatives (pages 172, 178, and 180). It has become quite popular in recent years, and can now be purchased in most grocery stores. Tahini varies wildly in texture, with some brands being as thick as peanut butter, while others are as runny as a milkshake. Adjust liquids in recipes accordingly.

Tamari: Tamari is a richly flavored, Japanese-style soy sauce. We use gluten-free reduced-sodium tamari, and then add salt to taste. If you cannot find tamari, use reduced-sodium soy sauce in its place. (Note that the Gluten-Free Potential icon won't apply anymore if gluten-free tamari is replaced with soy sauce.)

Textured Vegetable Protein: Textured Vegetable Protein, (TVP), is also known as Textured Soy Protein (TSP), texturized vegetable protein, or defatted soy protein. It is a common meat substitute, extender, and filler found in many everyday convenience foods, as well as in many meat substitutes. It can be purchased on its own and prepared very simply at home to create delicious and nutritious meat-free meals.

It is very important to source only organically produced TVP. Many commercial producers of TVP use a chemical called *hexane* in the production process. Hexane is classified as an air pollutant by the Environmental Protection Agency (EPA) and as a neurotoxin by the Centers for Disease Control and Prevention (CDC). It's unclear how much hexane, if any, remains in the food after processing because the Food and Drug Administration (FDA) does not monitor hexane in foods, nor does it require companies to test for it. Organically produced TVP does not use hexane in the manufacturing process, making it a much safer choice.

Vegan butter: In addition to making sure no animal-derived ingredients make their way into our foods, it is also our responsibility to make sure the source of ingredients is cruelty-free as well. In recent years, there has been an outcry against the use of palm oil in vegan foods as it has been reported that the harvesting of palm oil leads to the death and displacement of orangutans in tropical rain forests. While sustainable palm oil is an option, and companies such as Earth Balance can source their palm oil to non-native orangutan plantations, we feel it is important to give you vegan butter options that are free of palm oil, such as the recipe provided by Mattie Hagedorn of veganbaking.net (page 24). In addition, we have done our best when writing recipes to simply not use butter as an ingredient. We opt for other sources of fat instead, such as whole nuts, coconut butter, various oils, or nut butters.

Vegan milks: If you don't have the time to make your own milk (page 27), just check out the nut milk section of your favorite grocery store. You're bound to find a whole bounty of vegan milks in many flavors. Two of our favorites are the unsweetened, plain, almond milk and the almond-coconut blend. Remember to use unsweetened plain for savory applications. Use plain or vanilla-flavored milk (unsweetened or not) in sweet applications.

Whole-wheat pastry flour: We most frequently use this finely ground whole-grain flour instead of all-purpose flour (ratio of 1:1). It is more nutritious because it retains fiber, minerals, and vitamins. If you cannot find it, you can use an equal combination of (white or regular) whole-wheat flour and all-purpose flour, or only all-purpose flour instead.

Xanthan gum: Xanthan gum is a white, odorless, plant-based stabilizing and thickening agent derived from corn which, unlike cornstarch or arrowroot, isn't activated by heat. It's frequently found in salad dressings and sauces, and is also used in gluten-free baking. A very small amount goes a long way, so one bag should last you a while.

Recipe Icons

As you turn the pages of this book, you will come across recipes labeled as follows:

* Gluten-Free Potential
Recipes that can be safe to enjoy by those who need to eat gluten-free foods. Make sure to thoroughly check ingredients for safe use, and watch for cross-contamination by purchasing ingredients that are certified gluten-free. Contact the manufacturer, if needed, for up-to-date information.

* Nut-Free
Recipes that are absolutely free of nuts (including coconuts), or nut-derived products, provided nut-based milks aren't used wherever unspecified vegan milk is called for. Please thoroughly check labels, and contact the manufacturer if needed.

* No Added Sugar
Recipes where no refined sugar (including agave nectar, pure maple syrup, granulated sugar, or evaporated cane juice) is used.

* No Added Oil
Recipes where no extracted or refined oils of any kind are used.

* Quick and Easy
Recipes that take less than 30 minutes to whip up, provided you have intermediate cooking or baking skills.

* Soy-Free
Recipes that are free of any soy products, provided soymilk isn't used wherever unspecified vegan milk is called for. Please thoroughly check labels, and contact the manufacturer if needed. If using nonstick cooking spray, remember to check for soy lecithin, too. If you cannot find soy-free nonstick cooking spray, use an oil spray instead.

Note that at the time of printing, all the store-bought products we mention and recommend were indeed vegan. Please make sure to always double-check ingredient labels as sometimes companies change their recipes without warning.

Shakshouka, page 116 >

SECTION ONE

How to Best Substitute for Dairy

DAIRY IS TRADITIONALLY DEFINED as being of, or relating to, a type of farming that deals with the production of milk and foods made from milk—usually from cows or goats, but also buffalo, sheep, horses, or camels. We here at *Vegan Food Substitution Headquarters*, however, have taken matters into our own hands. We are taking back the word dairy, and our definition reads as follows:

Vegan Dairy (noun): Creamy, cruelty-free, delicious, and nutritious foods made with plant-based milks such as rice, soy, coconut, almond, or any other nut, seed, or grain. Vegan dairy foods are better for our health, better for the environment, and better for the animals.

THE GOOD NEWS is these foods are not hard to find. Just peruse the dairy aisles of any grocery store. From classics such as soy, rice, and almond milk, to new and exciting products such as hazelnut milk, cultured cashew Brie, tapioca-based shredded pepper jack cheese, dessert whipped toppings, coconut-based ice creams, and French vanilla coffee creamers, there really isn't any dairy product imaginable that hasn't been made vegan.

While all of the above products are convenient and fun, we want to provide you with the recipes and techniques to be able to make these items at home, using easy-to-find (and often more natural) ingredients. This will empower you to tackle just about any recipe, and give you absolute and complete control over the ingredients that go into your food.

In the following pages we will talk about animal-based milks and cheeses, and why, as compassionate vegans, you should do whatever you can to avoid them. Then we will give you the tools, tips, tricks, techniques, and, of course, *the recipes* to make cruelty-free, dairy substitutes in your very own kitchen.

Milk

Milk. It does a body good, right? But whose body? Truthfully, cow's milk is only good for one type of body: a baby cow's. It contains far too many of some nutrients and far too few of others to be healthful for a human baby. Furthermore, cow's milk is designed to grow a 25-pound (11.3 kg) newborn calf into a 600-pound (272 kg) cow, and in order to do so, it contains a lot of naturally occurring growth hormones that were never meant to be consumed by humans. (Don't even get us started on all of the added growth hormones and antibiotics that are injected into many dairy cows . . .)

The human body is an amazing piece of machinery. Case in point, the naturally occurring enzyme *lactase*, produced by our intestinal villi to break down the sugar found in mammal's milk known as *lactose*, will decrease in production as a baby is weaned off of her mother's milk, making it uncomfortable to digest. The body instinctively knows that this form of food is meant to be consumed only during infancy, when extreme nutrition is needed for optimum growth. Therefore, milk is only produced by mammals to feed and nourish baby mammals from the time of birth until the baby is weaned from its mother.

A mother will make milk as long as she has a baby to feed it to. Unfortunately for the dairy cow, that means she is constantly kept pregnant in order to keep her producing milk. If her baby is a female, she will most likely be raised into the same life as her mother, as a dairy cow. Most male calves are quickly whisked away from their mothers to be sold off to veal farms where they will live out their short lives in veal crates, being fattened up for slaughter.

As you can see, the only body milk does any good for is the baby of the mommy who makes it. Fortunately, there are so many options available to replace milk in our everyday lives that there really is no reason to exploit cows, goats, sheep, or any other living creature for their milk.

Cheese

Knowing what you already know about dairy, it's pretty obvious why one should give up dairy-based cheeses when becoming vegan. However, lots of folks hang on to cheese as one of the things they "could never give up." We get it. It's yummy and gooey, and it is the quintessential comfort food.

But the fact is that there are some nasty things that go into cheese. Things you might not have ever heard of, like thinly sliced pieces of dried stomach lining from young, un-weaned calves. When you look at the ingredients list and see the word rennet listed, unless it's specifically listed as vegetable rennet, you can bet your bottom dollar that's what it is. Rennet is full of all sorts of enzymes that assist in the coagulation of dairy milk and aid in the cheese-making process, but the stomachs have to come from young un-weaned calves because older animals do not produce the same enzyme, known as chymosin. Similarly, because young animals create enzymes designed to digest the milk of their mothers, goat or sheep cheeses will contain rennet made from the stomachs of kid goats and baby lambs.

You need not worry though. As we've already mentioned, the vegan world and this book have a lot to offer in the way of cheese substitutes, so keep on turning the pages.

Guidelines for Substituting for Dairy

Whether you want to make a quick substitute using store-bought products, or you plan on making your substitutes from scratch, the chart on the following page will help you decide what sub will work best in the to-be-veganized recipe.

The boldface entries reference from-scratch recipes in this book.

WHEN THE ORIGINAL RECIPE CALLS FOR . . .	REPLACE WITH . . .
¼ cup (56 g) butter	• ¼ cup (56 g) Mattie's Regular Vegan Butter (page 24) • ¼ cup (60 g) Coconut Butter (page 25) (for spreading on bread, and some other applications, see page 25) • ¼ cup (56 g) store-bought non-hydrogenated vegan butter, such as Earth Balance
1 cup (235 ml) buttermilk	• Place 2 teaspoons (10 ml) fresh lemon juice or apple cider vinegar at the bottom of a bowl. Top with 1 cup (235 ml) unsweetened, plain vegan milk of choice, then stir. Let stand 5 minutes to curdle.
1 cup (235 ml) heavy cream or creamer	• 1 cup (235 ml) plain Homemade Creamer (page 26) • 1 cup (235 ml) canned full-fat and unsweetened coconut milk or cream • 1 cup (235 ml) store-bought plain soy creamer, such as Silk or Wildwood • 1 cup (235 ml) store-bought plain coconut creamer, such as So Delicious • 1 cup (235 ml) almond creamer, such as Califia Farms or So Delicious
2 scoops ice cream (various flavors)	• 2 scoops Cherry Cheesecake Chocolate Chunk Ice Cream (page 61) or Strawberry Swirl Ice Cream (page 62) • 2 scoops store-bought soy, rice, almond, cashew, or coconut ice cream, such as So Delicious
1 cup (235 ml) milk (e.g., cow, goat, or sheep)	• 1 cup (235 ml) plain Almond Milk (page 27) • 1 cup (235 ml) unsweetened plain soy, almond, almond-coconut, rice, or hemp milk • 1 cup (235 ml) unsweetened plain canned or refrigerated coconut milk
½ cup (120 g) sour cream	• ½ cup (120 g) Sour Cream (page 30) • ½ cup (120 g) store-bought vegan sour cream, such as Tofutti, or Follow Your Heart
½ cup (30 g) whipped cream	• ½ cup (30 g) Whipped Coconut Cream (page 64) • ½ cup (30 g) store-bought vegan whipped soy or rice cream from a box, such as Soyatoo! (We cannot recommend the cans, as these rarely work properly.)

WHEN THE ORIGINAL RECIPE CALLS FOR . . .	REPLACE WITH . . .
½ cup (120 g) yogurt (e.g., cow, goat, or sheep)	• ½ cup (120 g) **Homemade Yogurt (page 28)** • ½ cup (120 g) store-bought vegan soy yogurt, such as WholeSoy • ½ cup (120 g) store-bought vegan coconut or almond yogurt, such as So Delicious (also available in Greek-style) • ½ cup (120 g) blended soft silken tofu, such as Mori-Nu, mixed with ½ teaspoon fresh lemon juice (only in baking applications, not for eating as is)
CHEESE ½ cup (57 g) cheese (e.g., shredded jack, Cheddar, or mozzarella)	• ½ cup (57 g) store-bought vegan shredded cheese, such as Daiya, Follow Your Heart, or Go Veggie Vegan
1 slice of cheese (for sandwiches)	• 1 slice **'Merican Cheese Slices (page 70)** • 1 slice of store-bought vegan cheese slices, such as Daiya, Tofutti, Vegusto, Go Veggie Vegan, or Chao
½ cup (120 g) cream cheese	• ½ cup (120 g) **Cashew and Yogurt Spread (page 33)** • ½ cup (120 g) **Cashew Coconut Spread (page 32)** • ½ cup (114 g) **Chia Seed Cream Cheese (page 76)** • ½ cup (120 g) store-bought vegan cream cheese, such as Tofutti, Follow Your Heart, Wayfare, or Daiya
½ cup (85 g) cotija or queso fresco	• ½ cup (85 g) **Cotija-Style Tofu Crumbles (page 73)**
½ cup (75 g) feta crumbles	• ½ cup (120 g) **Easy Tofu Feta (page 186)**
½ cup (50 g) Parmesan cheese, grated for added flavor (not as a binder)	• ½ cup (56 g) **Hemp Parm (page 72)** • ½ cup (50 g) store-bought vegan Parmesan, such as Go Veggie, Parmela, or Parma
½ cup (123 g) ricotta cheese	• ½ cup (113 g) **Almond Cashew Ricotta (page 73)** • ½ cup (123 g) store-bought vegan ricotta, such as Tofutti or Kite Hill
Artisan cheeses, to serve with crackers or wine	• Store-bought artisan vegan cheeses, such as Miyoko's Kitchen, Kite Hill, Treeline, Vromage, or Parmela

CHAPTER 1
Milk Substitutions

MAKING YOUR OWN SUBSTITUTES FOR DAIRY IS EASY! In this chapter, we will start off with recipes for simple dairy substitutions that you can make ahead of time and keep on hand, just as you would with any store-bought product. To prep for this, we recommend investing in a few good storage containers, such as mason jars in a variety of shapes and sizes to keep your milks, creamers, butters, and yogurts fresh in the refrigerator.

Our basic dairy recipes will be followed by recipes traditionally prepared *with* dairy ingredients, such as creamy vegetable dishes, velvety soups and sauces, puddings, and ice creams. We make them vegan by using our homemade substitutes, or sometimes by simply using a new combination of ingredients to whip up dishes so good no one would even bother wondering where the missing dairy went.

Practice Makes for Perfect Substitutions

The best way to demonstrate how easy it is to transform a nonvegan recipe into a cruelty-free wonder is to showcase how it's done. Let's go through a sample recipe step by step! Once you know the basics, it's easy to put them into practice on any recipe.

BASIC SPROUTED GRAIN MUFFINS

Non-Veganized

This recipe is an excerpt from *Back to Butter*, by Molly Chester and Sandy Schrecengost (Fair Winds Press, 2014). We will substitute vegan ingredients for the butter, honey, egg, and buttermilk, and re-write the directions accordingly.

½ cup (112 g) butter
½ cup (160 g) raw honey
3 cups (360 g) fresh-milled, sprouted whole-wheat pastry flour
1 teaspoon sea salt
2 teaspoons (9 g) baking soda
2 teaspoons (9 g) baking powder
1 egg, beaten
1 cup (235 ml) buttermilk

Preheat the oven to 400°F (200°C, or gas mark 6). Line 18 standard muffin cups with paper liners.

Combine the butter and honey in a small-size saucepan over medium heat, heating until just melted. Stir and set aside to cool.

In a large-size bowl, combine the flour, sea salt, baking soda, and baking powder, whisking briefly. In a separate bowl, add the egg to the buttermilk, and whisk to combine. Add the honey mixture and buttermilk mixture to the dry ingredients, whisking until just blended.

Using a large-size cookie scoop, fill each muffin cup three-fourths full. Bake for 13 minutes, or until a toothpick inserted into the center of a muffin comes out clean.

YIELD: 18 muffins

BASIC SPROUTED GRAIN MUFFINS Veganized!

We have four items to substitute for in this recipe: butter, honey, egg, and buttermilk. For the butter substitution, we simply use a lower amount of neutral-flavored oil. Honey is a quick swap for agave nectar or maple syrup. The egg is replaced with unsweetened, plain, vegan yogurt here, for binding and adding moisture. And finally, the buttermilk is created by combining apple cider vinegar and vegan milk, left to stand for a few minutes until curdled. The oven temperature is lowered a little bit, because both agave nectar and maple syrup have a tendency to make baked goods darken quickly. As these tasty muffins are true to their description and not overly sweetened or flavored, add-ins would be a great way to give them a touch of personality: Toasted nuts, raisins, and currants are but a few of our favorite additions.

2 teaspoons (10 ml) apple cider vinegar] — (**buttermilk substitute**)
1 cup (235 ml) plain Almond Milk (page 27) or other vegan milk

⅓ cup (80 ml) neutral-flavored oil] — (**butter substitute**)
½ cup (160 g) agave nectar or pure maple syrup] — (**honey substitute**)
¼ cup (60 g) unsweetened plain vegan yogurt, store-bought or homemade (page 28)] — (**egg substitute**)

3 cups (360 g) fresh-milled, sprouted whole-wheat pastry flour or regular whole-wheat pastry flour
1 teaspoon fine sea salt
2 teaspoons (9 g) baking soda
2 teaspoons (9 g) baking powder

Preheat the oven to 375°F (190°C, or gas mark 5). Line 18 standard muffin cups with paper liners.

Place the vinegar at the bottom of a medium bowl. Top with milk, then stir. Let stand 5 minutes to curdle. **This is your buttermilk substitute.**

Whisk the oil **(this is your butter substitute)**, agave **(this is your honey substitute)**, and yogurt **(this is your egg substitute)** into the buttermilk substitute.

In a large-size bowl, combine the flour, salt, baking soda, and baking powder, whisking briefly. Add wet ingredients to dry ingredients, whisking until just blended. If you find that the mixture is too dry, add extra vegan milk as needed, 1 tablespoon (15 ml) at a time, incorporating it while trying not to overmix.

Using a large-size cookie scoop, fill each muffin cup about two-thirds full. Bake for 13 minutes, or until a toothpick inserted into the center of a muffin comes out clean.

YIELD: 18 muffins

MATTIE'S REGULAR VEGAN BUTTER

* Gluten-Free Potential * No Added Sugar

Mattie Hagedorn of *Veganbaking.net* created this recipe for those opposing the use of palm oil, as well as for those who may not have easy access to vegan butter. This is regular ol' vegan butter that's designed to mimic your favorite commercial variant. Use it wherever you use butter or margarine. Like traditional butter, vegan butter is more solid than tub margarine and not as spreadable. This is so it can perform optimally in vegan baking applications. If you want a conveniently softer, spreadable vegan butter, swap out 1 tablespoon (14 g) of the coconut oil with 1 additional tablespoon (15 ml) canola, light olive oil, or rice bran oil.

- ¼ cup plus 2 teaspoons (70 ml) soymilk
- ½ teaspoon apple cider vinegar
- ½ teaspoon coconut vinegar (or an additional ½ teaspoon apple cider vinegar)
- ¼ plus ⅛ teaspoon salt
- ½ cup plus 2 tablespoons plus 1 teaspoon (130 g) refined coconut oil, melted
- 1 tablespoon (15 ml) canola oil, light olive oil or rice bran oil
- 1 teaspoon liquid soy lecithin *or* liquid sunflower lecithin *or* 2¼ teaspoons (5 g) soy lecithin granules
- ¼ teaspoon xanthan gum *or* ½ plus ⅛ teaspoon psyllium husk powder

Place the soymilk, vinegars, and salt in a small cup and whisk together with a fork. Let sit for 10 minutes so the mixture curdles.

Melt the coconut oil in a microwave so it's barely melted and as close to room temperature as possible. Measure and add it and the canola oil to a food processor. Making smooth vegan butter is dependent on the mixture solidifying as quickly as possible after it's mixed. This is why it's important to make sure your coconut oil is close to room temperature before you mix it with the rest of the ingredients.

Add the curdled soymilk mixture, soy lecithin, and xanthan gum to the food processor. Process for 2 minutes, scraping down the sides halfway through the duration. Pour the mixture into an ice cube mold and place it in the freezer to solidify. The butter should be ready to use within 1 hour. Store in an airtight container in the refrigerator for up to 1 month or in plastic wrap in the freezer for up to 1 year.

YIELD: About 1 cup (215 g)

COCONUT BUTTER

* Gluten-Free Potential * No Added Oil * No Added Sugar
* Quick and Easy * Soy-Free

This coconut butter is much more than just a flavorful substitute for nonvegan butter. Enjoy it by the spoonful with vegan dark chocolate, on top of toasted bread, drizzled on pancakes or waffles, as an addition to smoothies or soups, or in our Passion Fruit Curd (page 144), Coconut Butter Granola (page 38), Brioche Waffles (page 136) and Cinnamon Raisin Pull-Apart Loaves (page 137). Just don't use defatted coconut (indicated on the label of the package); the oils naturally contained in coconut are necessary to create a spreadable butter.

12 ounces (340 g) unsweetened shredded or flaked coconut

Place the coconut in a food processor or high-speed blender. Process until the coconut transforms into a runny mixture, similar to nut butter. Note that coconut butter will not be entirely smooth. Processing time takes between 10 and 15 minutes, depending on the machine. Stop the machine occasionally to scrape the sides with a rubber spatula. If the motor of the machine starts to overheat, power off to let it cool before continuing.

Once the coconut butter is ready, transfer to airtight jars, and store at room temperature. If the room temperature is cold, the coconut butter might harden: Heat it slowly in the microwave oven if you use one, or in a bain-marie on the stove. Stir before use.

YIELD: Generous 1¼ cups (340 g)

HOMEMADE CREAMER

* Gluten-Free Potential   * No Added Oil   * Soy-Free

We love to use this plain creamer in our Most Luscious Mashed Taters Ever (page 44), and in many other savory recipes throughout this book. We're also including a half-batch of vanilla and maple version for those who enjoy a little flavored goodness in their morning coffee. If you have efficient blending equipment, you shouldn't have to strain the cashews; they are so creamy once soaked that the pulp can just stay in. However, if you happen to find the creamer too gritty, just strain it. You wouldn't want to find floating bits of nuts in your morning cup of joe!

FOR PLAIN CREAMER:

1 cup (140 g) raw cashews
3¼ cups (765 ml) filtered water, divided
¼ cup (60 ml) full-fat coconut milk
Pinch fine sea salt

FOR VANILLA MAPLE CREAMER:

½ recipe (1 cup, or 235 ml) plain creamer
4 teaspoons (20 ml) pure vanilla extract, or to taste
1 tablespoon (12 g) maple sugar or (20 g) pure maple syrup, or to taste

To make the plain creamer: Place the cashews in a medium bowl or 4-cup (940 ml) glass measuring cup. Cover with 2 cups (470 ml) water. Cover with plastic wrap or a lid. Let stand at room temperature overnight (about 8 hours), to soften the nuts.

Drain the cashews (discard soaking water), and give them a quick rinse. Combine cashews with 1¼ cups (295 ml) fresh water, coconut milk, and salt in a blender and blend until perfectly smooth. If the results aren't smooth, use a nut bag and a fine-mesh sieve to filter the mixture. (Enjoy the leftover pulp in your morning bowl of oatmeal.)

Transfer plain creamer into a 1-pint (470 ml) mason jar. Screw the lid on tightly. Store in the refrigerator for up to 1 week, and shake well before use.

To make the vanilla maple creamer: Place plain creamer, vanilla, and sugar in 1 half-pint (8 ounces, or 235 ml) jar. Use a small whisk to thoroughly combine. Screw the lid on tightly. Store in the refrigerator for up to 1 week, and shake well before use.

YIELD: Approximately 2 cups (470 ml)

ALMOND MILK

* Gluten-Free Potential   * No Added Oil   * Soy-Free

It takes very little effort to make your own nut milk, and it offers the advantage of keeping the ingredients list to a minimum. No stabilizers or preservatives here! You can use raw almonds instead of a combination of raw and toasted, but we love the assertive, nutty flavor the toasted nuts give the milk. You can also replace almonds with any other nut, and adjust the amount of water to taste.

FOR PLAIN MILK:

½ cup (60 g) whole raw almonds
½ cup (60 g) toasted whole almonds
4 to 4½ cups (470 to 590 ml) filtered water, divided
Pinch fine sea salt

FOR LIGHTLY FLAVORED MILK:

2 teaspoons (6 g) maple sugar or date sugar, optional
Pure vanilla extract, optional and to taste

Place the almonds in a medium bowl or 4-cup (940 ml) glass measuring cup. Cover with 2 cups (470 ml) water. Cover with plastic wrap or a lid. Let stand at room temperature for 18 hours, changing the water halfway through, to soften the nuts.

Drain the almonds (discard soaking water), and give them a quick rinse.

To make plain milk: Combine almonds, 2 to 2½ cups (470 to 590 ml) fresh water, and salt in a blender. Blend until almonds are pulverized. Jump to filtering instructions.

Or, to make lightly flavored milk: Combine almonds, 2 to 2½ cups (470 to 590 ml) fresh water, salt, sugar, and vanilla in a blender. Blend until almonds are pulverized. Continue with the following instructions.

Place a fine-mesh sieve lined with an open nut milk bag on top of a large glass measuring cup. Slowly pour milk into the bag. Filter the milk by carefully squeezing the bag, allowing the liquid (milk) to pass through while keeping the pulp in the bag. Enjoy the leftover pulp in oatmeal or use it in baked goods (see pages 38 and 41). You can store it in the refrigerator for up to 2 weeks. Store the milk in an airtight bottle for up to 5 days. Shake well before use.

YIELD: 2 to 2½ cups (470 to 590 ml)

HOMEMADE YOGURT

* Gluten-Free Potential * No Added Oil * No Added Sugar * Nut-Free

Considering how tricky it can be to find store-bought, unsweetened, plain vegan yogurt, we included instructions for making your own at home. We've put a few different vegan milks to the test, but we've only been 100 percent satisfied with the texture and flavor obtained when using refrigerated (not UHT) soymilk. Affordable yogurt makers can be found on the market worldwide. If you'd rather make yogurt without a machine and in your oven instead, you will find useful instructions online.

FOR STARTER-BASED YOGURT:

1 quart (946 ml) unsweetened plain soymilk
2 tablespoons (16 g) tapioca flour (also known as tapioca starch)
1 packet vegan yogurt starter (about 0.03 ounce, or 0.9 g)

FOR YOGURT MADE FROM STORE-BOUGHT YOGURT:

27 ounces (798 ml) unsweetened plain soymilk
1½ tablespoons (12 g) tapioca flour (also known as tapioca starch)
½ cup plus 2 tablespoons (150 g) store-bought, plain vegan yogurt (unsweetened or sweetened)

For both methods: Place the milk in a stainless steel pot. Heat on medium-high heat, whisking occasionally, until milk reaches 180°F (82°C)—use a candy or digital thermometer to keep an eye on the temperature. Remove from heat, and let cool to 110°F (43°C). This might take up to 1 hour, so check occasionally with the thermometer. When the milk has cooled, place tapioca flour in a small bowl. Remove 3 tablespoons (45 ml) of milk, and whisk into the flour to dissolve. Add the resulting mixture back to the milk, and whisk to thoroughly combine.

To make the yogurt with a vegan starter: Place the vegan yogurt starter in the same small bowl you used for the tapioca mixture. Remove 1 tablespoon (15 ml) of milk, and whisk into the starter to dissolve. Add the mixture back to the milk, and whisk to thoroughly combine. Skip to "To culture the yogurt" instructions.

To make the yogurt with a store-bought vegan yogurt: Whisk store-bought vegan yogurt into the cooled milk to thoroughly combine. Continue with the following instructions.

To culture the yogurt: Pour milk into the yogurt maker and incubate for 8 to 10 hours, or until set. Be careful when removing the lid to check the yogurt, as condensation will have formed. Avoid letting the water drip into the yogurt. Let cool at room temperature for about 15 minutes before covering with a lid and storing in the refrigerator. Keep yogurt refrigerated for at least 24 hours after culturing, before use. Yogurt will keep for up to 1 week.

YIELD: 1 quart (960 g)

Celine Says

"You can purchase vegan yogurt starter in specialty vegan stores, or order it online.

Using store-bought, plain vegan yogurt is quite affordable, and yields scrumptious results. Given the choice between using a vegan starter and store-bought vegan yogurt, we'd choose the latter. The results have come out slightly firmer than when using vegan starter, but both options yield extremely pleasing flavors.

It's important to check on your yogurt. If the room temperature is high, chances are it will be ready sooner rather than later. When you check, be sure to be gentle; shaking the yogurt maker can disturb the cultures. If you notice that the yogurt starts to separate into curd and 'whey,' remove it from the yogurt maker and refrigerate it immediately. As long as the yogurt smells nice and tart, and no bad odors are present, the yogurt will be good for use. If it comes out thinner than you'd like, use it in smoothies or salad dressings. The health benefits from the cultures will still be present, even if the presentation isn't top notch.

If the yogurt doesn't come out exactly as you'd like, we recommend trying several soymilk brands until you find the perfect match. We found the Silk brand yielded great results. As for the store-bought vegan yogurt brands we've used to test these instructions, we can recommend So Delicious in Northern America, and Sojade in Europe.

We've managed to create at least two heirloom batches of yogurt with both methods, even when the starter is sold as 'direct-set,' which means it's only supposed to work once. This is something you will have to test for yourself as results can vary, and we cannot speak for the performance of all vegan yogurt and starter brands out there."

SOUR CREAM

* Gluten-Free Potential   * No Added Oil   * No Added Sugar

We're pleased to bring you a dead ringer for regular sour cream. It can even be made soy-free if using Cashew Coconut Spread! Use it as you would dairy-based sour cream: on baked potatoes, Mexican-style dishes, and the list goes on . . .

FOR PLAIN SOUR CREAM:

- ½ cup (120 g) Cashew and Yogurt Spread (page 33) or Cashew Coconut Spread (page 32)
- 3 to 4 tablespoons (45 to 60 ml) plain Homemade Creamer (page 26)
- ¾ teaspoon white balsamic vinegar
- Pinch salt, to taste

FOR ONION CHIVES SOUR CREAM:

- 1 recipe plain sour cream
- ¼ teaspoon onion powder
- 1 small clove garlic, grated or pressed
- 1½ tablespoons (4 g) minced fresh chives

To make the plain sour cream: Whisk the spread, 3 tablespoons (45 ml) of creamer, vinegar, and salt in a medium bowl, until thoroughly combined. Leave plain, or flavor as follows.

To make the onion chives sour cream: Whisk onion powder, garlic, and chives into the plain sour cream until thoroughly combined.

Refrigerate in an airtight container for at least 12 hours before use, so that the sour cream can develop its flavor. If you find that the sour cream is too thick for your taste, add up to 1 tablespoon (15 ml) of the remaining creamer, whisking to combine. Will keep for up to 4 days.

YIELD: About ⅔ cup (165 g)

Celine Says

"Fancy some Sour Cream Dressing for your salad? That's easy! Whisk to combine a full recipe of Onion Chives Sour Cream with 2½ tablespoons (38 ml) plain Almond Milk (page 27) or other unsweetened plain vegan milk, 2½ teaspoons (13 ml) white balsamic or apple cider vinegar, ¼ teaspoon mild Dijon mustard, and a pinch of kosher salt, to taste. Drizzle on your favorite salad, and store leftovers in the refrigerator for up to 4 days. Yields about 1 cup (235 ml)."

RANCH-Y DIPPING SAUCE

* Gluten-Free Potential * No Added Oil * No Added Sugar
* Quick and Easy * Soy-Free

Ranch dressing was one of the things Celine fell in love with when she moved to the United States. Try this vegan version with raw veggies and Sassy Hot Sauce Chickpea Sticks (page 227).

> ¾ cup (180 g) Cashew Coconut Spread (page 32)
> ¼ cup (60 ml) plain Homemade Creamer (page 26)
> 1 teaspoon onion powder
> 1 teaspoon dried parsley or 1 tablespoon (4 g) minced fresh parsley
> ¾ teaspoon dried dill or 1 to 1½ teaspoons minced fresh dill, to taste
> ½ teaspoon liquid smoke
> ¼ teaspoon fine sea salt
> 1 clove garlic, grated or pressed

Place all the ingredients in a medium bowl, and whisk to thoroughly combine. For the smoothest results, use a blender to do this. Cover and refrigerate until ready to use. Will keep for up to 4 days. Stir before use. If you find the sauce has thickened too much after refrigeration, slowly add extra creamer, 1 teaspoon at a time.

YIELD: 1 cup (235 ml)

SIMPLE YOGURT DIP

* Gluten-Free Potential * No Added Sugar * Quick and Easy

Our Homemade Yogurt shines through in this easy recipe that belongs with Moroccan Lentil Balls (page 224) and Scallion Kale Pudla (page 106).

> ½ cup (120 g) Homemade Yogurt (page 28) or store-bought
>   unsweetened plain vegan yogurt
> 2 tablespoons (32 g) tahini
> 1 tablespoon (15 ml) fresh lemon juice
> 1 teaspoon toasted sesame oil
> 1 large clove garlic, grated or pressed
> ¼ teaspoon fine sea salt

Combine all the ingredients in a small bowl until thoroughly mixed, and chill for at least 30 minutes before serving. Store leftovers in an airtight container in the refrigerator for up to 4 days.

YIELD: ¾ cup (180 ml)

CASHEW COCONUT SPREAD

* Gluten-Free Potential   * No Added Oil   * No Added Sugar   * Soy-Free

We know some people dislike the flavor of coconut, while others need or prefer to eat soy-free foods. We offer two versions of this versatile spread so that (hopefully) everyone can find their happiness. This recipe can easily be doubled for a larger batch, and is also used in many of our recipes (e.g., pages 46, 60, and 85).

Note that both cashew spreads are interchangeable wherever they're used in this book. The Cashew Coconut Spread offers the advantage of being soy-free, if this is something that's important to you.

1 cup (140 g) raw cashews

2 cups plus 2 tablespoons (500 ml) filtered water, divided

¼ cup (60 ml) coconut cream (scooped from the top of an unshaken, chilled can of full-fat coconut milk stored in the refrigerator for 24 hours before use)

1 tablespoon (15 ml) fresh lemon juice

Heaping ¼ teaspoon fine sea salt

Place the cashews in a medium bowl or 4-cup (940 ml) glass measuring cup. Cover with 2 cups (470 ml) of water. Cover with plastic wrap or a lid. Let stand at room temperature overnight (about 8 hours), to soften the nuts.

Drain the cashews (discard soaking water), and give them a quick rinse. Place in a food processor or high-speed blender, along with the coconut cream, 2 tablespoons (30 ml) water, lemon juice, and salt. Process until perfectly smooth, stopping to scrape the sides occasionally with a rubber spatula. This might take up to 10 minutes, depending on the power of the machine.

Transfer the spread into a medium bowl fitted with a lid or covered with plastic wrap. Let stand at room temperature for 24 hours, or until the spread smells tangy and has firmed up; this will depend on room temperature and might go more quickly in the summer. Place the spread in the refrigerator until ready to use. It will keep for up to 2 weeks.

YIELD: 1¼ cups (300 g)

CASHEW AND YOGURT SPREAD

* Gluten-Free Potential * No Added Oil * No Added Sugar

Now that you know how to make your own fantastically flavorful vegan yogurt at home, it's time to put it to great use here. This creamy and rich spread is a perfect fit on a toasted bagel, as well as in many of our recipes (e.g., pages 46, 60, and 85). Note that both cashew spreads are interchangeable wherever they're used in this book. The Cashew Coconut Spread offers the advantage of being soy-free, if this is something that's important to you.

1 cup (140 g) raw cashews
2 cups (470 ml) filtered water, for soaking
½ cup plus 1 tablespoon (135 g) Homemade Yogurt (page 28)
  or store-bought unsweetened plain vegan yogurt
1 tablespoon (15 ml) fresh lemon juice
Generous pinch fine sea salt

Place the cashews in a medium bowl or 4-cup (940 ml) glass measuring cup. Cover with the water. Cover with plastic wrap or a lid. Let stand at room temperature overnight (about 8 hours), to soften the nuts.

Drain the cashews (discard soaking water), and give them a quick rinse. Place in a food processor or high-speed blender, along with the yogurt, lemon juice, and salt. Process until perfectly smooth, stopping to scrape the sides occasionally with a rubber spatula. This might take up to 10 minutes, depending on the power of the machine.

Transfer the spread into a medium bowl fitted with a lid or covered with plastic wrap. Let stand at room temperature for 24 hours, or until the spread smells tangy and has firmed up; this will depend on room temperature and might go more quickly in the summer. Place the spread in the refrigerator until ready to use. It will last up to 2 weeks.

YIELD: Scant 1½ cups (345 g)

Celine Says

"This recipe can easily be doubled if you want a larger batch from the get-go. If the yogurt is a little thin, start with ⅓ cup plus 1 tablespoon (95 g) of it. Add the remaining 3 tablespoons (45 g) as needed if the mixture is hard to process."

SAVORY CASHEW SAUCE

* Gluten-Free Potential * No Added Oil * No Added Sugar * Soy-Free

How can something that is 100 percent dairy-free taste so decadent and addictive? It's the cashews. We believe they're quite magical when paired with the right flavors and spices. You can use this sauce stirred into pasta, as a layer in any lasagna recipe, as a quesadilla filling with your favorite veggies, and of course, in our Farrosotto (page 80), Eggplant Pizza (page 83), as well as part of the accompanying sauce for our Barley Bean Patties (page 228).

1 cup (140 g) raw cashews
2 cups (470 ml) filtered water, for soaking
1 cup (235 ml) water
1 tablespoon (8 g) Mushroom Broth Powder (page 218)
1 tablespoon (15 ml) fresh lemon juice
1 tablespoon (15 ml) white balsamic vinegar
2 teaspoons (10 g) maca powder
1 tablespoon (8 g) arrowroot powder
1½ teaspoons onion powder
½ teaspoon fine sea salt
Ground white or black pepper, to taste

Place the cashews in a medium bowl or 4-cup (940 ml) glass measuring cup. Cover with the filtered water. Cover with plastic wrap or a lid. Let stand at room temperature overnight (about 8 hours), to soften the nuts.

Drain the cashews (discard soaking water), and give them a quick rinse. Combine with all the remaining ingredients in a blender, and blend until perfectly smooth. The sauce will already be rather thick. Add to a medium saucepan, cook on medium heat until just slightly thicker and heated through, whisking constantly, about 4 minutes. Adjust seasoning as needed. Store cooled leftovers in an airtight container in the refrigerator for up to 4 days.

YIELD: 1¾ cups (460 g)

BREAKFAST RICE WITH PLUMS

* Gluten-Free Potential * No Added Oil * Quick and Easy * Soy-Free

While this nutritious hot breakfast bowl is of course entirely butterless and dairy-free, it remains 100 percent satisfying thanks to the use of almond milk and toasted almonds. The almonds are turned into a slightly coarse meal, giving the ensemble a flavor reminiscent of marzipan. Be sure not to use soymilk, if you want to keep the recipe soy-free.

4 fresh, firm plums, pitted and sliced thinly
¼ cup plus 2 teaspoons (93 g) pure maple syrup, divided
1 teaspoon pure lemon juice
2 to 3 cups (470 to 705 ml) Almond Milk (page 27) or other vegan milk (see headnote)
Pinch fine sea salt
⅔ cup (109 g) brown rice farina
⅓ cup (40 g) toasted almonds, ground not too finely
1 teaspoon pure vanilla extract

Place the plums in a warm skillet and combine with 2 teaspoons (13 g) syrup and lemon juice. Simmer and stir occasionally until the plums start to get a little more tender, about 2 minutes, or longer for a more tender fruit, to taste. Remove from heat and set aside.

Place the milk and salt in a medium saucepan, and bring to a low boil on medium-high heat. Lower heat and slowly whisk in the farina, stirring constantly to avoid lumps.

Simmer until thickened but still creamy, about 5 minutes. Add extra milk as needed to reach to-taste tenderness, and cook as needed. Remove from heat and stir in the ground almonds, remaining ¼ cup (80 g) syrup, and vanilla. Divide the rice among 4 bowls, and top each serving with cooked plums. Leftovers of the farina can be slowly reheated in a small saucepan, adding extra milk as needed to maintain the creaminess of the dish.

YIELD: 4 servings

Celine Says

"You can replace the rice farina with other types of farina (wheat, for example, but note that the outcome won't be gluten-free) if you prefer. Substitute apricots for plums, depending on the season.

If you like your cereal to keep some bite, use 2 cups (470 ml) of vegan milk. And if you like it creamier, start directly with 2¼ cups (295 ml), adding more as needed to get the creaminess you're looking for."

RED, WHITE, AND BLUE MUESLI

* No Added Oil

We find it so rewarding to know exactly what goes into our food in general. In our breakfast bowl (or jar), we have yogurt made from scratch, milk made from scratch, nutrient-packed grains, fruits, and nuts—all ensure that you're getting your day started right.

Generous 1 cup (165 g) halved fresh strawberries, chopped

1 cup (148 g) fresh blueberries

3 tablespoons (60 g) pure maple syrup or agave nectar, divided, more if needed

½ cup (40 g) rolled spelt flakes

½ cup (40 g) rolled oat flakes

1¼ cups (300 g) Homemade Yogurt (page 28) or store-bought plain vegan yogurt

¾ cup (180 ml) Almond Milk (page 27) or other plain vegan milk

½ teaspoon pure vanilla extract

½ cup (54 g) toasted slivered, sliced, or chopped whole almonds

Place the berries in a large bowl, drizzle with 1 tablespoon (20 g) syrup, and let marinate for 1 hour at room temperature. Place spelt and oat flakes in a large skillet. Toast on medium heat, stirring frequently until a nutty smell comes out of the pan and the flakes are light golden brown, about 6 minutes. Remove from heat, still stirring because the skillet will remain hot, and let cool completely.

In a large bowl, combine the yogurt, milk, remaining 2 tablespoons (40 g) syrup, and vanilla. Stir the cooled flakes into the yogurt mixture. Adjust sweetness to taste. Layer the berries and yogurt mixture into 4 serving dishes (such as mason jars), reserving a handful of each berry to top each portion. Cover and store in the refrigerator overnight to let the toasted flakes plump up and the flavors meld. Add 2 tablespoons (14 g) of toasted almonds on each portion before serving. Drizzle a little extra syrup on top if you like your muesli extra sweet.

YIELD: 4 portions

Celine Says

"If you have some of our Coconut Butter Granola (page 38) at the ready, use 1 generous cup (175 g) of granola instead of spelt and oat flakes. Omit the raisins in the granola so that it pairs up nicely with the muesli components. If using granola, adjust the amount of maple syrup to taste, or add none at all."

COCONUT BUTTER GRANOLA

* No Added Oil * Soy-Free

We love to keep our breakfast fully homemade whenever time permits, and usually serve the granola with Almond Milk (page 27) or Homemade Yogurt (page 28), and fresh berries or a big spoonful of Passion Fruit Curd (page 144) if we're feeling decadent.

> **½ cup (120 g) Coconut Butter (page 25)**
> **¼ cup (80 g) agave nectar**
> **¼ cup (80 g) brown rice syrup**
> **1 teaspoon pure vanilla extract**
> **¼ teaspoon fine sea salt**
> **4 cups (384 g) extra-thick rolled oats or old-fashioned rolled oats**
> **¼ cup (23 g) toasted leftover pulp from Almond Milk (see "Celine Says") or (30 g) almond meal**
> **¾ cup (120 g) raisins**

Preheat the oven to 300°F (150°C, or gas mark 2). Line a 12 x 17-inch (30 x 43 cm) rimmed baking sheet with parchment paper.

In a large bowl, combine coconut butter, agave, rice syrup, extract, and salt. Add oats and almond pulp, and stir until thoroughly combined.

Place on prepared sheet, and bake in 10-minute increments, using a spatula to flip the granola crumbles after each increment, until golden brown. Check more frequently during last 10 minutes, as the edges will brown a little more quickly. The total baking time should be approximately 30 minutes.

Let cool completely on the baking sheet. Stir raisins into the granola once cooled, and store in an airtight container at room temperature or in the refrigerator for up to 2 weeks.

YIELD: 5 cups (750 g)

Celine Says

"To toast the pulp that remains after making Almond Milk, place the pulp in a large skillet. Heat on medium, and toast, stirring constantly, until the pulp is quite fragrant and thoroughly dried. This can take up to 10 minutes. Remove from heat, and keep on stirring for a few moments, as the skillet will still be hot. Let cool before use and store in an airtight container in the refrigerator for up to 4 days. Yield will vary, but approximately 1⅔ cups (150 g)."

RISE AND SHINE MOCHA DRINK

* Gluten-Free Potential   * No Added Oil   * Quick and Easy

If you find your homemade yogurts are too thin for your taste, this refreshing morning jolt of a drink will be the perfect way to use them up. But any plain vegan yogurt will work well here. If you don't have espresso granules at hand, simply replace the milk with the same amount of strong, freshly brewed and cooled coffee.

> 1¼ cups (300 g) Homemade Yogurt (page 28) or store-bought plain vegan yogurt
> 1½ tablespoons (23 ml, or 18 g) favorite liquid or granulated vegan sweetener, adjust to taste
> 1½ teaspoons unsweetened cocoa powder
> 1 to 1¼ teaspoons instant espresso granules, to taste
> ½ teaspoon pure vanilla extract
> ½ cup (120 ml) plain vegan milk, store-bought or homemade (page 27)

Combine all the ingredients in a blender, and blend until perfectly smooth. Pour into 2 serving glasses, and enjoy immediately.

YIELD: 2 servings

SIMPLE FRUIT SMOOTHIE

* Gluten-Free Potential   * No Added Oil   * No Added Sugar
* Quick and Easy   * Soy-Free

Love mocha, but you prefer beverages that contain no refined sugar for the first meal of the day? Here's fruitiness, good energy, creaminess, and satisfaction, all packed in a glass. You can also replace ¼ cup (60 ml) of the milk with ¼ cup (60 g) of Homemade Yogurt (page 28) or store-bought vegan yogurt, for a tangier flavor. If using soy yogurt or soymilk, the recipe won't be soy-free anymore.

> ½ large frozen banana, sliced
> ½ cup (125 g) frozen raspberries
> ½ cup (78 g) frozen blueberries
> 1 cup (235 ml) plain Almond Milk (page 27) or other vegan milk
> 1 generous teaspoon Toasted Hazelnut Butter (page 220), optional

Combine all the ingredients in a blender, and blend until perfectly smooth. Pour in 2 serving glasses, and serve immediately. Note that the smoothies will be quite thick, almost like soft serve at first. You can enjoy them with a spoon, but as minutes pass, they do become smoothie-like and drinkable.

YIELD: 2 servings

HERBES DE PROVENCE CRACKERS

* No Added Sugar * Soy–Free

Thankfully, it has become increasingly easier to find vegan-friendly crackers on the market in recent years, and avoid those that come with dairy-based ingredients such as butter and Cheddar cheese. We still like to take matters into our own hands on occasion, and create delicious homemade crackers such as these. Be sure not to use soymilk, if you want to keep the recipe soy-free.

7 tablespoons (105 ml) plain Almond Milk (page 27) or other unsweetened plain vegan milk

½ teaspoon apple cider vinegar

1¼ cups (150 g) whole-wheat pastry flour

⅓ cup (30 g) toasted leftover pulp from Almond Milk (page 27) or ¼ cup (30 g) almond meal

½ teaspoon fine sea salt (slightly generous)

½ teaspoon herbes de Provence (slightly generous)

½ teaspoon garlic powder

½ teaspoon baking soda

½ teaspoon baking powder

2 tablespoons (30 ml) grapeseed or olive oil

Combine the milk with the vinegar in a small bowl. Stir, and let stand 5 minutes. It will curdle and become like buttermilk.

In a large bowl, combine flour, toasted almond meal, salt, herbes de Provence, garlic powder, baking soda, and baking powder. Drizzle the oil on top, and stir it in with a fork. Add ¼ cup (60 ml) of the soured milk, and stir to combine until a dough forms. It shouldn't be too dry or too wet, so add extra milk as needed, 1 tablespoon (15 ml) at a time. Cover the bowl, and let stand 30 minutes for the dough to be easier to work with.

Preheat the oven to 350°F (180°C, or gas mark 4). Line two large baking sheets with parchment paper. Divide the dough into four equal portions. Place a dough quarter on a piece of parchment paper, and roll out extremely thinly, about $\frac{1}{16}$ inch (1.6 mm). Using a 2-inch (5 cm) round cutter, cut the dough into crackers, and transfer to the prepared sheets. Prick 3 times with the tines of a fork. Roll out the dough scraps until you run out, and repeat with the remaining dough quarters. Bake for 16 minutes, or until golden brown. Keep an eye on the crackers after 14 minutes, as some of them might bake faster than others. Transfer to a wire rack, and let cool completely. Store in an airtight container at room temperature. The crackers will stay fresh for up to 4 days.

YIELD: Approximately 54 crackers

GRILLED APPLE AND CHARD CHOPPED SALAD WITH CREAMY DIJON DRESSING

* Gluten-Free Potential

Grilling the apples really brings out the sugars and balances nicely with the bitterness of the chard.

FOR THE SALAD:

> **2 Granny Smith apples, cored and thinly sliced with skin left on**
> **5 large leaves chard, finely chopped (about 3 cups, or 108 g)**
> **1 cup (160 g) diced red onion**
> **1 cup (99 g) pecans**

FOR THE CREAMY DIJON DRESSING:

> **½ cup (112 g) vegan mayonnaise, store-bought or homemade (page 118)**
> **2 tablespoons (40 g) agave nectar**
> **1 tablespoon (15 g) mild Dijon mustard**
> **1 tablespoon (15 ml) fresh lemon juice**

To make the salad: Preheat a grill or grill pan. Grill the apples for 3 to 4 minutes, or until grill marks are present. Flip and repeat on other side. Remove from grill and allow to cool.

While the apples are cooling, prepare the remaining salad ingredients and add them to a large mixing bowl.

To prepare the dressing: Whisk together the mayonnaise, agave, mustard, and lemon juice.

Add the dressing to the salad and toss to coat. Serve immediately. If you plan to serve at a later time, keep dressing separate and chill until ready to serve, then toss with dressing immediately before serving.

YIELD: 6 servings

 Joni Says

"Any bitter green works well in this salad—chard, collard greens, peppery arugula, chopped kale, even dandelion greens make a great backdrop for the sweet apples and tangy mustard dressing."

MOST LUSCIOUS MASHED TATERS EVER

* Gluten-Free Potential * No Added Oil * No Added Sugar * Soy-Free

Who said butter was necessary to create the most delicious mashed potatoes one could dream of? Not us! Celine's parents have been making these mashed potatoes in non-vegan form since she was too tiny to even remember, and then they seamlessly switched to using vegan ingredients without losing any of the flavor and texture. She's never met another mashed potato recipe she loves more than this. Try it, and see for yourself.

25 ounces (709 g) red potatoes, fingerling, Yukon Gold, or Agria, cut in large cubes, peeled or not

¾ cup (180 ml) plain Homemade Creamer (page 26)

¾ cup (180 ml) plain Almond Milk (page 27) or other unsweetened plain vegan milk

½ teaspoon fine sea salt, to taste

⅜ teaspoon freshly grated nutmeg

Place the cubed potatoes in a large pot. Cover with water. Bring to a boil, and cook 15 to 20 minutes, or until the potatoes break apart when forked. Drain well, and thoroughly mash with a potato masher.

Combine creamer and milk in a small saucepan, and heat on medium heat until warmed, about 4 minutes.

Add salt and nutmeg to the potatoes. Whisk while slowly adding the warm creamer and milk, a little at a time. You're looking for completely smooth results, and the quantity of milk needed will depend on the quality of the potatoes. This will be quite a workout for your arm muscles: Have a friend around if possible so she can lend a hand—or an arm in this case. Serve immediately.

YIELD: 6 servings

Celine Says

"The quantity of milk and creamer needed will depend on the type of potatoes used. You can always heat a little extra in the saucepan at the last minute if you notice more is needed.

Be sure not to use soymilk, if you want to keep the recipe soy-free.

For less decadent results, you can replace the creamer with another ¾ cup (180 ml) plain Almond Milk (page 27) or other unsweetened plain vegan milk.

Feeling lazy? Fit your stand mixer or hand mixer with the wire whip attachment, and let it do all the mashing and whisking for you."

LINGUINE IN TOMATO GARLIC CREAM SAUCE

* Quick and Easy

Classic, familiar flavors in a simple dish that comes together almost as quickly as the time it takes to cook the pasta.

> **1 pound (454 g) linguine noodles**
> **3 tablespoons (45 ml) olive oil**
> **3 tablespoons (17 g) minced garlic**
> **¼ cup (31 g) all-purpose flour**
> **1 cup (235 ml) vegetable broth, store-bought or homemade (page 218)**
> **1 cup (235 ml) unsweetened Almond Milk (page 27)**
> **½ cup plus 2 tablespoons (6 ounces, or 170 g) tomato paste**
> **¼ cup (30 g) nutritional yeast**
> **⅛ teaspoon nutmeg**
> **1 tablespoon (15 ml) fresh lemon juice**
> **5 large leaves fresh basil, julienne**
> **Salt and pepper, to taste**

Prepare the noodles according to package instructions.

While the noodles are cooking, preheat oil in a large, deep frying pan over medium-high heat.

Add garlic and sauté for 2 to 3 minutes, or until fragrant and lightly browned.

Add the flour to make a roux, and stir until all oil is absorbed. Continue to cook the paste until golden in color, about 2 minutes, stirring constantly. Carefully add the vegetable broth, and stir vigorously into the roux until completely dissolved.

Add the almond milk, stir, bring to a boil, then reduce to a simmer. Stir in the tomato paste, nutritional yeast, and nutmeg, and stir to combine until smooth. Add the lemon juice and prepared linguini to the pan and toss to combine with the sauce. Add fresh basil, salt and pepper to taste. Serve immediately.

YIELD: 4 main-dish servings

SPRINGTIME CARROTS AND PEAS

* Gluten-Free Potential   * No Added Sugar   * Quick and Easy

We've used just enough cashew-based spread in this colorful dish to add a little creaminess without overwhelming the goodness of the fresh vegetables, or overtaking the clean taste of any of the ingredients. It makes for an ideal side dish to many of our protein-based meals, such as our Barley Bean Patties (page 228) or Curry Quinoa Amaranth Patties (page 126).

2 teaspoons (10 ml) melted coconut oil
Scant ½ cup (70 g) minced shallot
2 large cloves garlic, grated or pressed
1 pound (454 g) carrots, trimmed, peeled, diced
1½ teaspoons Mushroom Broth Powder (page 218)
½ cup (120 ml) water, divided, more if needed
10 ounces (283 g) fresh shelled English peas
⅓ cup (80 g) Cashew and Yogurt Spread (page 33)
**   or Cashew Coconut Spread (page 32)**
1 tablespoon (5 g) packed fresh minced dill, more to taste
1 teaspoon fresh lemon juice, more to taste
Salt and pepper, to taste

Heat the oil in a large skillet on medium-high heat. Add shallots, garlic, and carrots. Cook for 3 minutes until the shallots soften.

Add broth powder and ¼ cup (60 ml) water, and lower heat. Cover with a lid, and cook 8 minutes, or until the carrots start to get tender. The cooking time will vary upon the type of carrot used.

Add the peas and 2 tablespoons (30 ml) water. Cook covered for 5 minutes, or until the carrots and peas are tender, yet still firm.

Combine the spread, dill, and lemon juice in a small bowl.

Add the spread mixture and remaining 2 tablespoons (30 ml) of water to the vegetables and stir, cooking on low heat uncovered, until just heated through. Adjust seasoning, and serve immediately with extra lemon and dill if desired.

YIELD: 4 to 6 side-dish servings

SAVORY FRUITED QUINOA

* Gluten-Free Potential * No Added Oil * No Added Sugar * Soy-Free

A similar version of this dish was made by a family friend many moons ago. It was made with white rice and a lot of butter. This version has no added oil, and with all of that delicious fruit, you are never going to miss the butter! This makes a great side dish at a holiday gathering, or even cold the next day as an easy pack-and-go lunch.

4 cups (940 ml) vegetable broth
2 cups (336 g) white quinoa
½ cup (80 g) diced red onion
¼ cup (61 g) dried cherries
¼ cup (62 g) dried apricots
¼ cup (40 g) raisins
½ cup (54 g) slivered or sliced almonds
½ cup (87 g) pomegranate arils (seeds)
1 apple, cored and cubed
1 pear, cored and cubed

Bring the vegetable broth to a boil in a pot with a tight-fitting lid. Stir in the quinoa, onion, cherries, apricots, and raisins. Return to a boil, reduce to a simmer, cover and simmer for 20 minutes, or until liquid is absorbed and the quinoa is tender and the tails have sprung.

Remove from heat and stir in the almonds, pomegranate arils, apple, and pear. Serve.

YIELD: 8 servings

CREAM OF ASPARAGUS

* Gluten-Free Potential * No Added Sugar * Quick and Easy
* Soy-Free

Celine came up with this recipe especially for her parents. Every year during the far too short-lived asparagus season, they eat as many of the tasty spears as they can afford to. For a super-decadent outcome, you can replace the almond milk with the same quantity of plain Homemade Creamer (page 26), or go with half milk and half creamer. Be sure not to use soymilk, if you want to keep the recipe soy-free.

1 tablespoon (15 ml) olive oil

2 pounds (908 g) fresh, thin green asparagus, trimmed, chopped into 1-inch (2.5 cm) pieces

½ cup (80 g) chopped shallot

3 cloves garlic, grated or pressed

2 tablespoons (16 g) Mushroom Broth Powder (page 218)

½ teaspoon fine sea salt, to taste

2 tablespoons (30 ml) dry vegan white wine or vegetable broth

2 cups (470 ml) water

2 cups (470 ml) plain Almond Milk (page 27) or other unsweetened plain vegan milk

1½ tablespoons (6 g) fresh minced dill

1 to 2 teaspoons (5 to 10 ml) white balsamic vinegar, to taste

Ground white pepper, to taste

Heat the oil in a large pot. Add the asparagus, shallot, and garlic, and sauté until the shallot softens, about 3 minutes. Add broth powder and salt, and stir to combine. Deglaze with the wine while stirring. Add water, cover with a lid, and lower heat. Simmer 15 to 20 minutes until the asparagus is tender.

Add the milk, and use a handheld blender (or carefully transfer to a blender) to purée until smooth. Transfer back into the pot if needed, and add dill, vinegar, and pepper. Simmer uncovered for another 5 minutes. Adjust seasoning if needed.

YIELD: 6 servings of 1 generous cup (250 ml) each

CAULIFLOWDER

* Gluten-Free Potential   * No Added Sugar   * Nut-Free   * Soy-Free

Chowder made with cauliflower. Get it? Such a simple list of ingredients makes a thick, creamy, rich soup that you wouldn't suspect was free from any added milks.

- **¼ cup (60 ml) olive oil**
- **1 cup (160 g) diced shallot (2 small, or 1 large)**
- **3 tablespoons (26 g) minced garlic**
- **2 pounds (908 g) cauliflower, chopped**
- **½ teaspoon salt, more or less to taste**
- **¼ teaspoon black pepper**
- **3 cups (705 ml) vegetable broth**
- **1 tablespoon (4 g) fresh parsley or 1 teaspoon dried parsley**

Heat the oil in a soup pot with a lid over medium-high heat. Add the shallot and garlic and sauté 3 to 5 minutes, or until fragrant and translucent.

Add the cauliflower, salt, and pepper and toss to mix. Cover and cook for 5 minutes, stirring a few times. The cauliflower will reduce in size and release a lot of moisture. Add broth, stir, bring to a boil, reduce to a simmer, cover and simmer for 30 minutes. Remove from heat and add the parsley. Using an immersion blender, purée to the desired consistency. If it is too thick, feel free to add a little more broth.

YIELD: 4 servings

Joni Says

"Looking for a lower-fat option? Replace the oil in this recipe with a white wine and shallot reduction. Add ¼ cup (60 ml) vegan white wine to the pot and heat over medium-high heat. Add the shallot and garlic and cook 3 to 5 minutes, until shallots are browned. Add ¼ cup (60 ml) more wine and cook until reduced by half. Then follow the recipe."

VEGGIE NOODLE CURRY

* Gluten-Free Potential * No Added Oil * No Added Sugar
* Quick and Easy * Soy-Free

Loaded with veggies, flavor, and great texture, this is the ideal soup to prepare when you crave comfort food that needs to be ready in moments. Its full-bodied flavor comes partially thanks to the use of coconut milk. To boost the protein profile of this dish, top it with crispy, panfried tofu cubes, or add cooked chickpeas at the same time as the noodles (so that they're heated through).

4 carrots, trimmed, peeled, and chopped (10 ounces, or 283 g)
5 tablespoons (50 g) chopped shallot
1 medium jalapeño pepper, seeded and minced
4 cloves garlic (½ ounce, or 14 g), minced
1 tablespoon (6 g) grated fresh gingerroot or ½ teaspoon ginger powder
2 tablespoons (30 ml) fresh lime juice
1 tablespoon (6 g) mild or medium curry powder
1 heaping tablespoon (10 g) Mushroom Broth Powder (page 218)
½ teaspoon fine sea salt, to taste
3 cups (705 ml) water
1 can (14 ounces, or 414 ml) full-fat coconut milk or coconut cream
2 packed cups (140 g) small fresh broccoli florets (avoid tougher stem)
3 ounces (85 g) brown rice pad Thai noodles, broken into 3-inch (8 cm) pieces
Fresh Thai basil, fresh mint, or fresh cilantro, chopped, to taste
Red pepper flakes, to taste

Place the carrots, shallot, jalapeño, garlic, ginger, lime juice, curry powder, broth powder, and salt in a large pot. Sauté on medium-high heat for 4 minutes, or until the shallots are translucent, stirring occasionally.

Add water and coconut milk, stirring to combine. Bring to a boil, immediately lower heat, cover with a lid, and simmer for 15 minutes, until the carrots can be pierced with a fork without being mushy, stirring occasionally. (The cooking time will vary depending on the type of carrot.)

Add broccoli florets and noodles, stirring to combine. Cover again, and simmer for another 6 minutes, until the noodles are cooked, and the broccoli is tender without being mushy and still bright green. Remove from stove, and let stand for 5 minutes before serving. Divide among bowls, and top with herbs of choice, and a pinch of red pepper flakes.

YIELD: 4 servings

COCONUT, ONION, HERB, AND GARLIC SOUP

* Gluten-Free Potential * No Added Sugar * Quick and Easy
* Soy-Free

This one-pot soup is bright, vibrant, and full of fresh herb flavor. It's super simple to make, and the finished product makes a great, light meal all on its own, or an excellent start to dinner.

> **2 tablespoons (30 ml) olive oil (If you are on a no-added-oil diet, and you have a good nonstick pot, you can simply leave it out)**
> **1 medium yellow onion, diced**
> **2 leeks, thinly sliced**
> **4 stalks celery, chopped**
> **3 tablespoons (26 g) minced garlic**
> **4 cups (940 ml) vegetable broth**
> **1 can (13.5 ounces, or 400 ml) full-fat coconut milk**
> **2 tablespoons (4 g) fresh chopped thyme**
> **2 tablespoons (8 g) fresh chopped tarragon**
> **2 tablespoons (8 g) fresh chopped parsley**
> **1 tablespoon (3.5 g) fresh chopped dill**
> **1 tablespoon (15 ml) lime juice**
> **Salt and pepper, to taste**

Heat the oil (if using) in a pot over medium-high heat. Add the onions, leeks, celery, and garlic. Sauté until fragrant and soft, about 5 minutes.

Add the vegetable broth and coconut milk and stir. Bring to a boil, reduce to a simmer, and simmer uncovered for 20 minutes.

Remove from heat, and stir in the fresh chopped herbs and lime juice. Add salt and pepper to taste. Serve immediately.

YIELD: 4 servings

CHOCOLATE CHIA SEED PUDDING

* Gluten-Free Potential   * No Added Oil   * Soy-Free

When you find yourself craving a chocolate treat that's reminiscent of tapioca pudding, this treat is it! The puddings have the added bonus of being packed with fiber and protein thanks to the chia seeds. Store servings individually in mason jars at the ready in the refrigerator for a quick and happy snack for when you arrive home from work or school. Be sure not to use soymilk if you want to keep the recipe soy-free.

14 ounces (414 ml) full-fat canned coconut milk
1²/₃ cups (395 ml) plain Almond Milk (page 27) or other vegan milk
½ cup (100 g) evaporated cane juice or vegan granulated sugar
¼ cup plus 2 tablespoons (30 g) unsweetened cocoa powder
2 teaspoons (10 ml) pure vanilla extract
1 teaspoon pure hazelnut extract
Pinch fine sea salt
⅓ to ½ cup (53 to 80 g) white chia seeds, to taste

Combine the milks, evaporated cane juice, cocoa powder, extracts, and salt in a blender. Blend until completely smooth and combined. Place in a large bowl, and thoroughly combine with chia seeds. Refrigerate overnight to let the puddings firm up thanks to the seeds that will soften and swell. Stir before serving. Serve as is, or with fresh berries, a squiggle of Whipped Coconut Cream (page 64), and a few cacao nibs or chopped chocolate on top. Store leftovers in an airtight container in the refrigerator for up to 4 days.

YIELD: 6 servings

 Celine Says

"Add the chia seeds according to your personal textural preference and taste. The mixture will thicken just fine with the lesser amount."

COCONUT PANNA COTTA WITH FRESH BERRIES

★ Gluten-Free Potential   ★ No Added Oil   ★ Soy-Free

This rich, not-too-sweet dessert is the perfect backdrop for fresh berries or any of your favorite toppings. The Strawberry Lime Coulis (page 65) or the Passion Fruit Curd (page 144) would be lovely here.

4 cups (940 ml) full-fat coconut milk, divided
½ ounce (14 g) agar powder
¾ cup (90 g) powdered sugar, divided
¼ cup (84 g) agave nectar
1 teaspoon vanilla extract
½ teaspoon salt
2 cups (290 g) fresh blueberries (or any of your favorite toppings)

Place 2 cups (470 ml) of the milk in a pot and whisk in the agar powder.

Bring to a boil, reduce to a simmer, and simmer for 5 full minutes to dissolve and activate the agar. Add ½ cup (60 g) of the powdered sugar and whisk to dissolve.

Remove from heat and whisk in the remaining coconut milk, agave, vanilla, and salt.

Pour into dessert cups so that they are half full to leave room for the berries, and cool for 10 minutes. Refrigerate until set, about an hour. Top with fresh berries and sprinkle with remaining powdered sugar.

YIELD: 4 to 6 servings depending on the size of your cups

 Joni Says

"To make a traditional panna cotta, pour your mixture into an oiled or silicone mold instead of dessert cups. Once set, the panna cotta is firm enough to invert onto a plate and keep its shape."

RASPBERRY CRANACHAN

* No Added Oil

This subtly boozy and quite decadent Scottish dessert can be made with any berry you love the most. We're just suckers for anything raspberry, although we can also recommend strawberries here. Cranachan is traditionally made with heavy or double cream, and honey as a sweetener. Rest assured that our vegan version makes for a great doppelganger. It's the perfect finishing touch to a light meal, with a cup of tea or a shot of espresso as a sidekick.

> **6 tablespoons (30 g) rolled oats (quick-cooking or old-fashioned both work well)**
>
> **3 to 4 tablespoons (45 to 60 ml) vegan whiskey, divided**
>
> **¼ cup (80 g) Lyle's golden syrup or agave nectar or brown rice syrup, plus extra**
>
> **1 pound (454 g) fresh raspberries, divided**
>
> **½ teaspoon evaporated cane juice or vegan granulated sugar**
>
> **14 ounces (1⅔ cups, or 414 ml) chilled coconut cream (scooped from 1 to 2 cans of chilled coconut cream or full-fat coconut milk)**
>
> **⅓ cup (80 g) Cashew and Yogurt Spread (page 33) or Cashew Coconut Spread (page 32)**

Refrigerate the bowl and beaters used for whipping the cream and spread overnight.

Have ready 6 half-pint (8 ounces, or 235 ml) mason jars, or 6 small dessert ramekins.

Place the oats in a heavy-bottomed saucepan. Toast on medium heat, stirring constantly, until the oats are light golden brown and smell nutty. This will take about 6 minutes. Remove from heat, let cool a couple of minutes. Add 3 tablespoons (45 ml) of whiskey and the syrup, stirring to combine, and set aside to cool completely.

Place 10 ounces (283 g) of raspberries in a bowl, and the evaporated cane juice on top. Crush coarsely, and set aside.

Place cooled oats, chilled cream, and spread in a large bowl. Using a handheld electric mixer with a whisk attachment, whisk until thoroughly combined and thickened, about 5 minutes. Have a taste and see if you want to add the remaining 1 tablespoon (15 ml) of whiskey into this mixture. Add crushed raspberries and the cream mixture (in two layers each) into 6 mason jars.

Cover each jar or ramekin, and chill overnight before serving. The longer the dessert sits, the more the flavors will meld and develop. Top with the remaining 6 ounces (170 g) fresh and whole raspberries. Drizzle a little extra syrup on top of each serving.

YIELD: 6 servings

CINNAMON BROWN SUGAR POPS

* Gluten-Free Potential   * Nut-Free

It's hard to believe there is no ice cream in these rich and creamy popsicles.

> **3 medium-size ripe bananas**
> **6 ounces (170 g) firm silken tofu**
> **2 tablespoons (30 ml) neutral-flavored oil**
> **2 teaspoons (10 ml) fresh lemon juice**
> **2 teaspoons (10 ml) agave nectar or other liquid sweetener**
> **¼ cup (55 g) tightly packed brown sugar, divided**
> **1 teaspoon ground cinnamon**

In a food processor, purée bananas, tofu, oil, lemon juice, agave, and 2 tablespoons (23 g) of the brown sugar until very smooth. In a small bowl, combine remaining 2 tablespoons (23 g) brown sugar with cinnamon.

Fill molds one-quarter full with banana mixture, then sprinkle a layer of cinnamon sugar, then more banana mixture, then more cinnamon sugar. Continue until molds are full, you should have 4 layers in total. Place sticks in the molds and freeze until solid.

Run warm water over the molds to loosen, then gently pull out the pops.

YIELD: 6 to 8 pops, depending on mold size

....

PASSION FRUIT CURD AND CREAM POPS

* Gluten-Free Potential   * No Added Oil

These pretty pops are cheesecake-like, tart, and refreshing, too. We used a combination of cashew spread and creamer to take the place of dairy.

> **¼ cup (60 g) either Cashew Spread (page 32 or 33)**
> **½ cup plus 2 tablespoons (150 ml) plain Homemade Creamer (page 26)**
> **3 tablespoons (60 g) agave nectar**
> **¼ teaspoon pure vanilla extract**
> **6 tablespoons (106 g) Passion Fruit Curd (page 144)**

Using a blender, blend the spread, creamer, nectar, and vanilla until smooth. Drop 1½ teaspoons of curd each at the bottom of six 2¼-ounce (67 ml) shot glasses. Fill each shot glass halfway with creamer mixture. Drop another 1½ teaspoons curd in each glass. Divide the remaining creamer mixture between the glasses, and gently swirl to slightly mix the curd and creamer mixtures. Freeze for 2 hours, or until the preparation is solid enough to hold the stick upright. Insert sticks in the center of all pops. Freeze overnight. To release the pops from their molds easily, run tepid water on the outside of the molds for a few seconds.

YIELD: 6 shot-size pops

CHERRY CHEESECAKE CHOCOLATE CHUNK ICE CREAM

* Gluten-Free Potential   * No Added Oil   * Soy-Free

Composed of creamer for richness, cashew-based spread for a slight tang, and cherries to impart their inimitable flavor, we were told our testers couldn't help themselves and ate most of the batter before it even made it into the ice cream maker. Oops.

1 recipe (2 cups, or 470 ml) plain Homemade Creamer (page 26)
4 teaspoons (11 g) cornstarch (preferably organic)
½ cup plus 2 tablespoons (120 g) evaporated cane juice or vegan granulated sugar, more if needed
1½ teaspoons pure vanilla extract
¼ teaspoon pure almond extract
⅓ cup plus 1½ tablespoons (100 g) Cashew Coconut Spread (page 32)
1 cup (154 g) fresh pitted cherries, divided
¼ cup (44 g) chopped vegan chocolate

Freeze the tub part of the ice cream machine for at least 24 hours prior to making ice cream.

Combine the cornstarch with 2 tablespoons (30 ml) of creamer in a small bowl. Stir this slurry into the rest of the creamer, and place with the evaporated cane juice in a small saucepan. Cook on medium-high heat, whisking constantly, until just thickened, about 5 minutes. Remove from heat, whisking occasionally, and let cool.

Place cooled creamer, extracts, spread, and ½ cup (77 g) cherries in a blender. Blend until completely smooth. Taste the mixture, and add extra sugar as needed, if desired.

Following the manufacturer's instructions, churn the ice cream until it is firm. While the ice cream is churning, halve the remaining ½ cup (77 g) cherries. Add cherries and chopped chocolate during the last 5 minutes of churning. Place in the freezer for a couple of hours to firm up. The ice cream will be reluctant to be scooped out straight out of the freezer after more than a few hours. Leave it at room temperature for about 15 minutes before serving.

YIELD: 1 quart (946 ml)

LEMONY CREAM AND STRAWBERRY SWIRL ICE CREAM

* Gluten-Free Potential * No Added Oil * Soy-Free

This ice cream is absolutely scrumptious, and it's also quite the looker. We haven't eaten dairy-based ice cream for years, but we daresay this one is the closest we've ever gotten to mimicking it.

> **1 cup (140 g) raw cashews, soaked overnight and rinsed (see instructions in Homemade Creamer, page 26)**
> **1¼ cups (295 ml) water**
> **1 cup (235 ml) coconut cream**
> **4 teaspoons (11 g) cornstarch (preferably organic)**
> **½ cup (160 g) agave nectar**
> **1 tablespoon (15 ml) pure vanilla extract**
> **¼ teaspoon pure lemon extract**
> **Pinch fine sea salt**
> **¾ cup (180 ml) Strawberry Curd (page 144)**

Freeze the tub part of the ice cream machine for at least 24 hours before making ice cream. Place an 8-inch (20 cm) loaf pan in the freezer, too.

Place cashews, water, and coconut cream in a blender. Process until perfectly smooth. If the results aren't smooth, use a nut bag and a fine-mesh sieve to filter the mixture. (Enjoy the leftover pulp in your morning bowl of oatmeal.)

Combine the cornstarch with 2 tablespoons (30 ml) of cashew mixture in a small bowl. Stir this slurry into the rest of the mixture, and place with the agave in a medium saucepan. Cook on medium-high heat, whisking constantly, until just thickened, about 5 minutes. Remove from heat, and add the extracts and salt. Whisk occasionally, until cool enough to chill in the refrigerator for about 2 hours. Pass through a fine-mesh sieve to avoid clumps.

Following the manufacturer's instructions, churn the ice cream until firm.

Add 3 tablespoons (45 ml) of curd during the last 2 minutes of churning so that it is distributed throughout.

Transfer half of the ice cream to the chilled pan, and add approximately half of the remaining curd on top. Spoon the remaining ice cream on top, then add the remaining curd on top. Using a butter knife, gently swirl the curd into the ice cream. Cover the pan with plastic wrap, and place in the freezer for a few hours to firm up.

The ice cream is best enjoyed within a day of preparation. It might be hard to scoop out after more than a few hours, so leave it at room temperature for about 20 minutes before serving.

YIELD: 3½ cups (825 ml)

WHIPPED COCONUT CREAM

* Gluten-Free Potential   * No Added Oil   * Soy-Free

Because vegan desserts often call for a fancy final touch to take them from really good to great, just like nonvegan desserts do!

FOR WHIPPED CREAM BASE:

1 to 2 cans (14 ounces, or 414 ml) each, full-fat coconut milk

FOR BASIC WHIPPED CREAM:

¼ cup (30 g) organic powdered sugar, sifted
½ teaspoon pure vanilla extract

FOR CHOCOLAT PRALINÉ WHIPPED CREAM:

¼ cup (30 g) organic powdered sugar, sifted
2 tablespoons (10 g) unsweetened cocoa powder
½ teaspoon pure hazelnut extract
¼ teaspoon pure vanilla extract

FOR MAPLE WHIPPED CREAM:

3 tablespoons (36 g) superfine maple sugar
½ teaspoon pure vanilla extract
⅛ teaspoon pure maple extract

Let contents of coconut milk cans settle at room temperature. Refrigerate for 24 hours with the bowl and whisk attachment used to whip the cream. Pick a flavor, and use 1 can per flavor.

To make basic whipped cream: Place the sugar and vanilla in the bowl.

To make chocolate praline whipped cream: Place the sugar, cocoa powder, and extracts in the bowl.

To make maple whipped cream: Place the sugar and extracts in the bowl.

For all flavors: Scoop the hardened cream from the top of the can, and place it on the other ingredients in the bowl. You should get 7 ounces (198 g) of cream per can. If not, open second can and scoop out more cream. (Keep the liquid for soups!)

Using a handheld electric mixer with a whisk attachment, whisk slowly at first, then speed up, until fluffy and thickened, about 5 minutes. Refrigerate in an airtight container for at least 1 hour before use. Cover and refrigerate leftovers for up to 2 days.

YIELD: Approximately 8 ounces (1 cup, or 227 g)

CHOCOLATE SYRUP

* Gluten-Free Potential * No Added Oil * Quick and Easy * Soy-Free

This creamy syrup also tastes great as a coffee creamer. Don't use soymilk if you want to keep it soy-free!

½ cup (40 g) unsweetened cocoa powder
¾ cup (144 g) evaporated cane juice or vegan granulated sugar
1 cup (235 ml) Almond Milk (page 27) or other vegan milk, divided
1 ounce (28 g) raw cocoa butter, optional
Pinch kosher salt
1 teaspoon pure vanilla extract

Whisk cocoa powder, evaporated cane juice, and ½ cup (120 ml) of milk in a small saucepan until smooth. Add remaining ½ cup (120 ml) of milk, whisking to combine.

Bring the mixture to a low boil, add cocoa butter and salt. Lower heat to medium. Cook for 4 minutes, or until slightly thickened, whisking to dissolve sugar and melt cocoa butter.

Remove from heat, and whisk in the vanilla extract. Let cool before transferring to an airtight container. Refrigerate for up to 1 week.

YIELD: 1½ cups (355 ml)

STRAWBERRY LIME COULIS

* Gluten-Free Potential * No Added Oil * Quick and Easy

Swirl this coulis into yogurts, drizzle it over pancakes, or Strawberry Clafoutis (page 142).

¾ cup (180 g) puréed super ripe strawberries, from a scant
  1¼ cups (180 g) halved strawberries
2 to 3 tablespoons (40 to 60 g) agave nectar, to taste
2 tablespoons (30 g) Cashew Coconut Spread (page 32)
  or Cashew and Yogurt Spread (page 33)
2 tablespoons (30 ml) bottled lime juice
¼ teaspoon pure vanilla extract
1 tablespoon (10 g) white chia seeds, ground into a fine meal

To avoid seeds, strain the puréed strawberries in a fine-mesh sieve. Combine all the ingredients in blender, or use an immersion blender, and blend until smooth. Do not overblend, or the mixture might get a little goopy. Store in an airtight container or jar in the refrigerator until ready to use, for up to 1 week. Stir before use.

YIELD: 1¼ cups (295 ml)

CHAPTER 2
Cheese Substitutions

FANCY ARTISAN CHEESES ARE NO LONGER RELEGATED to the lactose-laden world. With new ingredient combinations and a few cool new techniques, downright impressive homemade vegan cheeses are a reality. Get ready to enjoy sharp Cheddar cheese balls rolled in sliced almonds; smoked truffle Gouda sliced on crackers; a dish of cottage cheese topped with fruit compote; or an ooey-gooey grilled cheese sandwich.

This chapter will show you how to make a few homemade cheese substitutes to use in other recipes, or simply to have on hand for everyday use. Then we have all sorts of recipes that use those substitutes, or are simply downright cheesy on their own.

Practice Makes for Perfect Substitutions

The best way to demonstrate how easy it is to transform a nonvegan recipe into a cruelty-free wonder is to showcase how it's done. Let's go through a sample recipe step by step! Once you know the basics, it's easy to put into practice on any recipe.

< *Smoked Truffle Gouda–Style Almond Cheese, page 77*

ROASTED CORN OFF THE COB WITH CHILI LIME SAUCE & MEXICAN CHEESE

Non-Veganized

This recipe is an excerpt from *Clean Eating For Busy Families*, by Michelle Dudash, R.D. (Fair Winds Press, 2012). We will substitute vegan ingredients for the light mayonnaise, low-fat milk, and crumbly cheese, and rewrite the directions accordingly.

FOR CORN:

4 ears of corn, husks and silks removed
2 teaspoons (10 ml) expeller-pressed grapeseed or canola oil
⅛ teaspoon salt
⅛ teaspoon freshly ground black pepper

FOR AIOLI:

¼ cup (60 g) light mayonnaise
1 tablespoon (15 ml) low-fat milk
1 teaspoon (5 ml) lime juice
1 pinch chili powder
1 pinch garlic powder

FOR SERVING:

3 tablespoons (28 g) crumbly Mexican–style cheese, such as queso fresco or cotija (or feta)

Preheat the oven to 450°F (230°C, or gas mark 8) and line a sheet pan with parchment paper or a silicone baking mat.

To roast the corn: Brush the corn with the oil and sprinkle with salt and pepper. Bake until blistered, about 15 minutes, turning halfway through cooking. Cool slightly. Stand the cobs on a cutting board and holding the cobs firmly, cut off the kernels.

To make the aioli: Stir the sauce ingredients together in a small bowl.

To serve: Place the corn in serving dishes, drizzle with aioli, and sprinkle on the cheese.

YIELD: 4 servings

ROASTED CORN OFF THE COB WITH CHILI LIME SAUCE & MEXICAN CHEESE

Veganized!

We have three items to substitute for in this recipe: light mayonnaise, low-fat milk, and Mexican–style cheese. The light mayonnaise is a straightforward substitution: Use Silky Tofu Mayo (page 118), or store-bought regular or low-fat vegan mayonnaise, such as Vegenaise. As for the milk, this is also as easy as can be: plain Almond Milk (page 27), or any favorite store-bought unsweetened plain vegan milk will work perfectly. The specific cheese called for in this recipe is also a breeze thanks to the Cotija–Style Tofu Crumbles on page 73.

FOR CORN:

4 ears of corn, husks and silks removed
2 teaspoons (10 ml) expeller-pressed grapeseed or canola oil
⅛ teaspoon fine sea salt
⅛ teaspoon freshly ground black pepper

FOR AIOLI:

¼ cup (60 g) Silky Tofu Mayo (page 118) or store-bought regular or low-fat vegan mayonnaise — mayonnaise substitute
1 tablespoon (15 ml) plain Almond Milk (page 27) or other unsweetened plain vegan milk — low-fat milk substitute
1 teaspoon (5 ml) fresh lime juice
1 pinch chili powder
1 small garlic clove, grated or pressed or 1 pinch garlic powder

FOR SERVING:

3 tablespoons (28 g) Cotija–Style Tofu Crumbles (page 73) — crumbly–style Mexican cheese substitute

Preheat the oven to 450°F (230°C, or gas mark 8) and line a sheet pan with parchment paper or a silicone baking mat.

To make the corn: Brush the corn with the oil and sprinkle with salt and pepper. Bake until blistered, about 15 minutes, turning halfway through cooking. Cool slightly. Stand the cobs on a cutting board and holding the cobs firmly, cut off the kernels.

To make the aioli: Stir the Silky Tofu Mayo **(this is your mayonnaise substitute)**, Almond Milk **(this is your milk substitute)**, lime juice, chili powder, and garlic together in a small bowl.

To serve: Place the corn in serving dishes, drizzle with aioli, and sprinkle on Cotija–Style Tofu Crumbles **(this is your Mexican–style cheese substitute)**.

YIELD: 4 servings

'MERICAN CHEESE SLICES

* No Added Sugar   * Gluten-Free Potential

Make your own cheese slices at home! This recipe is very basic and, while we think it tastes great on its own, it lends itself quite well to add-ins. Try chopped peppers, liquid smoke, herbs, and spices—pretty much anything you can think of. If you do use add-ins, after you have boiled the mixture for the full 7 minutes, add them in, stir, and pour immediately.

> **2 cups (470 ml) original (not unsweetened) almond milk**
> **2 tablespoons (30 ml) neutral-flavored oil**
> **1 tablespoon (18 g) miso**
> **¼ cup (30 g) nutritional yeast**
> **¼ teaspoon paprika**
> **¼ teaspoon turmeric**
> **½ teaspoon sea salt**
> **1 ounce (28 g) agar-agar (Powder is best to prevent graininess, but any type will work.)**

Line a rimmed 9 x 13-inch (23 x 33 cm) baking sheet with waxed paper.

Add all the ingredients to a pot and whisk until well mixed. Bring to a boil over medium-high heat, stirring regularly with a rubber spatula to prevent any from sticking to the bottom of the pot and scorching. Boil for 7 minutes, stirring regularly.

Carefully pour onto the lined baking sheet and smooth out into a thin even layer. Take another piece of waxed paper and smooth over the top. Place in the refrigerator to set for a few hours, or overnight.

Leaving the paper on both sides, carefully remove the whole thing from the pan and lay on a flat surface. Using a pair of clean scissors, trim the edges square. Then carefully cut into 12 even squares of individually wrapped slices of cheese.

Store in an airtight container in the refrigerator until ready to use. Should last at least 2 weeks in the refrigerator.

YIELD: 12 slices

SHARP ALMOND CHEESE BALL

* No Added Oil * No Added Sugar

A cheeseball just like mama used to make, complete with almonds! Serve with crackers. Pairs well with a nice merlot. Just sayin'.

8 ounces (227 g) extra-firm tofu, drained and pressed
½ cup (120 ml) vegan milk
½ cup (60 g) almond meal (finely ground almonds)
¼ cup (30 g) nutritional yeast
2 tablespoons (16 g) arrowroot powder
1 to 2 tablespoons (18 to 36 g) miso, to taste
  (the more the miso, the sharper the cheese)
1 tablespoon (15 ml) apple cider vinegar
1 tablespoon (15 ml) tamari
½ teaspoon garlic powder
¼ teaspoon paprika
¼ onion powder
¼ cup (20 g) quick-cooking oats
½ cup (45 g) sliced almonds

Place all the ingredients, except the oats and sliced almonds, into a blender or food processor, and process until smooth. The mixture should be thick, not runny, about the same consistency as creamy peanut butter.

Transfer to a pot and mix in the oats. Heat over medium-high heat for 10 minutes, constantly scraping and turning with a rubber spatula to prevent the mass from sticking to the bottom and scorching. The mixture will not boil. Ten minutes over medium-high heat should be plenty of time to cook the oats and activate the arrowroot, as well as evaporate excess moisture.

Remove from heat and cool completely in the refrigerator to thicken. Place sliced almonds on a plate. Once cold, roll the mass in the palms of your hands into a ball about the size of a navel orange. It will be sticky, but manageable.

Set the ball on the plate of almonds, then wash hands clean. Press almonds all over the ball by rolling the ball in the almonds on the plate. Keep refrigerated until ready to serve.

YIELD: 1 cheese ball, 8 servings

HEMP PARM

* Gluten-Free Potential * No Added Oil * No Added Sugar
* Quick and Easy * Soy-Free

This stand-in for dairy Parmesan is perfect for adding saltiness and a flavor-packed punch to virtually any savory dish. It's also ready in minutes, and loaded with protein from the nuts, nutritional yeast, and maca powder to boot.

½ cup (60 g) toasted whole almonds
½ cup (60 g) toasted walnut halves
¼ cup (30 g) nutritional yeast
2 tablespoons (30 g) maca powder or 2 extra tablespoons (15 g) nutritional yeast

1 teaspoon herbes de Provence, or other blend of dried herbs, optional
½ teaspoon onion powder
¼ teaspoon garlic powder
¼ teaspoon fine sea salt, to taste
¼ cup (40 g) shelled hemp seeds

Place all the ingredients except the hemp seeds in a food processor. Pulse until the almonds and walnuts are coarsely ground, to the consistency of panko bread crumbs. Add the hemp seeds and pulse twice, just to roughly mix with the other ingredients. Store in an airtight container in the refrigerator for up to 2 weeks. Use anywhere you would use Parmesan cheese.

YIELD: 2 cups (225 g)

· ·

COTTAGE-STYLE CHEESE

* Gluten-Free Potential * No Added Oil * No Added Sugar

Use this cheese as a high protein snack, topped with fruit compote or jam, or simply eat it plain, maybe sprinkled with a little salt and pepper, served with crackers.

1 cup (235 ml) unsweetened plain soymilk
2 tablespoons (16 g) arrowroot powder
1 pound (454 g) extra-firm or super firm tofu, drained

¼ cup (60 g) unsweetened plain vegan yogurt, store-bought or homemade (page 28), or Cashew Coconut Spread (page 32)
¼ cup (60 ml) apple cider vinegar, divided
¾ teaspoon fine sea salt

Add the soymilk and arrowroot to a pot and whisk until smooth. Add the tofu and crumble until it resembles cottage cheese. Add yogurt, 2 tablespoons (30 ml) vinegar, and salt, and stir to combine. Heat over medium-high heat until it begins to bubble. Simmer for 10 to 15 minutes, stirring regularly, until thickened.

Cool for 15 minutes, then refrigerate to cool completely. Add the remaining vinegar to taste upon serving.

YIELD: 2½ cups (565 g)

ALMOND CASHEW RICOTTA

* Gluten-Free Potential

This slightly tangy and nut-based cheese works wonders in lasagnas, stuffed manicotti, or anywhere a ricotta is called for.

- ½ cup (120 ml) Almond Milk (page 27)
- ¼ cup (60 ml) olive oil
- 2 tablespoons (30 g) plain vegan yogurt, store-bought or homemade (page 28)
- 1 teaspoon lemon juice
- 1 cup (140 g) raw cashews
- 1 cup (120 g) raw almonds
- 2 tablespoons (15 g) nutritional yeast
- ½ teaspoon salt

Add all the ingredients to a blender and purée until almost perfectly smooth. Store in an airtight container in the refrigerator for up to 2 weeks, or in the freezer for up to 6 months.

YIELD: 1 pound (454 g)

COTIJA-STYLE TOFU CRUMBLES

* No Added Oil   * No Added Sugar   * Nut-Free

Traditional Cotija is a bland, salty, crumbly, Mexican cheese similar in texture to feta. It is most often used as a topping for soups, salads, enchiladas, and tacos.

- 1 block (12 ounces, or 340 g) extra-firm or super-firm tofu, drained and pressed
- ½ teaspoon salt
- ½ teaspoon garlic powder
- ½ teaspoon onion powder
- ½ teaspoon dried oregano
- ¼ teaspoon ground cumin
- ¼ teaspoon chipotle powder
- 1 tablespoon (15 ml) rice vinegar

In a mixing bowl, using your fingers, crumble the tofu until it resembles crumbled feta. Mix in the spices and vinegar until well incorporated.

Allow to sit overnight before using to allow the flavors to absorb into the tofu.

YIELD: 2 cups (340 g)

HERB-CRUSTED CASHEW CHEESE LOG

* Gluten-Free Potential * No Added Sugar

This mild, creamy, spreadable cheese is perfect for crackers. This recipe makes quite a bit, but it freezes well, so you can make a batch, freeze it before crusting and use it with whatever spice mixture fits your needs. The spice mixture included in this recipe is an all-purpose herb crust that is perfect for wine and cheese parties. For a sharper cheese, add 1 tablespoon (18 g) miso paste when blending.

FOR THE CHEESE:

- **1 pound (454 g) raw cashews**
- **6 ounces (170 g) plain vegan yogurt, store-bought or homemade (page 28)**
- **2 tablespoons (15 g) nutritional yeast**
- **2 tablespoons (20 g) chia seeds**
- **2 tablespoons (30 ml) neutral-flavored oil**
- **2 teaspoons (10 ml) fresh lemon juice**
- **¾ teaspoon salt**

FOR THE HERB CRUST (ENOUGH TO COAT 1 CHEESE LOG):

- **1 tablespoon (2 g) dried parsley**
- **1 teaspoon dried basil**
- **1 teaspoon dried dill**
- **½ teaspoon garlic powder**
- **½ teaspoon onion powder**
- **½ teaspoon salt**
- **¼ teaspoon black pepper**

To make the cheese: Add the cashews to a pot and fill the pot with enough water to cover the nuts by 3 inches (13 cm). Bring to a boil, reduce to a simmer, and simmer for 1 hour. Drain all excess water and cool the cashews under cool running water.

Add the cooled and drained cashews and the remaining cheese ingredients to a food processor or high-speed blender, and purée until very smooth. Stop to scrape down sides as needed. The final product should be the texture of thick, creamy peanut butter.

Divide the mixture into 4 equal portions. Place each portion in the center of a square of plastic wrap and wrap into a log shape. Place in the freezer for at least 2 hours to harden. This step is necessary to make the log firm enough to roll in the herbs. After it is rolled in the herbs, it will keep its shape and can be rewrapped and kept in the refrigerator, as it is supposed to be a soft spreadable cheese.

To make the herb crust: Mix the herbs together in a small dish, then spread them out evenly on a plate or another sheet of plastic wrap.

Once hardened, carefully unwrap a log and roll in the herb mixture until coated.

Serve, or rewrap and place back into the refrigerator until ready to serve.

YIELD: 4 logs, approximately 2 pounds (908 g)

CHIA SEED CREAM CHEESE

* Gluten–Free Potential   * No Added Sugar

This super-simple, super-versatile spread works just like any other cream cheese. Use it whenever you want a creamy, tangy spread—on bagels or toast, even in frostings. We've included a few flavor combinations that work well, but your options are limitless. Stir in some Coconut Bacon and scallion, or some cinnamon and vanilla, or cocoa powder, or sun-dried tomatoes and basil. Seriously, make it your own! If you are not a fan of coconut oil, or are worried about the flavor coming through, you can substitute olive oil, or other neutral-flavored, oil. Just be aware that it will have a softer set, as coconut oil is solid when chilled.

FOR PLAIN CREAM CHEESE:

- **½ cup (120 ml) melted coconut oil**
- **1 block (12 ounces, or 340 g) soft silken tofu, drained**
- **3 tablespoons (45 ml) lemon juice**
- **1 cup (224 g) whole raw cashews**
- **¼ cup (40 g) chia seeds**
- **1 teaspoon salt**

FOR STRAWBERRY:

- **½ cup (83 g) fresh sliced strawberries or ⅓ cup (107 g) strawberry preserves**

FOR GARLIC AND HERB:

- **2 stalks scallion, chopped**
- **1 tablespoon (9 g) minced garlic**
- **2 teaspoons (1 g) dried parsley or 2 tablespoons (8 g) finely chopped fresh parsley**
- **1 teaspoon dried dill or 1 tablespoon (4 g) chopped fresh dill**
- **1 teaspoon onion powder**
- **½ teaspoon dried tarragon or 1½ teaspoons finely chopped fresh tarragon**
- **¼ teaspoon black pepper**

FOR SPICY CHIPOTLE:

- **1 whole chipotle in adobo, finely chopped (more or less to taste)**
- **1 tablespoon (15 ml) adobo sauce from the can**
- **2 stalks scallion, finely chopped**
- **2 tablespoons (2 g) finely chopped cilantro**

Add all the ingredients, except variations, to a blender and blend on high for 3 minutes.

If using optional add-ins, add the additional ingredients to the blender and pulse a few times to incorporate, but not purée. Alternatively, you can make an entire batch of plain, then stir in the add-ins in small batches and have a variety of spreads on hand. Adjust the amount of ingredients used accordingly.

Transfer to an airtight container and refrigerate overnight to set. Store in the refrigerator until ready to use. Keeps for up to 2 weeks in the refrigerator.

YIELD: 2½ cups (20 ounces, or 568 g)

SMOKED TRUFFLE GOUDA–STYLE ALMOND CHEESE

* No Added Sugar

This classy cheese is perfect for slicing on crackers, or adding a certain *je ne sais quoi* to a very grown-up grilled cheese.

- **3 cups (705 ml) unsweetened Almond Milk (page 27)**
- **1 ounce (28 g) agar flakes or powder**
- **2 tablespoons (36 g) miso**
- **2 tablespoons (30 ml) olive oil**
- **1 tablespoon (15 ml) lemon juice**
- **1 teaspoon black truffle oil**
- **½ teaspoon liquid smoke**
- **2 cups (240 g) almond meal (finely ground almonds)**
- **¼ cup (30 g) nutritional yeast**
- **½ ounce (14 g) dried shiitake mushrooms, finely chopped**

Oil a 9 x 5-inch (23 x 13 cm) loaf pan, or other mold and set aside.

Stir the milk together with agar in a pot. In a small bowl mix together the miso, olive oil, lemon juice, truffle oil, and liquid smoke. Set aside.

In a separate mixing bowl, mix together the almond meal, nutritional yeast and chopped mushrooms. Set aside. Bring the milk and agar mixture to a boil over medium-high heat and boil for a full 5 minutes to ensure agar is dissolved and activated. Remove from heat and stir in the miso mixture until thoroughly mixed in. Stir in the almond mixture, and stir until well combined.

Immediately and carefully pour mixture into loaf pans or molds. Allow to cool for 15 minutes, then refrigerate to cool and harden completely. You can leave in the mold and slice right in the mold for easy storage, or simply invert onto a dish for a nicer presentation and easier slicing.

YIELD: 2½ pounds (1.1 kg)

SPICY CHIA CASHEW SAUCE

* Gluten-Free Potential * No Added Oil * No Added Sugar * Soy-Free

This sauce is rich, cheesy, and spicy. It's the ideal topping for Mexican-style baked dishes, and also a great creamy addition to quesadillas, burritos, tacos, and more.

1 cup (140 g) raw cashews

2⅔ cups (630 ml) filtered water, divided

1 medium jalapeño pepper, trimmed and seeded or not (the sauce will be spicier if the seeds are used)

2 scallions, trimmed and chopped (25 g)

1 to 2 cloves garlic, to taste

⅜ teaspoon fine sea salt

⅓ cup (7 g) packed fresh cilantro leaves

1 tablespoon (15 ml) fresh lime juice

1 tablespoon (10 g) white chia seeds

2 tablespoons (15 g) nutritional yeast

1½ teaspoons maca powder

Place the cashews in a medium bowl or 4-cup (940 ml) glass measuring cup. Cover with 2 cups (470 ml) water. Cover with plastic wrap or a lid. Let stand at room temperature overnight (about 8 hours), to soften the nuts.

Drain the cashews (discard soaking water), and give them a quick rinse.

Combine the soaked cashews, remaining ⅔ cup (160 ml) water, and remaining ingredients in a food processor or high-speed blender, and process until mostly smooth. The chia seeds will look bumpy, but there should be no cashew pieces left. Store in an airtight container in the refrigerator.

The sauce needs to be heated in a small saucepan over medium-high heat before serving if it isn't baked in the final dish. Whisk frequently until warmed throughout, about 6 to 8 minutes. Lower heat if needed to avoid scorching. See instructions in Mexican Polenta Bake (page 233), and in the headnote to Cauliflower Taco Crumbles (page 174) for suggested uses.

YIELD: 1¾ cups (475 g)

SAVORY BUTTERNUT PIELETS

* No Added Sugar

It's one of our golden rules in life to never turn down tiny vegan pies. These are packed with butternut squash, giving them a pleasing orange hue. They're made a little cheesy flavorwise by using cashew-based spread and maca powder in the filling.

12 ounces (340 g) cubed butternut squash

3 cloves garlic, halved

¼ cup (40 g) chopped shallot

1 teaspoon Mushroom Broth Powder (page 218)

½ cup (120 ml) water, divided, as needed

½ cup (120 g) Cashew Coconut Spread (page 32)
or Cashew and Yogurt Spread (page 33)

1 tablespoon (15 g) maca powder or (8 g) nutritional yeast

⅛ teaspoon ground nutmeg

Generous ¼ teaspoon fine sea salt, to taste

Ground white pepper, to taste

⅛ to ¼ teaspoon cayenne pepper, to taste

1 tablespoon (12 g) potato starch or (8 g) cornstarch (preferably organic)

¼ teaspoon baking powder

Nonstick cooking spray or oil spray

1 recipe dough Herbes de Provence Crackers (page 41,
made right up to and including 30-minute rest)

Smoked paprika, to sprinkle tops

Place the butternut squash, garlic, shallot, broth powder, and 1 tablespoon (15 ml) water in a large skillet. Cook on medium-high heat for 2 minutes. When squash starts sticking to the skillet when you stir it, add water, 1 tablespoon (15 ml) at a time. Lower heat, cover, and cook until tender, about 15 minutes, adding more water as needed. Once tender, place squash, spread, maca powder, nutmeg, salt, white pepper, and cayenne pepper in a food processor. Process until smooth and combined, stopping to scrape the sides if needed. Add the potato starch and baking powder, and process until combined. Set aside.

Preheat the oven to 375°F (190°C, or gas mark 5). Lightly coat a 24-cup mini muffin pan with cooking spray.

Place a packed 1½ teaspoons of dough in each muffin cup, pressing down to fit the bottom and sides of the cup. Add 1 tablespoon (15 ml) of filling per crust. Don't worry if it looks like too much. Sprinkle each top with a pinch of paprika.

Bake for 24 minutes, or until the tops are firm. Remove from pan, transfer to a wire rack, and serve warm or at room temperature.

YIELD: 24 pielets

FARROSOTTO

* No Added Sugar   * Soy-Free

This autumnal dish will fool the most hardcore risotto fan out there, thanks to the collaboration of our creamy Savory Cashew Sauce and flavor-rich Hemp Parm. While it might be tempting to grab seconds of the *molto* savory farrosotto alone, we highly recommend pairing a plateful of it with roasted, quartered Brussels sprouts or cubed butternut squash instead.

0.7 ounce (20 g) dried shiitake or other dried mushroom

4 cups (940 ml) prepared broth from Mushroom Broth Powder (page 218), divided, as needed

1 tablespoon (15 ml) olive oil, divided

½ cup (80 g) chopped shallot

4 large cloves garlic, minced

Fresh rosemary leaves from 1 small sprig, rinsed and minced

1¾ cups (350 g) dry pearled farro

¼ cup (60 ml) dry vegan white wine

½ cup (120 g) Savory Cashew Sauce (page 34)

Salt and freshly ground white peppercorn, to taste

Hemp Parm (page 72), for serving, optional

Soak the mushrooms in 1 cup (235 ml) of broth for 10 minutes. Being careful to retain the soaking broth, drain and mince the mushrooms. Add soaking broth to the remaining 3 cups (705 ml) of broth.

Heat 1 teaspoon of oil in a large skillet on medium-high heat. Add the mushrooms, and cook for 2 minutes to brown them slightly. Remove from skillet, and set aside. Heat the remaining 2 teaspoons (10 ml) of oil in the same skillet. Add shallots, garlic, and minced rosemary. Lower heat to medium, and cook for 3 to 4 minutes until the shallots soften. Add farro, and cook another 3 to 4 minutes to toast the grain. Deglaze with white wine, stirring to combine.

Add 3 cups (705 ml) of broth, bring to a boil, then cover and simmer 25 minutes, adding the mushrooms, and extra broth if needed. (If you have leftover broth once the dish is cooked, do not discard it: It can be used to cook other grains and vegetables if safely stored in an airtight container in the refrigerator, for up to 1 week.) Stir occasionally, and check the farro for doneness. It should be tender, yet still firm. Add the cashew sauce, stirring to combine, until heated through. Adjust seasoning to taste. Garnish with Hemp Parm upon serving.

YIELD: 6 servings

PESTO POLENTA SQUARES

* Gluten-Free Potential * No Added Sugar * Soy-Free

The addition of fresh basil pesto to already creamy grits makes for a rich and decadent spin on this classic dish.

FOR THE PESTO:

- ½ cup (120 ml) olive oil
- 1 tablespoon (15 ml) lemon juice
- 2 ounces (56 g) spinach leaves
- 2 ounces (56 g) fresh basil, about 40 large leaves
- ¼ cup (30 g) pine nuts
- ½ teaspoon salt

FOR THE POLENTA:

- 6 cups (1.4 L) vegetable broth
- ¼ cup (60 ml) olive oil
- 2 cups (280 g) yellow or white corn grits
- ¼ cup (30 g) nutritional yeast
- 2 tablespoons (15 g) pine nuts

To make the pesto: Add all the ingredients to a blender and purée until smooth. This recipe yields about 1½ cups (355 ml) pesto.

To make the polenta: Have ready a 9 x 13-inch (23 x 33 cm) baking dish. Bring the vegetable broth to a boil. Reduce heat to low and add the oil.

Carefully stir in the grits and nutritional yeast, and stir until well combined. The mixture will bubble and pop at first, then thicken up as it simmers. Cover and gently simmer for 20 minutes, stirring often to prevent sticking, until most of the liquid has been absorbed.

While the polenta is simmering, preheat the oven to 400°F (200°C, or gas mark 6).

Remove from heat and stir in 1 cup (235 ml) of pesto into the polenta. Stir until well combined. Spread evenly in the baking dish. Top with remaining ½ cup (120 ml) pesto and smooth over the top.

Bake for 20 minutes. Remove from oven. Sprinkle the top with pine nuts and allow to cool to set. The longer it cools the stiffer the polenta will be. Cut into squares and serve.

YIELD: 8 servings

 Joni Says

"For a lower-fat option: In the pesto, use only ¼ cup (60 ml) of oil. Replace the rest with ¼ cup (60 ml) water and 1 tablespoon (8 g) Mushroom Broth Powder (page 218). In the polenta, simply nix the oil. Instructions remain the same."

EGGPLANT PIZZA

* No Added Sugar   * Soy-Free

This is the kind of pizza that will make you wonder why you ever craved dairy-rich pizzas in the first place. Gooey and cheesy in its own right, this pie has got everything you're looking for in a savory pizza. There should be ½ cup (120 g) of leftover cilantro sauce, which is put to great use in our Barley Bean Patties (page 228).

FOR THE CILANTRO SAUCE:

 ½ cup (10 g) packed fresh cilantro leaves
 ¼ cup (60 ml) water
 Juice of 2 fresh limes (about ¼ cup, or 60 ml)
 8 scallions, white and light green parts, chopped (about ¾ cup, or 120 g)
 4 to 6 cloves garlic, grated or pressed, to taste
 2 medium jalapeño peppers, trimmed, seeded or not, chopped
 1½ tablespoons (9 g) grated fresh ginger root
 ¼ cup (64 g) natural creamy or crunchy peanut butter
 ½ teaspoon fine sea salt
 1 tablespoon (8 g) Mushroom Broth Powder (page 218)

FOR THE PIZZA:

 Olive oil, for baking sheet
 1 eggplant (20 ounces, or 570 g), trimmed and peeled if desired
 Flour, for baking sheet
 1 pound (454 g) vegan pizza dough, store-bought or homemade (page 187)
 ½ cup (60 g) Savory Cashew Sauce (page 34)
 Hemp Parm (page 72), to taste

To make the cilantro sauce: Place all the sauce ingredients in a large food processor. Pulse to chop until mostly smooth.

To make the pizza: Preheat the oven to 450°F (230°C, or gas mark 8). Have a large, lightly oiled baking sheet handy.

Cut the eggplant in two widthwise and then lengthwise in ½-inch (1.3 cm) slices. You should get 10 slices. Brush each side with cilantro sauce. Place the eggplant on the baking sheet. Bake for 8 minutes, flip the slices, and bake for another 6 minutes, until golden brown. The eggplant should not be too soft. Remove from oven, and set aside.

Lightly flour a second baking sheet. Roll the pizza dough into a 12 x 10-inch (30 x 25 cm) rectangle. Evenly apply ¼ cup (60 g) of cilantro sauce all over the dough. Evenly apply ¼ cup (60 g) cashew sauce on top of the cilantro sauce. Top with eggplant slices. Drizzle remaining ¼ cup (60 g) cashew sauce on top of the eggplant slices. Bake for 16 minutes, or until the pizza is golden brown. Serve immediately, sprinkled with Hemp Parm.

YIELD: 8 servings, 1¼ cups (300 g) cilantro sauce

SWEET SPUD-STUFFED SQUASH

* Gluten-Free Potential * No Added Sugar

Our beautifully stuffed squash is made extra flavorful with the use of Hemp Parm. The cashew-based spread mixed into the mashed potato adds richness. This dish has convinced former squash-haters to love the poor misunderstood vegetable, which says a lot.

> 2 large sweet potatoes (27 ounces, or 765 g), peeled and cubed
> 1½ tablespoons (12 g) Mushroom Broth Powder (page 218)
> 3 cups (705 ml) water
> 3 large squareneck yellow squashes (31 ounces, or 885 g)
> ½ cup (120 g) Cashew Coconut Spread (page 32) or
>   Cashew and Yogurt Spread (page 33)
> Scant ½ teaspoon fine sea salt, plus more for sprinkling
>   on squash
> Ground rainbow peppercorn, to taste
> 1 teaspoon onion powder
> 1 teaspoon chili powder
> 1 teaspoon fresh lime juice
> 2 cloves garlic, grated or pressed
> Nonstick cooking spray or oil spray
> ¼ cup (28 g) Hemp Parm (page 72), more if needed

Place the potato cubes and broth powder in a large pot, and cover with water. Bring to a boil, lower heat, and simmer until tender, about 20 minutes. Use a large slotted spoon to remove the potato cubes from the broth. Place them in a colander to drain. Do not discard the broth.

Add the whole yellow squashes to the broth. Bring back to a boil, lower heat, and simmer until tender enough to be pricked with a fork, yet still firm, about 8 minutes.

Mash the potatoes with the cashew spread, scant ½ teaspoon salt, ground peppercorn, onion powder, chili powder, lime juice, and garlic. Set aside. Preheat the oven to 375°F (190°C, or gas mark 5). Lightly coat a 9 x 13-inch (23 x 33 cm) baking pan with cooking spray.

Drain the squash, and cool slightly. Trim the stems, and cut the squashes in half lengthwise. Carefully remove and discard seeds with a small spoon. Place the shells upside down on paper towels to remove excess moisture.

Place the shells in the pan, and lightly sprinkle with salt. Fill each shell with a generous ½ cup (137 g) mashed sweet potato mixture. Sprinkle with Hemp Parm. Bake for 20 minutes, or until set and golden brown.

YIELD: 6 stuffed squash shells

How to Best Substitute for Eggs

COMPANIES SUCH AS HAMPTON CREEK are working hard to ensure that egg-free egg products including mayo, premade cookie dough, and even a commercial egg replacer that produces a spot-on scrambled egg are making their way into the hands of mainstream consumers. Their products are appearing on the shelves of discount markets (think dollar stores) and warehouse stores such as Costco. As we all wait for the mainstream demand to catch up with vegan demand, it is necessary to make our own substitutions at home.

THERE ARE SEVERAL REASONS TO AVOID USING EGGS IN THE KITCHEN. It's just so easy to replace them with plant-based sources that not only taste great, but offer a better nutritional profile than that of any egg. Indeed, plant-based foods are naturally free of cholesterol, whereas one large egg contains approximately 185 mg of cholesterol. Also comparatively, 100 g (3.5 ounces) of scrambled egg contains 13 g of protein, while the same weight of tempeh contains 19 g.

Remember, eggs, all neatly packaged up in a perfectly compact shell are "Nature's Perfect Food" . . . for chicken embryos. That's the whole point of eggs: A place for an unborn baby chick to live and grow and prepare itself for life in the real world outside of the mother hen's nest. We aren't quite sure whatever compelled us humans to steal these little packages of sustenance from the chickens, but it has led to the suffering of billions of them. Trapped in horrible conditions, hens are being forced to lay far more eggs than they would in the wild.

Chickens are naturally social animals who love to live in family groups, not cramped in warehouses, by the thousands . . . and these are the conditions in the cage-free facilities. It's far worse for the poor hens stuck in cages so small they can't even spread their wings or turn around, and even worse for the unfortunate chicks that happen to be born boys in the hatcheries, as male chicks are considered undesirable and summarily disposed of.

Although egg substitutes can accomplish a lot, it's undeniable that they, like virtually anything, present a few challenges and limitations. It is, for example, impossible to re-create absolutely every single delicate egg-based recipe that involves a lot of eggs. Most veganization attempts that go over 3 or 4 eggs get a little hairy. Egg whites are especially challenging—fluffy meringues and angel-food cakes are still elusive to the vegan chef. Nevertheless, it is far more important to realize that by living without just a few dishes, we are sparing the lives of these intelligent birds, while still being able to enjoy healthy, satisfying, and nourishing foods.

The Purpose of the Egg(s)

The main factor to look at when veganizing an egg recipe is the role of the egg. Is the egg used to add moisture or leavening? Or is it used to bind the recipe ingredients?

Here are a few clues to pay attention to when you plan on veganizing an egg-based recipe:

The overall liquid content (such as fruit juice, water, or milk) in the recipe is low, but leavening agents (such as baking soda, baking powder, or a combination of the two) are included. This indicates the egg is used mainly as a **moisturizing agent**.

The recipe doesn't contain leavening agents (such as baking soda, baking powder, or a combination of the two), but acidic ingredients (such as lemon juice, apple cider vinegar, or buttermilk) are included. There are usually two to three eggs in the recipe. This indicates the egg is used mainly as a **leavening agent**.

The recipe contains a fair amount of liquid (such as fruit juice, water, or milk), as well as leavening agents (such as baking soda, baking powder, or a combination of the two), unless these aren't needed (such as in patties or meatballs). The number of eggs is usually limited to one. This indicates that the egg is used mainly as a **binding agent**.

Eggs in Savory Dishes

As we mentioned, eggs play many roles in cooking. They bind foods such as veggie burgers, and moisten foods as in a fluffy quiche or frittata. In many cases, they are simply the star of the show, whether it be scrambled eggs in a breakfast burrito or hard-boiled eggs in a cobb salad.

Luckily, thanks to the enthusiastic research and recipe-developing habits of many vegan chefs, bakers, and cooks, eggs in all their various forms and uses are getting increasingly easier to replace in vegan-friendly recipes.

Tofu has always been a trusted stand-by, but it doesn't have to be your only option, especially if you are trying to cut down on your soy intake. You'll find that chickpea flour, combined with other ingredients of course, is a brilliant soy-free alternative that yields stunningly egglike results, especially when complemented with black salt (also known as *kala namak*), which imparts recipes with the type of pungent sulfuric scent and flavor eggs are (in)famous for.

With dishes such as scrambled eggs, quiches, frittatas, and omelets, where eggs are used in large amounts and are present in the forefront, taste- and texture-wise, quite a bit of tweaking is usually called for in order to straight-up veganize an existing recipe. But don't fret, you will still be able to partake! You can find vegan versions of such items (see chart on page 90) with flavors you can easily tweak to match the recipes you already know and love, and which you want to try cruelty-free style.

Thankfully, it's far simpler to work on veganizing foods such as burgers, meatballs, patties, pancakes, all of which use eggs mostly as a binding agent, and not in such an intimidating quantity. You will see in the chart that there are quite a lot of options to choose from to successfully re-create such savory foods.

Eggs in Baking and Sweets

While eggs used in baking and sweets applications are probably the trickiest to veganize, it is still possible to get entirely convincing (and tasty!) results with some knowledge and a little practice. The information in the following chart is here to help you keep the trial-and-error experience to a minimum.

With such a wide array of vegan egg substitutes, ranging from vegan yogurt, to flax eggs, chia eggs, and fruit or vegetable purées, it's also easy to find fat-free and soy-free options, while simultaneously turning your baked goods or sweets into cruelty-free works of art.

Two of the recommendations we feel are important to give ambitious, newbie, vegan bakers is first that for items such as macarons, puff pastry, and other similarly delicate confections, it is best to work from a tried-and-true, already-vegan recipe rather than attempt to veganize an existing nonvegan recipe.

Secondly, we also recommend playing around with easily made–vegan recipes (such as cookies), or already-vegan recipes before throwing yourself into veganizing the trickiest baking recipes, in order to get a feel for how vegan ingredients work. We're giving you good bases here, but practicing always helps when it comes to, well, pretty much all things in life, including vegan baking.

On the subject of desserts that contain eggs such as curds and custards, it's easiest to work with already-vegan recipes than it is to veganize them one item at a time. A whole slew of tried-and-true vegan recipes are available online and in our books (including this volume, on pages 62 and 144, to name a couple).

Most commonly, the eggs in such items are made obsolete with the use of vegan milks that are flavored and sweetened appropriately, either before or after being thoroughly combined with starches (such as cornstarch or arrowroot powder) or other thickeners (such as agar powder or flakes), and cooked until satisfyingly thickened. The typically richer and creamier outcome one looks for in such desserts can be obtained by using Homemade Creamer (page 26), or canned coconut milk or cream, instead of (or in addition to) lighter vegan milks, such as Almond Milk (page 27).

Blended silken tofu is also a great alternative to egg whites in flourless desserts (such as in our Chocolate Almond Soufflés, on page 152), provided soy can be consumed. Another noteworthy point is that all of these recipes can be used as a base, or starting point, and then easily tweaked to the desired flavor you're looking for.

So let's get cracking, shall we? Whether you want to make a quick substitute using store-bought products, or you plan on making your substitutes from scratch, the following chart will help you decide what sub will work best in the to-be-veganized recipe. **The boldface entries reference from-scratch recipes in this book.**

WHEN THE ORIGINAL RECIPE CALLS FOR . . .	REPLACE WITH . . .
IN SAVORY DISHES **1 egg**	• 1 flax egg: 1 tablespoon (7 g) freshly ground golden flaxseeds combined with 3 tablespoons (45 ml) water, whisked and left to stand for a few minutes, until thickened and viscous. *Purpose: binding agent, leavening agent if combined with ¼ teaspoon baking powder. Works best in: veggie burgers, meatloaf, meatballs, fritters, and patties. Less expensive than chia seeds; slightly nuttier outcome.* • 1 chia egg: 1 tablespoon (10 g) white chia seeds, ground to a meal in coffee grinder, combined with 3 tablespoons (45 ml) water, whisked and left to stand for a few minutes, until thickened and viscous. *Purpose: binding agent, thickening agent. Works best in: veggie burgers, meatloaf, meatballs, fritters, and patties, as well as dressings and sauces. Note that the seeds don't need to be ground for binding purposes, but they become less visible—an advantage in certain dishes.*

WHEN THE ORIGINAL RECIPE CALLS FOR . . .	REPLACE WITH . . .
(continued)	• 3 tablespoons (48 g) natural creamy or crunchy peanut butter, or other nut or seed butter (such as tahini, cashew, or almond), or **Cashew Coconut Spread (page 32)**, or **Cashew and Yogurt Spread (page 33)**. *Purpose: binding agent; moisturizing agent. Works best in: veggie burgers, meatloaf, meatballs, fritters, and patties.*
	• ¼ cup (60 g) blended soft silken tofu. *Purpose: binding agent, moisturizing agent. Works best in: dressings, sauces, and to give body and lift to veggie burgers, matzo balls, and potato pancakes. Note that this option can create heavier results, so adding ¼ to ½ teaspoon of baking powder (the quantity depends on how leavened the recipe needs to be) can be indicated if using as a leavening agent. Use caution: An excess of leavening can alter both consistency and flavor.*
	• ¼ cup (60 g) unsweetened plain vegan yogurt, store-bought or **homemade (page 28)**. *Purpose: binding agent, moisturizing agent. Works best in: dressings, sauces, and to give body and lift to veggie burgers, matzo balls, and potato pancakes. Note that this option can create heavier results, so adding ¼ to ½ teaspoon of baking powder (the quantity depends on how leavened the recipe needs to be) can be indicated if using as a leavening agent. Use caution: An excess of leavening can alter both consistency and flavor.*
	• 2 tablespoons (16 g) cornstarch, preferably organic (or potato starch or arrowroot powder) whisked with 2 tablespoons (30 ml) water. *Purpose: binding agent. Works best in: veggie burgers, meatloaf, meatballs, and potato pancakes.*
	• ¼ cup (60 g) puréed or mashed cooked vegetable (such as beans, sweet potato, regular potato). *Purpose: binding agent, moisturizing agent. Works best in: veggie burgers, meatloaf, meatballs, fritters, and patties. Note that this option can create heavier results, so adding ¼ to ½ teaspoon of baking powder (the quantity depends on how leavened the recipe needs to be) can be indicated if using as a leavening agent. Use caution: An excess of leavening can alter both consistency and flavor.*

WHEN THE ORIGINAL RECIPE CALLS FOR . . .	REPLACE WITH . . .
Egg Yolks	• **Hard-Boiled Egglike Crumbles (page 122)** • **Egg yolk from Shakshouka recipe (page 116)** • Commercial egg yolk replacer, such as The Vegg or Beyond Eggs
Egg Whites	• **Egg white from Shakshouka recipe (page 116)** • Plain tofu, cubed for egg-salad type use (page 122)
Scrambled eggs	• **Bánh Mi Scramble (page 124)** • **Chickpea Scramble (page 112)** • **Plain Scrambled Eggs (page 114)** • Commercial scrambled egg replacer, such as Beyond Eggs
Frittata or Quiche	• **Chives and Scallion Soy-Free'ttatas (page 108)** • **Hash Brown–Quiche Bites (page 110)**
French toast	• **Savory *Pain Perdu* (page 104)** • **Tapenade French Toast Sandwiches (page 130)**
Egg-in-a-Hole	• **(Vegan) Egg-in-a-Hole (page 111)**
Omelet	• **Tofu Omelet (page 102)** • **Scallion Kale Pudla (page 106)**
Mayonnaise	• **Silky Tofu Mayo (page 118)** • Store-bought vegan mayonnaise, such as Vegenaise or Just Mayo
IN BAKING AND SWEETS **1 egg**	• 1 flax egg: 1 tablespoon (7 g) freshly ground golden flaxseeds combined with 3 tablespoons (45 ml) water, whisked and left to stand for a few minutes, until thickened and viscous. *Purpose: binding agent, leavening agent if combined with ¼ teaspoon baking powder. Works best in: most baked goods, such as cookies, cakes, muffins, waffles, pancakes, and yeast breads; less expensive than chia seeds, slightly nuttier in outcome.* • 1 chia egg: 1 tablespoon (10 g) white chia seeds, ground to a meal in coffee grinder, combined with 3 tablespoons (45 ml) water, whisked and left to stand for a few minutes, until thickened and viscous. *Purpose: binding agent, leavening agent if combined with ¼ teaspoon baking powder. Works best in: most baked goods, such as cookies, cakes, muffins, waffles, pancakes, and yeast breads. Note that the seeds don't need to be ground for binding purposes, but they become less visible—an advantage in certain baked goods.*

WHEN THE ORIGINAL RECIPE CALLS FOR . . .	REPLACE WITH . . .
(continued)	• 3 tablespoons (48 g) natural creamy or crunchy peanut butter, or other nut or seed butter (such as tahini, cashew, or almond) *Purpose: binding agent, moisturizing agent. Works best in: cookies and muffins.* • ¼ cup (60 g) unsweetened plain vegan yogurt, store-bought or **homemade (page 28)**. *Purpose: binding agent, moisturizing agent. Works best in: cookies, cakes, muffins, waffles, pancakes, and yeast breads. Note that this option can create heavier results, so adding ¼ to ½ teaspoon of baking powder (the quantity depends on how leavened the recipe needs to be) can be indicated if using as a leavening agent. Use caution: An excess of leavening can alter both consistency and flavor.* • ¼ cup (60 g) thoroughly blended soft or firm silken tofu. *Purpose: binding agent, moisturizing agent. Works best in: cookies, cakes, muffins, waffles, pancakes, and yeast breads. Note that this option can create heavier results, so adding ¼ to ½ teaspoon of baking powder (the quantity depends on how leavened the recipe needs to be) can be indicated if using as a leavening agent. Use caution: An excess of leavening can alter both consistency and flavor.* • 2 tablespoons (16 g) cornstarch, preferably organic (or potato starch or arrowroot powder) whisked with 2 tablespoons (30 ml) water. *Purpose: binding agent. Works best in: cookies, cakes, muffins, waffles, and pancakes.* • ¼ cup (60 g) unsweetened applesauce or other puréed or mashed fruit (such as banana, pumpkin, or avocado.) *Purpose: binding agent, moisturizing agent. Works best in: most baked goods, such as soft cookies, cakes, muffins, waffles, pancakes, and anywhere the potential added flavor and color won't be an issue. Applesauce can make for cake-y cookies, so for chewy cookie results, this substitute isn't recommended. Note that this option can create heavier results, so adding ¼ to ½ teaspoon of baking powder [the quantity depends on how leavened the recipe needs to be] can be indicated if using as a leavening agent. Use caution: An excess of leavening can alter both consistency and flavor.*

How to Best Substitute for Eggs   93

WHEN THE ORIGINAL RECIPE CALLS FOR . . .	REPLACE WITH . . .
1 egg *(continued)*	• ¼ cup (60 ml) water plus 1½ teaspoons cornstarch, preferably organic. Dissolve cornstarch in 2 teaspoons (10 ml) of the water, whisk the rest of the water into this slurry, and cook until gelatinous and cloudy, about 30 seconds to 1 minute, see instructions on pages 135 and 136. *Purpose: gives excellent structure without adding flavor, binding agent, leavening agent. Works best in: fluffy baked goods such as brioche, cakes, and muffins. (To boost lift, adding ¼ to ½ teaspoon of baking powder [the quantity depends on how leavened the recipe needs to be] can be indicated if using as a leavening agent. Use caution: An excess of leavening can alter both consistency and flavor.)*
	• 1 teaspoon psyllium seed husk (look for *whole psyllium husks*, not the powder, and not the whole seed; available at health food stores) combined with 3 tablespoons (45 ml) water, left to stand 3 minutes. Use promptly as it continues to thicken if left to stand. *Purpose: binding agent. Works best in: cookies, crackers, and waffles.*
	• ¼ cup (30 g) chickpea flour combined with ¼ cup (60 ml) water or vegan milk of choice. *Purpose: binding agent, moisturizing agent. Works best in: cookies, clafoutis, and cakes. Do not taste the preparation before baking or cooking, because chickpea flour doesn't taste good raw.*
	• 1½ teaspoons Ener-G or Bob's Red Mill egg replacer powder whisked with 2 tablespoons (30 ml) warm water, until frothy. *Purpose: binding agent, leavening agent. Works best in: cookies, but can make for chalky baked goods. Not our first choice, but works in a bind.*
	• 1 tablespoon (7 g) Neat Egg mix mixed into 2 tablespoons (30 ml) water. *Purpose: binding agent. Works best in: cookies, pancakes.*
1 egg yolk	• Commercial egg yolk replacer, such as The Vegg or Beyond Eggs. Note that not all of these products claim to replace the functional properties of eggs in baking applications. Always check the brand before purchase and use, for up-to-date information.

WHEN THE ORIGINAL RECIPE CALLS FOR . . .	REPLACE WITH . . .
1 egg white	• ¼ teaspoon xanthan gum whisked with ¼ cup (60 ml) water, let stand 5 minutes, whip until frothy. *Purpose: binding agent, leavening agent. Works best in: cookies, cakes, and muffins. This works well for 1 to 2 egg whites, but it isn't recommended to use to veganize an egg white–heavy recipe (such as macarons) and expect good results.*
	• 1½ teaspoons Ener-G or Bob's Red Mill egg replacer powder whisked with 2 tablespoons (30 ml) warm water, until frothy. *Purpose: binding agent, leavening agent. Works best in: cookies, but can make for chalky baked goods. Not our first choice, but works in a bind.*
	• ¼ cup (60 ml) water plus 1½ teaspoons cornstarch, preferably organic. Dissolve cornstarch in 2 teaspoons (10 ml) of the water, whisk the rest of the water into this slurry, and cook until gelatinous and cloudy, about 30 seconds to 1 minute, see instructions on pages 135 and 136. *Purpose: gives excellent structure without adding flavor, binding agent, leavening agent. Works best in: fluffy baked goods such as brioche, cakes, and muffins. (To boost lift, adding ¼ to ½ teaspoon of baking powder [the quantity depends on how leavened the recipe needs to be] can be indicated if using as a leavening agent. Use caution: An excess of leavening can alter both consistency and flavor.)*

CHAPTER 3
Eggs Substitutions in Savory Dishes

Tofu-based scrambles, quiches, and frittatas are all great options when it comes to making savory egglike dishes in an egg-free manner. Recipes for such things are available all over the Internet, and even in many of the books we wrote. But it was time to delve a little deeper in this volume, so we've included a lot of recipes for what we consider (and hope you will too) to be pretty clever tricks for partaking in jiggly vegan egg yolks, a completely soy-free frittata, chickpea scramble, and even a recipe for the diner classic known as the Egg-in-a-Hole!

Like mad scientists in a laboratory (maniacal laugh included), the two of us had our food scales, grinders, blenders, and other kitchen gadgets working hard to come up with new and interesting ways to replicate eggs. Our aim was to create egg substitutions not solely for their function in recipes, but to make our dishes look and taste just like their animal-based counterparts.

The recipes that follow continue to prove that as time passes there are fewer and fewer limitations to what can be accomplished in the cruelty-free cooking realm. You really can feel no deprivation and still have fun with your food after making the decision to follow a vegan lifestyle.

Practice Makes for Perfect Substitutions

The best way to demonstrate how easy it is to transform a nonvegan recipe into a cruelty-free wonder is to showcase how it's done. Let's go through a sample recipe step by step! Once you know the basics, it's easy to put into practice on any recipe.

< *Scallion Kale Pudla, page 106*

CREAMY DEVILED EGGS

This recipe is an excerpt from *Back to Butter*, by Molly Chester and Sandy Schrecengost (Fair Winds Press, 2014). We will substitute vegan ingredients for the hardboiled eggs, mayonnaise, cream cheese, and honey, and rewrite the directions accordingly.

8 eggs
3 tablespoons (42 g) mayonnaise
1 tablespoon (15 g) cream cheese
2 tablespoons (30 g) pickle relish
⅛ teaspoon sea salt
⅛ teaspoon white pepper
1 teaspoon mild Dijon mustard
2 teaspoons (2 g) chopped fresh chives
1 teaspoon honey
Paprika, for garnish

Place the eggs in a medium-size pot and add enough water to cover by 2 inches (5 cm). Cover the pot and bring to a boil over high heat. Once boiling, remove the lid and boil for 10 minutes. If necessary, lower the heat to medium-high to keep the water from spilling over. After 10 minutes, turn off the heat and drain. Allow the eggs to cool to the touch before peeling.

Meanwhile, in a small-size bowl, combine the mayonnaise, cream cheese, relish, sea salt, pepper, mustard, chives, and honey. Whisk to combine.

Once the eggs are cooled, peel and cut in half lengthwise. Carefully remove the yolk of each egg half and place in a small-size flat-bottomed bowl. Mash the yolks well with a potato masher. Add the mayonnaise mixture to the mashed yolks. Stir well with a spoon to combine. Taste, adding additional sea salt as desired.

Using a teaspoon, carefully fill the cavity of each egg with the yolk mixture. Gently sprinkle the top of each with a dash of paprika. Cover and refrigerate for several hours or overnight before serving.

YIELD: 8 servings

CREAMY DEVILED EGGS

Veganized!

V

We have four items to substitute for in this recipe: hardboiled eggs, mayonnaise, cream cheese, and honey. We picked tofu to mimic the hardboiled eggs; it involves very little work for the white part of the "egg." We used a combination of ingredients (such as black salt and turmeric) for the egg yolk. Mayonnaise, cream cheese, and honey all are easy to substitute with their straightforward vegan counterparts.

1 block (12 ounces, or 340 g) extra-firm or super firm tofu, divided ⎤
¼ teaspoon black salt (kala namak) ⎬─(egg substitute)
¼ teaspoon turmeric ⎦

3 tablespoons (42 g) Silky Tofu Mayo (page 118) or store-bought vegan mayonnaise ⎤─(mayonnaise substitute)

1 tablespoon (14 g) plain Chia Seed Cream Cheese (page 76) or Cashew and Yogurt Spread (page 33) or store-bought vegan cream cheese ⎤─(cream cheese substitute)

2 tablespoons (30 g) pickle relish
⅛ teaspoon sea salt
⅛ teaspoon white pepper
1 teaspoon mild Dijon mustard
2 teaspoons (2 g) chopped fresh chives
1 teaspoon agave nectar ⎤─(honey substitute)
Paprika, for garnish

Cut the block of tofu into 8 equal-size blocks. Cut each block in half, for a total of 16 pieces. Using a spoon, scoop out a shallow hole in the center of 8 of the pieces. **This is your cooked egg white substitute.**

Add the remaining 8 pieces and the scooped-out centers to a food processor or blender and pulse until the tofu resembles ricotta or cottage cheese. Transfer to a mixing bowl.

In a separate small bowl, mix together the vegan mayonnaise **(this is your mayonnaise substitute)**, vegan cream cheese **(this is your cream cheese substitute)**, relish, black salt, turmeric, sea salt, pepper, mustard, chives, and agave **(this is your honey substitute)**. Add to the crumbled tofu and use your hands to mash to combine. **This is your egg yolk filling substitute.** Add additional sea salt as desired.

Using a teaspoon, carefully fill the cavities of the remaining tofu blocks with crumbled tofu mixture. If you like to get extra fancy, you can pipe the filling in using a large star tip.

Gently sprinkle the top of each with a dash of paprika. Cover and refrigerate for several hours or overnight before serving.

YIELD: 8 servings

RED POTATO BREAKFAST SCRAMBLE

* Soy-Free   * Gluten-Free Potential   * No Added Sugar

No need for tofu in this breakfast scramble. It makes a wonderful breakfast side, but also makes a terrific breakfast burrito when layered in with some Veggie Bacon (page 207), plain Sour Cream (page 30), and avocado.

1½ pounds (681 g) red potatoes
1 cup (160 g) rice flour
2 tablespoons (15 g) nutritional yeast
½ teaspoon paprika
½ teaspoon turmeric
½ teaspoon black salt (kala namak)
¼ cup (60 ml) neutral-flavored oil
1 red or green bell pepper, seeded and chopped
½ of a medium yellow onion, roughly chopped
1 tablespoon (9 g) minced garlic
Salt and pepper, to taste

Wash and cut the potatoes into small cubes. Soak the potatoes in cool water for 10 to 15 minutes, then rinse in cool clean water. Drain excess water.

Add rice flour, nutritional yeast, paprika, turmeric, and black salt to a resealable plastic bag. Add potato cubes to the the bag and shake to coat.

Heat oil in a large cast iron skillet or pan over medium-high heat. Add coated potatoes and fry for 8 to 10 minutes. Flip to ensure all sides of the potatoes get cooked evenly. Continue to cook an additional 8 to 10 minutes. Add the bell peppers, onions, garlic, salt and pepper, and finish cooking for a final 5 to 7 minutes, or until peppers and onions are translucent, and potatoes are fork tender.

YIELD: 4 servings

BREAKFAST STROMBOLI

What's better than pizza for breakfast? A Breakfast Stromboli. This recipe will give you the basics. Once you get the technique down, you'll be making everything into a Stromboli. Even dessert!

1 recipe *Fantastica* Pizza and Stromboli Dough (page 187)
½ cup (130 g) Savory Cashew Sauce (page 34)
1 recipe Plain Scrambled Eggs (page 114)
½ medium red onion, julienne cut
1 red or green bell pepper, seeded and diced
1 cup (102 g) Bacon Bits (page 210)
Extra-virgin olive oil, for brushing
¼ teaspoon garlic powder
⅛ teaspoon paprika
Salt and pepper, to taste

Preheat the oven to 450°F (230°C, or gas mark 8).

Roll the dough into an oval that fits onto a rimmed baking sheet, lined with parchment or a reusable silicon baking mat.

Using a pizza cutter (or a sharp knife) cut 10 equal slits in both sides of the dough, leaving plenty of intact space in the center for your fillings.

Layer the fillings in the following order: Spread the cashew sauce all over the center of the uncut portion of the dough. Top with an even layer of Scrambled Eggs, layer in the onions and peppers, then sprinkle on an even layer of Bacon Bits.

Braid the bread. It really is so easy, but looks so extravagant when it's all done. To do this, start at one end and fold up the rounded edge. Then start braiding. Kind of like lacing your shoes, take one slit, and bring it to the center, then one on the opposite side, then repeat, finally tucking in the other end.

Brush the entire top with olive oil, and sprinkle the top with garlic powder, paprika, salt, and pepper. Bake for 15 to 18 minutes, or until golden brown. Let it sit for a few minutes before slicing into it.

YIELD: 8 slices

TOFU OMELET

* Gluten-Free Potential * No Added Sugar * Nut-Free * Quick and Easy

There are many recipes out there for tofu omelets. Shoot, we even have one in the original *Complete Guide to Vegan Food Substitutions*. But this one . . . you guys . . . this one is flexible and versatile! The recipe here is just for the omelet. You can fill it with your own choice of toppings.

12 ounces (340 g) soft silken tofu
1¼ cups (295 ml) water
2 tablespoons (30 ml) neutral-flavored oil
¼ cup (30 g) nutritional yeast
½ teaspoon onion powder
½ teaspoon garlic powder

½ teaspoon black salt (kala namak)
¼ teaspoon turmeric
½ ounce (14 g) agar flakes or powder
Additional oil, as needed, for frying
Salt and pepper, to taste

Add all the ingredients, except additional oil, salt, and pepper, to a blender and blend until smooth. Preheat a small amount of oil, just enough to coat the bottom of a small (8-inch, or 20 cm) cast iron skillet or nonstick frying pan, over medium heat.

Carefully pour one-quarter of the omelet mixture into the pan and cook for a full 5 minutes. It will bubble a bit. Remove from heat and carefully slide onto a glass or ceramic plate. Place desired toppings on top. Allow to cool for a few minutes to fully set, before folding in half. Sprinkle with salt and pepper to taste. Repeat.

YIELD: Four 8-inch (20 cm) omelets

POTATO AND BLACK BEAN BREAKFAST TACOS

* Gluten-Free Potential   * No Added Oil   * Nut-Free   * Soy-Free

Everyone loves tacos! Why not enjoy tacos for breakfast, the way they do in Austin, Texas? Seriously! Austin-ites take their breakfast tacos very seriously. Traditionally made with scrambled eggs, hash browns, bacon or sausage, and topped with salsa. Even the vegan versions were made with the usual suspects: tofu scramble and veggie bacon. This version throws tradition (Are breakfast tacos even a tradition?) out the window and loses the eggs altogether. To keep this meal oil-free, simply top with salsa or a sliced avocado. If you don't mind a little added fat, try drizzling the Special Sauce from the Dinner Plate Bowl (page 128) all over the top.

2 cups (470 ml) vegetable broth
1½ pounds (681 g) red potatoes with skin on, cubed
1 can (15 ounces, or 425 g) black beans, drained and rinsed
½ cup (80 g) finely diced yellow onion
1 Roma tomato, seeded and diced
1 chile pepper, such as Anaheim, pasilla, Hatch, or even jalapeño pepper, seeded and diced
1 tablespoon (9 g) minced garlic
½ teaspoon dried oregano
½ teaspoon paprika
¼ teaspoon red chili flakes
¼ teaspoon ground coriander
¼ teaspoon cumin
¼ teaspoon chipotle powder
Salt and pepper, to taste
12 (6-inch, or 15 cm) corn tortillas
2 stalks scallion, finely chopped
¼ cup (4 g) fresh cilantro, finely chopped

In a large frying pan, bring the vegetable broth to a boil. Carefully add the potatoes and simmer potatoes for 18 to 20 minutes, or until potatoes are tender and almost all of the broth has been absorbed.

While the potatoes are simmering, add the remaining ingredients through the salt and pepper to a mixing bowl. Toss to coat. Once the potatoes are ready, stir in the bean mixture. Cook over medium heat until completely warmed through and onions are translucent. About 5 to 7 minutes, tossing often.

Warm your tortillas. We like to do this in a dry pan over medium-high heat. Heat tortillas until lightly browned on each side, about 30 seconds per side. Scoop the mixture into the tortilla and garnish with scallions and cilantro.

YIELD: 12 tacos

SAVORY PAIN PERDU

* No Added Sugar * Quick and Easy

We're putting fantastic chickpea flour in the spotlight here again. Not only is it rich in protein, fiber, and completely free of soy, it also contributes a nice, eggy flavor to dishes. As a kid, Celine used to eat savory *pain perdu* ("lost bread," known in America as a version of French toast) with a lightly dressed mix of greens and tomato salad.

> **1 cup (235 ml) plain Almond Milk (page 27) or other unsweetened plain vegan milk, at room temperature so that the coconut oil doesn't seize**
> **1 tablespoon (15 ml) white balsamic vinegar**
> **1 tablespoon (15 ml) melted coconut oil**
> **1 large clove garlic, grated or pressed, optional**
> **¾ cup (90 g) chickpea flour**
> **¼ teaspoon baking soda**
> **⅜ teaspoon black salt (kala namak)**
> **¼ teaspoon fine sea salt, to taste**
> **2 tablespoons (15 g) nutritional yeast**
> **1 tablespoon (15 g) maca powder**
> **8 to 10 slices of any stale vegan bread, size will vary and so will yield**
> **Nonstick cooking spray or oil spray**

Combine the milk, vinegar, oil, and garlic in a bowl. Add flour, baking soda, salts, nutritional yeast, and maca powder on top. Whisk to thoroughly combine. Let stand 5 minutes.

Heat a large nonstick pan on medium-high heat. Lower heat to medium. Lightly coat the pan with cooking spray or oil spray once hot, away from the heat. Dip each slice of bread into the batter, letting some of the excess drip back down in the bowl. Cook 2 slices of bread at a time until golden brown, about 3 to 4 minutes on each side. Repeat with remaining slices, or until you run out of bread or batter. Lightly coat the pan with cooking spray between each batch. Serve immediately, or keep warm in an oven preheated to 325°F (170°C, or gas mark 3).

YIELD: 8 to 10 slices

Celine Says

"Remember: Don't taste the batter before it is cooked, because chickpea flour doesn't have a pleasant taste when eaten raw."

SCALLION KALE PUDLA

* Gluten-Free Potential   * No Added Sugar   * Quick and Easy

We were giving ourselves high-fives the first time we "created" what we later found out is quite a common dish in India. Pudla is an easy-to-make, chickpea-based, omelet-like dish that we love to pack with as much flavor as possible. Our favorite way to serve these pancake look-alikes is with an assortment of lightly-dressed, refreshing salads: shredded carrots, thinly sliced cucumber, or even more kale all partner up wonderfully with pudla. Once you taste these and find yourself besotted too, you must try our Sweet Date Pudla (page 139).

- **1 cup (235 ml) plain Almond Milk (page 27) or other unsweetened plain vegan milk, more if needed**
- **2 tablespoons (30 ml) seasoned rice vinegar**
- **¾ cup (90 g) chickpea flour**
- **2 tablespoons (15 g) nutritional yeast**
- **¼ teaspoon baking soda**
- **Scant ¼ teaspoon fine sea salt**
- **1 tablespoon (15 ml) tamari (use certified gluten-free, if needed)**
- **1 tablespoon (15 ml) toasted sesame oil**
- **1 tablespoon (15 ml) sriracha**
- **⅓ cup (30 g) chopped scallion**
- **½ cup (30 g) packed minced kale leaves**
- **2 large cloves garlic, grated or pressed**
- **Nonstick cooking spray or oil spray**

Combine the milk and vinegar in a medium bowl. Let stand for 2 minutes to let the milk curdle. This is your "buttermilk." (We're using more vinegar than in other buttermilk substitutes here. We want the extra acidity in this particular recipe.)

Whisk together the flour, nutritional yeast, baking soda, and salt in a large bowl. Add tamari, oil, sriracha, scallions, kale, and garlic to the buttermilk. Stir the wet ingredients into the dry until well combined, but do not overmix. Let stand 5 minutes.

Heat a large nonstick pan on medium-high heat. Lower heat to medium. Lightly coat the pan with cooking spray or oil spray once hot, away from the heat. Add a scant ½ cup (117 ml) of batter to the skillet. The batter should spread itself to an approximately 5-inch (13 cm) circle. Let cook for about 4 minutes, until the center bubbles and looks not too dry but not too moist either. Carefully lift the edges of the pudla to make sure it is light golden brown, which is another sign it is ready to flip. Carefully flip with a spatula, and let cook for another 4 minutes, or until golden brown. Lightly coat the pan again each time before cooking the remaining 3 pudla. Serve immediately.

YIELD: 2 to 4 servings

SAUSAGE AND EGG BREAKFAST SANDWICH

* Nut-Free

Think Sausage McMuffin, but without sausage or the Mc. This homemade version of a fast-food favorite is sure to make you feel much better about indulging. If you have the components made up ahead of time, you can throw one together in no time!

4 vegan English muffins, sliced
2 tablespoons (28 g) Vegan Butter (page 24), optional
4 slices 'Merican Cheese (page 70)
4 prepared Sausage Breakfast Patties (page 164), heated
1 recipe Plain Scrambled Eggs (page 114), heated

Toast the English muffins and spread with Vegan Butter, if using. On each muffin, sandwich 1 slice of cheese, 1 sausage patty, and a generous scoop of Plain Scrambled Eggs.

YIELD: 4 sandwiches

Joni Says

"Don't be afraid to let loose! Why not serve this sammie up on sourdough toast with tomato, avocado, and some greens thrown in for good measure?"

CHIVES AND SCALLION SOY-FREE'TTATAS

* No Added Sugar   * Soy-Free

When *The Complete Guide to Vegan Food Substitutions* came out, we received requests for dishes containing less or no soy. Challenge accepted! Here's a vegan frittata, usually heavy on tofu, that is rich and soy-free. You can increase the fiber content and add up to 1 cup (weight will vary) of chopped, lightly steamed veggies to the batter.

Nonstick cooking spray (make sure it contains no soy lecithin) or oil spray

1 recipe Ranch-y Dipping Sauce (page 31), made with Cashew Coconut Spread (page 32)

½ cup (120 ml) plain Almond Milk (page 27) or other unsweetened plain vegan milk (not soymilk, if you want to keep it soy-free)

3 tablespoons (9 g) minced fresh chives

⅓ cup (30 g) minced scallion

2 tablespoons (15 g) nutritional yeast

1 tablespoon (15 g) mild Dijon mustard

3 cloves garlic, grated or pressed

1 teaspoon Mushroom Broth Powder (page 218)

½ teaspoon fine sea salt

½ teaspoon onion powder

¼ teaspoon turmeric

¼ teaspoon ground rainbow, white, or black peppercorn, to taste

1 cup (235 ml) water

¾ cup (90 g) chickpea flour or garbanzo fava bean flour

2 tablespoons (16 g) cornstarch (preferably organic)

¼ teaspoon baking powder

Preheat the oven to 400°F (200°C, or gas mark 6). Lightly coat two prepared jumbo muffin pans (or 12 3-inch [7.6 cm] standard pans) with cooking spray.

In a large bowl, whisk to combine the dipping sauce, milk, chives, scallion, nutritional yeast, mustard, garlic, broth powder, salt, onion powder, turmeric, and ground pepper. Add the water, whisk to combine. Add flour, cornstarch, and baking powder, whisk to thoroughly combine, making sure no clumps are left. Set aside for 15 minutes.

Add ¼ cup (60 ml) of batter per cup in prepared pans. Bake for 30 minutes, or until golden brown on top, set, and the edges pull away from the pan. Let stand in the pan for 15 minutes before carefully removing and serving.

YIELD: 12 mini free'ttatas

HASH BROWN–QUICHE BITES

* Gluten-Free Potential   * No Added Sugar   * Nut-Free

We're suckers for things made in cupcake tins. This recipe makes for a fun breakfast to serve when you have company or are having a brunch. You can (read: *should*) bake the potatoes ahead of time, so preparation of the quiche bites is much quicker the morning of.

FOR THE HASH BROWN CRUST:
- **4 to 6 medium-size russet potatoes**
- **Salt and pepper, to taste**
- **Nonstick cooking spray**

FOR THE QUICHE:
- **12 ounces (340 g) extra-firm tofu, drained and pressed**
- **1 teaspoon onion powder**
- **1 teaspoon garlic powder**
- **¼ teaspoon turmeric**
- **1 tablespoon (15 g) yellow prepared mustard**
- **¼ cup (30 g) nutritional yeast**
- **¼ cup (30 g) chickpea flour**
- **¼ cup (60 ml) neutral-flavored oil**
- **½ teaspoon black salt (kala namak)**
- **1 green or red bell pepper, seeded and finely diced**
- **½ cup (80 g) diced red onion**
- **½ cup (51 g) Bacon Bits (page 210)**
- **¼ cup (25 g) diced scallion, for garnish**

To make the hash brown crust: Preheat the oven to 400°F (200°C, or gas mark 6). Prick the potatoes with a fork to allow steam to escape. Place unpeeled potatoes on a baking sheet and bake until almost tender. You don't need them to be soft and ready to eat, you want them to still be firm. This should take about 45 minutes to 1 hour. Allow potatoes to cool completely.

Carefully peel the cooled potatoes and grate them using a hand grater. You will need about 3 cups (600 to 700 g), weights will vary based on the mositure content of your potatoes. Add salt and pepper to taste, and mix to combine. Set aside. Coat a standard cupcake tin liberally with cooking spray. Divide the grated potatoes evenly into each hole. Using your fingers, press the potatoes to form a crust, approximately ¼-inch (6 mm) thick. Bake for 15 minutes, or until light golden brown. Remove from oven.

To make the quiche mix: While the hash brown crusts are baking, in a mixing bowl, crumble the tofu and add all of the other quiche ingredients up to the bell pepper, and mash it together using your hands. Mix until well incorporated. Fold in the bell pepper, red onion, and Bacon Bits.

Carefully spoon an equal amount of quiche mix into each hash brown crust, return to the oven, and bake for an additional 15 to 20 minutes. Take them out of the oven when the quiche tops begin to brown, and the crusts are dark golden brown.

Top with scallions before serving.

YIELD: 12 pieces

EGG-IN-A-HOLE

* Nut-Free

Not sure who the crafty cook was who invented this dish, but it is quite cute. And vegans love cute—just look at the ridiculous amount of cat photos we post to our Facebook pages! So, why shouldn't we be able to have a vegan version of Egg-in-a-Hole? Now we can.

8 slices of vegan bread of choice
1 recipe egg yolks mixture from Shakshouka (page 116)
1 recipe egg whites mixture from Shakshouka (page 116)
½ cup (120 ml) water
3 grams (0.1 ounce) agar flakes or powder (about 1 tablespoon flakes, or 1 teaspoon powder)
Vegan Butter (page 24) or Bacon Grease (page 211) as needed for frying
Salt and pepper, to taste

Remove a hole in the center of each piece of bread using a pint glass or a round cookie cutter. Discard the cut-out piece, or toast with the bread and serve alongside to use for dipping.

Prepare the yolks and whites according to recipe instructions and have them ready.

Place water in a small pot and add agar. Stir to dissolve. Bring to a boil, reduce to a simmer and simmer for 5 full minutes, stirring regularly. Carefully stir in the egg white mixture and reduce heat to low. Keep warm until ready to use.

Heat a nonstick frying pan, or cast iron skillet over medium-high heat. Melt enough Vegan Butter or Bacon Grease in the bottom of the pan to coat. Add 2 slices of bread and toast on one side. Flip over.

Carefully pour about ¼ cup (60 ml) of the egg white mixture into the center of the toast. Cook for about 1 minute, then carefully add a dollop (about 1 tablespoon, or 15 ml) of the egg yolk mixture to the center of the whites and continue to cook for another minute.

Sprinkle with salt and pepper to taste.

Using a spatula or turner, very carefully transfer the Egg-in-a-Hole to a glass or ceramic plate, one at a time.

Allow to cool for a few minutes before serving to give the "egg" a chance to set. You can certainly eat it straight away, but it will be a bit runny.

YIELD: 4 servings (2 pieces per serving)

CHICKPEA SCRAMBLE

* Gluten-Free Potential * Nut-Free * Quick and Easy * Soy-Free

Sure, tofu scrambles are awesome, but sometimes you just want something different. And this chickpea scramble delivers just as much breakfast flavor as any other. For fun, sometimes we like to wrap this up in a soft tortilla for a quick-and-easy breakfast burrito.

1 can (15 ounces, or 425 g) chickpeas, drained and rinsed
1 cup (160 g) finely diced white onion
1 teaspoon minced garlic
½ teaspoon turmeric
¼ teaspoon black pepper
¼ teaspoon paprika
2 tablespoons (30 ml) neutral-flavored oil
¼ teaspoon black salt (kala namak)
2 cups (60 g) baby spinach leaves
2 stalks scallion, finely chopped
Salt, to taste

In a medium bowl, toss together the chickpeas, onion, garlic, turmeric, black pepper, and paprika until well combined.

Preheat oil in a frying pan or cast iron skillet over medium-high heat.

Add the chickpea mixture to the pan and sauté for 5 to 7 minutes, tossing often, until onions are soft and tender. Add black salt and toss to combine. Remove from heat.

Stir in baby spinach. The heat of the chickpeas will wilt the spinach.

Garnish with scallions. Add salt to taste.

YIELD: 2 main-dish or 4 side-dish servings

 Joni Says

"Oil-free option: Substitute vegetable broth for the oil. You can substitute kale, chard, arugula, or any of your favorite greens for the baby spinach in this recipe."

CREAMY CILANTRO COLESLAW

* Gluten-Free Potential * Nut-Free * Quick and Easy

This coleslaw is the classic deli variety with a little added cilantro for good measure.

½ cup (112 g) vegan mayonnaise, store-bought or homemade (page 118)

1 tablespoon (15 ml) lemon juice

1 teaspoon agave nectar

1 tablespoon (3.5 g) fresh chopped dill, or 1 teaspoon dried dill

3 cups (7 ounces, or 199 g) finely shredded green cabbage

¼ cup (27 g) shredded carrots

¼ cup (25 g) finely chopped scallion

¼ cup (4 g) chopped cilantro

Salt and pepper, to taste

In a medium bowl, whisk together the mayonnaise, lemon juice, agave, and dill.

Add the cabbage, carrots, scallion, and cilantro. Toss to coat. Add salt and pepper to taste. Chill before serving.

YIELD: 2 cups (12 ounces, or 340 g)

PLAIN SCRAMBLED EGGS

* Gluten-Free Potential * No Added Sugar * Nut-Free * Quick and Easy

The recipe is simple and straightforward. It is a base recipe that can take any amount of additions. In fact, they taste pretty darned tasty, fried up in some Bacon Grease (page 211). So have fun with it! Use it in a breakfast burrito, as an addition to Fried Rice with Scrambled Eggs (page 115), or anywhere else scrambled eggs are called for.

½ cup (120 ml) water

2 tablespoons (15 g) nutritional yeast

2 tablespoons (16 g) cornstarch (preferably organic)

¼ teaspoon black salt (kala namak)

¼ teaspoon turmeric

2 tablespoons (30 ml) neutral-flavored oil

1 block (12 ounces, or 340 g) firm or extra-firm tofu, drained and pressed

Salt and pepper, to taste

Using an immersion blender (or a very fast wrist and a whisk) blend together the water, nutritional yeast, cornstarch, black salt, and turmeric. Set aside.

Preheat oil over medium-high heat in a frying pan. Crumble the tofu and add to the hot oil and sauté for 2 to 3 minutes, tossing constantly. Slowly stir in the cornstarch mixture and continue to stir until thickened, about 3 to 5 minutes, until desired consistency is reached. Add salt and pepper to taste. Serve immediately.

YIELD: 4 servings

FRIED RICE WITH SCRAMBLED EGGS

* Gluten-Free Potential   * No Added Sugar   * Nut-Free

Perfect for a Chinese-style take-out meal at home, make it even easier by making the rice and the Scrambled Eggs the day before. We think the texture of the rice is even better when you do it this way.

2 tablespoons (30 ml) neutral-flavored oil

8 ounces (1 cup, or 227 g) daikon radish, diced

1 large green chile, such as Anaheim, Hatch, or pasilla, seeded and diced

8 ounces (1 cup, or 227 g) carrots, diced

4 cloves garlic, thinly sliced

1 cup (134 g) green peas (fresh, frozen, or canned)

2 cups (316 g) cooked long grain white or (390 g) brown rice, chilled overnight

2 tablespoons (30 ml) tamari (use certified gluten-free)

1 recipe Plain Scrambled Eggs (page 114)

2 tablespoons (30 ml) sesame oil

1 cup (100 g) chopped scallions

Salt and pepper, to taste

Heat oil in a wok or a very large frying pan, over medium-high heat.

Add the daikon, chile, and carrots to oil and sauté for 3 minutes. Add the garlic and peas and cook for 3 more minutes, stirring regularly. Add the rice and tamari and toss to combine. Continue cooking until the rice is warmed all the way through.

Add the Plain Scrambled Eggs and sesame oil. Toss to combine and continue to cook until heated completely through. Remove from heat and mix in scallions. Add salt and pepper to taste.

YIELD: 4 main-dish or 8 side-dish servings

Joni Says

"Not a fan of daikon? Substitute onion, celery, water chestnuts, or any other crunchy vegetable in its place."

SHAKSHOUKA

* Gluten-Free Potential   * No Added Sugar   * Nut-Free

Shakshouka is a traditional dish of tomatoes and eggs, similar to a ragout. Tunisia, Libya, Algeria, Morocco, Egypt, and Israel all have their own spin on the dish. Some regions add beans, some add olives, some add potatoes. It should be served with bread to mop up the sauce and runny soft poached "eggs."

FOR THE EGG WHITES:

- 1 box (12 ounces, or 340 g) soft silken tofu
- 3 tablespoons (45 ml) neutral-flavored oil
- 2 tablespoons (16 g) cornstarch (preferably organic)
- ½ teaspoon salt
- ¼ teaspoon onion powder
- ¼ teaspoon garlic powder

FOR THE EGG YOLKS:

- 2 tablespoons (15 g) nutritional yeast
- 1½ teaspoons cornstarch (preferably organic)
- ½ teaspoon xanthan gum
- ¼ teaspoon black salt (kala namak)
- ¼ teaspoon turmeric
- ½ cup (120 ml) water

FOR THE SHAKSHOUKA:

- 3 tablespoons (45 ml) neutral-flavored oil
- 1 cup (160 g) diced yellow onion
- 2 tablespoons (17 g) minced garlic
- 1 pound (454 g) russet potatoes, cubed and rinsed in cool water
- 1 green chile, such as Anaheim, pasilla, or Hatch, seeded and diced
- 1 teaspoon ground cumin
- 2 cups (488 g) tomato sauce
- 1 cup (252 g) diced tomatoes
- 1 cup (150 g) chopped artichoke hearts
- ¼ cup (4 g) chopped cilantro (or parsley for you cilantro haters)
- Salt and pepper, to taste

To make the egg white mixture: Blend all the ingredients together until smooth, and set aside.

To make the egg yolks: Place all the ingredients, except water, in a spice grinder or coffee grinder, and grind into a fine powder. Place the powder in water and blend with an immersion blender until thickened and jiggly. Set aside.

To make the Shakshouka: In a large pan with a lid, heat oil over medium-high heat. Add the onions and sauté 5 to 7 minutes, until translucent and fragrant. Add garlic and continue to cook for 2 to 3 more minutes. Add the potatoes, pepper, and cumin. Continue to cook for 5 more minutes, until potatoes are browned.

Stir in the tomato sauce, diced tomatoes, and artichoke hearts. Simmer for 10 minutes, uncovered, stirring occasionally. Make an indentation in one-quarter of the mixture and pour in one-quarter of the egg white mixture. Repeat 3 more times with the remaining mixture.

Add one-quarter of the yolk mixture to the center of each white. Reduce to medium-low heat, cover and simmer for 20 minutes. Remove from heat, and allow to sit for 10 minutes before serving. Garnish with cilantro, salt, and pepper and serve.

YIELD: 4 main-dish servings

 Joni Says

"Keep in mind this dish is loose, not solid. It's like a very thick soup or ragout, and even the 'eggs' stay soft, so take care when serving. I found that a spatula works well. I use the edge of the spatula to divide the pan into four and then carefully scoop each serving out."

SILKY TOFU MAYO

* Gluten-Free Potential * Nut-Free * Quick and Easy

This easy recipe makes the perfect mayo to keep on hand to use in salad dressings, as a sandwich spread, or as an ingredient in many of the recipes right in this book. We find the texture is much lighter and more whipped when we use our immersion blender than when we use a tabletop blender.

> **1 block (12 ounces, or 340 g) soft silken tofu**
> **½ cup (120 ml) grapeseed or other neutral-flavored oil**
> **2 teaspoons rice vinegar**
> **1 teaspoon lemon juice**
> **1 teaspoon agave nectar**
> **½ teaspoon ground mustard seed**
> **½ teaspon salt**

Add all the ingredients to a blender and purée until smooth.

YIELD: 2 cups (448 g)

. . . .

DILL-Y TARTAR SAUCE

* Gluten-Free Potential * Nut-Free * Quick and Easy

This simple sauce works perfectly as a dipping sauce for the Panko Fried Artichokes (page 200) and as a topper for the Flaky Fish-y Tacos (page 194).

> **¾ cup (168 g) vegan mayonnaise, store-bought or homemade (page 118)**
> **1 tablespoon (15 g) sweet pickle relish**
> **1 teaspoon lemon juice**
> **½ teaspoon minced garlic**
> **½ teaspoon onion powder**
> **¼ teaspoon dried dill, or ¾ teaspoon fresh dill**

Whisk together all the ingredients and store in an airtight container in the refrigerator until ready to use.

YIELD: Just over ¾ cup (178 g)

TOMATILLO CHILAQUILES

* No Added Sugar   * Nut-Free

Breakfast nachos! This Mexican breakfast treat is traditionally made with corn tortillas. We give them a fun twist by using chips instead. Feel free to get creative with toppings. The ones we have listed here are only guidelines. All sorts of ingredients work well. Fresh avocado slices, guacamole, your favorite salsa, black beans, chopped tomatoes, or anything else that sounds yummy will taste great piled on top.

FOR THE TOMATILLO SAUCE:
- ½ cup (32 g) pumpkin seeds
- ½ teaspoon whole cumin seeds
- ½ teaspoon dried oregano
- 1 tablespoon (15 ml) neutral-flavored oil
- 1 yellow onion, roughly chopped
- 1 tablespoon (9 g) minced garlic
- 2 jalapeño peppers, or a milder green chile of choice, seeded and chopped
- ½ cup (120 g) canned crushed tomatillos
- 1½ cups (355 ml) vegan chicken-flavored broth, store-bought or homemade (page 167)
- 1 tablespoon (15 ml) lime juice
- ½ cup (8 g) chopped fresh cilantro
- ½ cup (50 g) chopped scallion
- 1 teaspoon salt

FOR THE CHILAQUILES:
- 8 large handfuls of tortilla chips, you will need 2 handfuls per serving
- 1 recipe Plain Scrambled Eggs (page 114)
- 1 cup (154 g) yellow corn, roasted or grilled
- 1 cup (170 g) prepared Cotija-Style Tofu Crumbles (page 73)
- Chopped cilantro, as needed for garnish

To make the tomatillo sauce: Heat a cast iron skillet or saucepan over medium-high heat. Toast the pumpkin seeds, cumin seeds, and oregano, for 3 to 4 minutes, constantly tossing to prevent burning. Remove from heat and allow to cool completely. Using a spice grinder (or a clean coffee grinder) grind the toasted seeds and spices into a fine powder and set aside.

Use the same skillet or pan and heat the oil over medium-high heat. Add the onion, garlic, and jalapeños, and sauté 3 to 5 minutes, or until lightly browned and fragrant.

Carefully transfer the sautéed mixture into a blender and add the remaining sauce ingredients. Purée until smooth. Carefully pour the mixture back into the skillet and add the ground spice mixture. Bring to a boil, and reduce to a simmer. Cover and simmer for 20 minutes, stirring every few minutes. Remove from heat.

To make the chilaquiles: Add tortilla chips to the sauce and toss to coat. Divide the coated chips evenly on serving plates. Top each pile of chips with Plain Scrambled Eggs, roasted corn, and top with Cotija Crumbles. Garnish with cilantro. Serve immediately.

YIELD: 4 servings

SPICY NO-MAYO MAC SALAD

* No Added Sugar * Nut-Free * Quick and Easy * Soy-Free

This spicy mac salad has all the flavor of a mayo-based salad without the mayo. The dressing is made from creamy white beans!

FOR THE SALAD:

- **1 pound (454 g) elbow or salad macaroni, prepared and cooled**
- **1 cup (2 ounces, or 56 g) chopped bitter greens such as kale, chard, or arugula**
- **½ cup (80 g) diced red onion**
- **½ cup (120 g) cherry tomatoes, quarters**
- **¼ cup (4 g) chopped cilantro**
- **1 jalapeño pepper, seeded and diced (or 6 slices of jarred jalapeño peppers, diced)**
- **Salt and pepper, to taste**

FOR THE DRESSING:

- **1 can (15 ounces, or 425 g) white beans, drained and rinsed**
- **¼ cup (60 ml) neutral-flavored oil**
- **¼ cup (60 ml) vegetable broth or water (or use ¼ teaspoon Mushroom Broth Powder [page 218] mixed with ¼ cup [60 ml] water)**
- **1 chipotle pepper in adobo sauce**
- **1 tablespoon (15 ml) adobo sauce**
- **1 tablespoon (15 ml) apple cider vinegar**
- **1 tablespoon (8 g) minced garlic**
- **1 tablespoon (1 g) chopped cilantro**
- **¼ teaspoon ground cumin**
- **¼ teaspoon salt**

To make the salad: In a large mixing bowl, add all salad components, except salt and pepper.

To make the dressing: Prepare the dressing by placing all the ingredients in a blender and blending until smooth. Add the dressing to the salad and toss to coat.

Add salt and pepper to taste. Keep refrigerated until ready to serve.

YIELD: A nice big bowl, perfect for parties or potlucks. About 8 servings.

 Joni Says

"Sprinkle in some pine nuts, sunflower seeds, or pumpkin seeds to add a little crunch!"

ROASTED FINGERLING POTATO SALAD WITH FRESH HERBS

* Gluten-Free Potential * No Added Sugar * Nut-Free * Soy-Free

This sophisticated potato salad takes roasted potatoes and dresses them in a light, tangy, mayo-free dressing teaming with fresh herbs.

FOR THE POTATOES:

2 tablespoons (30 ml) olive oil
1 cube vegetable bouillon
1 teaspoon dried parsley
½ teaspoon dried marjoram
½ teaspoon garlic powder
½ teaspoon onion powder
¼ teaspoon paprika
¼ teaspoon black pepper
1½ pounds (681 g) fingerling potatoes

FOR THE DRESSING:

2 tablespoons (30 ml) olive oil
1 tablespoon (15 ml) white balsamic vinegar
1 teaspoon lemon juice
1 tablespoon (4 g) fresh dill
1 tablespoon (3 g) fresh chopped tarragon
1 teaspoon minced garlic
⅓ cup (33 g) chopped scallion

To make the potatoes: Preheat the oven to 375°F (190°C, or gas mark 5.) Line a rimmed baking sheet with parchment or a reusable silicone baking mat.

Add oil to a small measure and dissolve the bouillon cube in the oil. Add the rest of the ingredients, except potatoes, and stir to combine. Set aside.

Cut the fingerlings in half and add to a mixing bowl. Add the oil mixture and toss to coat. Arrange the potatoes in a single layer on the pan and roast for 35 minute, or until fork tender. Remove from oven and allow to cool completely.

To make the dressing: Whisk all the dressing ingredients together in a mixing bowl. Add cooled potatoes to the dressing and toss to coat.

YIELD: 4 servings

MEXICAN COBB SALAD

* Gluten-Free Potential

This salad takes the best things about a traditional cobb salad and throws in a Mexican dressing, that's just a little *caliente*, to kick it up a notch—or *dos*! Make the components ahead of time, that way you can put it together quickly for easy dinners.

FOR THE ROASTED CHILE, AVOCADO, AND CILANTRO DRESSING:

- 2 green chiles such as Hatch, Anaheim, or pasilla
- Flesh from 1 large or two small avocados
- ¼ cup (4 g) cilantro leaves
- 1 cup (47 g) chopped romaine lettuce
- ¼ cup (60 ml) olive oil
- 2 tablespoons (30 ml) soy or Almond Milk (page 27)
- 2 teaspoons (10 ml) fresh lime juice
- Salt and pepper, to taste

FOR THE HARD-BOILED EGGLIKE CRUMBLES:

- 8 ounces (227 g) extra or super firm tofu, drained and pressed
- ½ teaspoon mild Dijon mustard
- ½ teaspoon turmeric
- ½ teaspoon black salt (kala namak)
- ¼ teaspoon garlic powder

FOR THE SALAD:

- 1 head romaine lettuce, chopped (about 8 cups, or 376 g)
- ½ cup (35 g) Coconut Bacon, store-bought or homemade (page 209)
- 1 recipe Dill-y Chickpeas (page 226)
- 2 Roma tomatoes, seeded and diced
- ¼ cup (16 g) pepitas (pumpkin seeds)

To make the dressing: Preheat the oven to 400°F (200°C, or gas mark 6), line a baking sheet with parchment or a reusable baking mat. Place the chiles uncovered on the baking sheet and roast for 20 minutes, or until browned and blistered. Allow to cool completely, then remove the stem and seeds. Place the flesh in a blender along with all of the other ingredients and purée until smooth. Place in an airtight container and refrigerate until ready to use.

To make the eggs: Cut the tofu in half. Cut one half into tiny cubes; this will be your "whites." Set aside. In a small bowl, crumble the remaining tofu and add the remaining ingredients. Mix until well incorporated. This will be your "yolks." Keep whites and yolks separated until ready to use.

Assemble the salad: Place about 2 cups (94 g) of chopped romaine in four salad bowls. On the top of the lettuce, arrange the ingredients in a traditional cobb salad pattern: a row of Coconut Bacon, a row of Dill-y Chickpeas, a row of hard-boiled egglike crumbles, and a row of tomatoes. Drizzle with dressing and garnish with pumpkin seeds.

YIELD: 4 main-dish servings

BÁNH MI SCRAMBLE

* Quick and Easy

Are scrambled eggs one of the foods that make you reticent to commit fully to veganism? We're confident you won't miss a thing with this refreshing tofu scramble. It's a good fit for any-hour meals, and that allows you to enjoy the flavors of the traditional Vietnamese sandwich in an "unsandwiched" way.

FOR THE PICKLED SLAW:

- **12 ounces (340 g) broccoli slaw (half shredded carrots, half shredded broccoli stalks)**
- **¼ cup (60 ml) seasoned rice vinegar**
- **2 teaspoons (13 g) agave nectar**
- **1 to 2 teaspoons (5 to 10 ml) sriracha, to taste**

FOR THE SCRAMBLED TOFU:

- **1 tablespoon (15 ml) melted coconut or peanut oil**
- **1 pound (454 g) super firm tofu, crumbled**
- **3 tablespoons (24 g) Mushroom Broth Powder (page 218)**
- **1 tablespoon (15 ml) tamari**
- **1 tablespoon (15 ml) seasoned rice vinegar**
- **1½ tablespoons (23 ml) fresh lime juice (juice from 1 lime)**
- **3 tablespoons (27 g) minced jalapeño pepper (1 medium)**
- **¼ cup (20 g) minced scallion**
- **2 packed teaspoons grated fresh ginger root**
- **4 cloves garlic, grated or pressed**
- **½ cup (10 g) loosely packed fresh cilantro leaves**
- **1 fresh, crusty vegan baguette, sliced**

To make the slaw: In a large bowl, thoroughly combine all the ingredients. Cover and store in the refrigerator for at least 30 minutes before, or up to 2 hours before.

To make the tofu: Heat the oil in a large skillet on medium-high heat. Add the tofu, sprinkle the broth powder on top, and stir well. Cook until browned and crisped, about 10 minutes, regularly scraping the flavor-packed browned bits at the bottom of the skillet with a wooden spatula.

In a small bowl, combine the tamari, vinegar, lime juice, jalapeño pepper, minced scallion, ginger, and garlic. Add on top of the browned tofu. Cook on high heat for another 2 minutes, or until mostly absorbed. Stir frequently. Evenly place on top of the pickled slaw, and sprinkle with cilantro leaves just upon serving. Serve with slices of baguette. This recipe tastes great at room temperature, too, which makes it ideal to take for lunch at work or for picnics.

YIELD: 4 servings

CURRY QUINOA AMARANTH PATTIES

* No Added Sugar

Flax meal and flour join hands to make eggs completely obsolete by playing the role of binder in these fork-and-knife (not handheld), healthy patties.

1 teaspoon olive oil
2 carrots, peeled and minced (5 ounces, or 142 g)
2 shallots, minced
½ medium jalapeño pepper, seeded
2 large cloves garlic, minced
1 tablespoon (15 ml) fresh lemon juice
1 tablespoon (16 g) tomato paste
2½ teaspoons (5 g) mild to medium curry powder
½ teaspoon ground coriander
1 tablespoon (8 g) Mushroom Broth Powder (page 218)
1½ cups (355 ml) water, plus more to deglaze
½ cup (85 g) dry ivory quinoa, rinsed
¼ cup (45 g) dry amaranth, rinsed
¼ teaspoon fine sea salt, to taste
Ground black pepper, to taste
2 tablespoons (2 g) minced fresh cilantro
3 tablespoons (23 g) whole-wheat pastry flour
3 tablespoons (21 g) ground flaxseed
Nonstick cooking spray or oil spray
1 recipe Sour Cream Dressing (see "Celine Says," page 30)

Place the oil, carrots, shallot, jalapeño, garlic, lemon juice, tomato paste, curry, coriander, and broth powder in a large skillet. Cook on medium-high heat until softened, about 4 minutes. Add water, 1 tablespoon (15 ml) at a time, if the veggies are sticking. Add the quinoa and amaranth, and stir to combine. Add 1½ cups (355 ml) of water, and bring to a boil. Stir, lower heat, and cover with a lid. Simmer for 20 to 25 minutes, or until tender and the liquid is mostly absorbed. Check and stir occasionally, adding more water if needed. Remove from heat, and add salt and pepper to taste. Fold the cilantro, flour, and flaxseed into the mixture. It should hold together when pressed with a rubber spatula. Refrigerate covered for at least 3 hours, or overnight.

Preheat the oven to 375°F (190°C, or gas mark 5). Lightly coat a baking sheet with cooking spray, or use 2 whoopie pie pans. Gather 2 packed tablespoons (40 g) of the mixture and shape into 2-inch (5 cm) patties. Lightly coat the top with cooking spray, and repeat with remaining mixture. You should get 18 patties in all. Bake for 15 minutes, gently flip the patties, and bake for another 10 minutes, until firm and golden brown. Gently transfer to a cooling rack, and let stand 10 minutes before serving with dressing.

YIELD: 18 patties

DINNER PLATE BOWL

* No Added Sugar   * Nut-Free

There is something about putting your whole meal into a bowl that just makes it, well, taste better. And this one is no exception. We call it the Dinner Plate Bowl because inside is all the components of a traditional dinner plate. We like to make all of the components ahead of time, and assemble the bowl and reheat as needed for a quick-and-easy lunch or dinner. In fact, Joni has been known to make huge batches of these ingredients just for the purpose of "bowling" all week long.

FOR THE POTATOES:

2 pounds (908 g) baby red potatoes, halved
2 tablespoons (30 ml) olive oil
1 tablespoon (9 g) minced garlic
1 teaspoon dried rosemary or 1 tablespoon (2 g) fresh
Salt and pepper, to taste

FOR THE BALSAMIC ONIONS:

1 tablespoon (15 ml) neutral-flavored oil
1 large red onion, cut into thin rings
1 tablespoon (15 ml) balsamic vinegar
Salt and pepper, to taste

FOR THE SPECIAL SAUCE:

1 cup (225 g) vegan mayonnaise, store-bought or homemade (page 118)
1 tablespoon (15 ml) apple cider vinegar
1 tablespoon (17 g) ketchup
1 teaspoon garlic powder
1 teaspoon onion powder
½ teaspoon chipotle powder
½ teaspoon dried dill, or 1½ teaspoons fresh
Salt and pepper, to taste

FOR THE TOFU:

1 block (10 ounces, or 284 g) extra or super firm tofu, drained and pressed
1 tablespoon (8 g) nutritional yeast
½ teaspooon garlic powder
½ teaspoon onion powder
¼ teaspoon black pepper
¼ teaspoon paprika
1 tablespoon (15 ml) neutral-flavored oil
Salt, to taste

FOR THE BOWL:

1 bunch (about 10 ounces, or 284 g) Dino Lacinto kale, julienne cut
4 cups (632 g) cooked white or (780 g) brown jasmine rice, warm
1 cup (134 g) green peas, heated (fresh, frozen, or canned is fine)
2 stalks scallion, small chop on the bias

To make the potatoes: Preheat the oven to 400°F (200°C, or gas mark 6).

In a medium bowl, toss the halved potatoes with oil, garlic, and rosemary to coat. Arrange in a single layer on baking sheet, and bake for 30 to 45 minutes, or until tender and edges are browned. When done, remove from oven, and add salt and pepper to taste. Keep warm until ready to serve.

To prepare the balsamic onions: Heat the oil in a small frying pan over medium heat. Add the onions and sauté until soft. About 5 minutes, tossing regularly. Add the balsamic vinegar, salt and pepper, and continue to cook down until onions are very soft and caramelized, 7 to 10 minutes.

To make the special sauce: Whisk together all the ingredients in a small bowl until well combined. Set aside, or refrigerate until ready to serve.

To make the tofu: Add all the ingredients, except oil and salt, to a small bowl and toss to coat. Preheat oil in a frying pan over medium-high heat. Add the tofu mixture and sauté for about 5 minutes or until golden brown. Add salt to taste.

To assemble the bowl: Layer the ingredients in the following order: Kale on bottom, rice over the kale, potatoes over the rice, tofu over the potatoes, peas over the tofu, balsamic onions all over the top, drizzle liberally with sauce, then garnish with chopped scallion. Serve immediately, or package for easy-to-reheat lunches and dinners throughout the week.

YIELD: 4 bowls

Joni Says

"If you are avoiding or cutting back on soy products, feel free to substitute your favorite protein source. Seitan and the Dill-y Chickpeas (page 226) both sub in nicely here."

TAPENADE FRENCH TOAST SANDWICHES

* No Added Sugar

We occasionally replace the bell pepper with 8 ounces (227 g) sliced mushrooms, cooked with salt in a pan. If using large bread slices, double the batter.

8 large (2 ounces, or 57 g) pitted olives of choice, minced
1 packed tablespoon (8 g) julienne-cut soft sun-dried tomato, minced
1 tablespoon (15 ml) capers with brine, minced
4 ounces (113 g) diced red bell pepper
2 tablespoons (20 g) minced shallot
¼ teaspoon smoked paprika
¼ teaspoon red pepper flakes
½ cup (120 ml) plain vegan milk, store-bought or homemade, (page 27)
1 teaspoon fresh lemon juice
¼ teaspoon vegan Worcestershire sauce
¼ teaspoon mild Dijon mustard
1½ tablespoons (11 g) Hemp Parm (page 72)
2 tablespoons (15 g) whole-wheat pastry flour
1 tablespoon (8 g) chickpea flour or garbanzo fava bean flour
¼ teaspoon baking powder
⅛ teaspoon fine sea salt
Ground peppercorn, to taste
¼ cup plus 2 tablespoons (90 g) either cashew spread (page 32 or 33)
8 slices stale vegan whole-grain sourdough or other bread
Nonstick cooking spray or oil spray

Combine olives through pepper flakes in a medium bowl, using your hand to squeeze and mix. Let stand 30 minutes at room temperature.

In a shallow pan, whisk to combine the milk through peppercorn.

Apply 2 teaspoons (10 g) of spread on each slice of bread, or enough to generously cover. Squeeze to remove moisture from ¼ cup (41 g) tapenade before evenly placing on one of the slices. Press down slightly so nothing falls out while cooking. Top with another slice, spread-side down. Repeat with remaining sandwiches. Heat a skillet on medium-high heat. Once hot, move it away from the heat to coat with cooking spray. Dip the whole sandwich in the batter, letting the excess drip into the pan. Place in the skillet, lower heat to medium, and fry for 4 minutes, until golden brown. Flip and fry for another 4 minutes, until golden brown. Apply cooking spray away from the heat between each batch. Repeat with remaining sandwiches. Serve immediately.

YIELD: 4 sandwiches

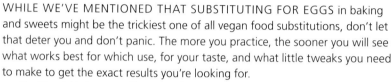

CHAPTER 4
Eggs Substitutions in Baking and Sweets

WHILE WE'VE MENTIONED THAT SUBSTITUTING FOR EGGS in baking and sweets might be the trickiest one of all vegan food substitutions, don't let that deter you and don't panic. The more you practice, the sooner you will see what works best for which use, for your taste, and what little tweaks you need to make to get the exact results you're looking for.

It will quickly become like second nature, and you will get to reward yourself for your newly-acquired, mad, vegan baking skills by enjoying a big spoonful of raw vegan cookie dough—if that's something you were always tempted to do with regular cookie dough, but never attempted due to the perils of eating raw eggs. Welcome to the dark side: This is just a fraction of what vegan baking can do for you.

Practice Makes for Perfect Substitutions

The best way to demonstrate how easy it is to transform a nonvegan recipe into a cruelty-free wonder is to showcase how it's done. Let's go through a sample recipe step by step! Once you know the basics, it's easy to put into practice on any recipe.

< *Cinnamon-Raisin Pull-Apart Loaves, page 137*

CITRUS-FLAVORED OLIVE OIL CAKE

Non-Veganized

This recipe is an excerpt from *Make-Ahead Meals Made Healthy*, by Michele Borboa (Fair Winds Press, 2011). We will replace the honey and the eggs with vegan substitutions, and rewrite the directions accordingly.

Juice of 2 oranges (about ⅔ cup, or 160 ml)
½ cup (170 g) warmed honey
¼ cup (60 ml) extra-virgin olive oil
2 large eggs, separated
2 tablespoons (12 g) finely grated orange zest
1⅔ cups (208 g) all-purpose flour, sifted
½ cup (100 g) granulated sugar
1 teaspoon baking powder
½ teaspoon baking soda

Preheat the oven to 350°F (180°C, or gas mark 4). Lightly grease and flour bottom and sides of a 9-inch (23 cm) springform pan. Set aside.

In a standup mixer fitted with the paddle attachment, mix orange juice, honey, olive oil, egg yolks, and orange zest on medium speed until well blended.

In a medium bowl, whisk together flour, sugar, baking powder, and baking soda. In a small bowl, beat egg whites until soft peaks form.

With mixer on low speed, add flour mixture to orange juice mixture, blending until just moistened. With a spatula, gently fold in egg whites. Pour batter into prepared pan.

Bake for 35 minutes or until a cake tester inserted in the center comes out clean. Cool 10 minutes on a wire rack and then remove sides from pan and cool completely. Just before serving, sprinkle with confectioners' sugar.

YIELD: One 9-inch (23 cm) cake

CITRUS-FLAVORED OLIVE OIL CAKE Veganized!

We've replaced the honey with agave nectar, which prompted us to lower the original oven heat because agave nectar makes baked goods darken quickly. A cooked combination of water and cornstarch is used instead of the eggs, which makes for a springy cake with outstanding texture, like the egg whites would yield. The amount of flour was increased by ⅓ cup (40 g), as the batter came out quite thin. Finally, the amount of baking powder was increased by ½ teaspoon to make up for the added flour, and to further boost the lift of the water and cornstarch combination, just like whipped egg whites would provide.

Nonstick cooking spray or oil spray
½ cup (120 ml) water ⎤
1 tablespoon (8 g) cornstarch (preferably organic) ⎦—(**egg substitute**)
⅔ cup (160 ml) fresh orange juice
½ cup (160 g) agave nectar ⎤—(**honey substitute**)
½ cup (100 g) evaporated cane juice or vegan granulated sugar
¼ cup (60 ml) extra-virgin olive oil
2 tablespoons (12 g) finely grated orange zest or 1 teaspoon
** pure orange extract**
1 teaspoon pure vanilla extract
2 scant cups (240 g) all-purpose flour
1½ teaspoons baking powder
½ teaspoon baking soda
Pinch fine kosher salt

Preheat the oven to 325°F (170°C, or gas mark 3). Lightly coat a 9-inch (23 cm) springform pan with cooking spray.

Place the cornstarch in a small microwave-safe bowl. Add 2 tablespoons (30 ml) water and stir to dissolve completely. Add the remaining 6 tablespoons (90 ml) water, and bring to a boil either in the microwave for 50 seconds, or in a small saucepan until it is slightly gelatinous and cloudy, about 1 minute. Whisk to make sure there are no lumps, and set aside for 5 minutes. **This is your egg substitute.**

In a large bowl, whisk the orange juice, agave **(this is your honey substitute)**, evaporated cane juice (or sugar), oil, zest, vanilla, and egg substitute until combined.

In a medium bowl, whisk together flour, baking powder, baking soda, and salt. Whisk dry ingredients into wet ingredients until moistened and free of lumps. Pour batter into pan.

Bake for 30 to 35 minutes, or until golden brown and firm to the touch in the center. Cool 20 minutes on a wire rack. Remove from pan and cool completely. Store in the refrigerator. Just before serving, sprinkle with confectioners' sugar.

YIELD: One 9-inch (23 cm) cake

BRIOCHE WAFFLES

You might recognize this brioche recipe as the one Celine developed a few years back. We wanted to replace the vegan butter from the original with coconut butter. Success! We've used a combination of cooked water and cornstarch to stand for the eggs.

½ cup (120 ml) water
1 tablespoon (8 g) cornstarch (preferably organic)
½ cup (120 ml) full-fat coconut milk at room temperature
3 tablespoons (36 g) evaporated cane juice or vegan granulated sugar
½ teaspoon fine sea salt
2 cups (250 g) all-purpose flour
1 tablespoon (12 g) instant yeast
¼ cup (60 g) Coconut Butter (page 25), warmed slightly if hardened
Nonstick cooking spray or oil spray
Organic powdered sugar, for serving

Place the cornstarch in a small bowl. Add 2 tablespoons (30 ml) water and stir to dissolve completely. Add the remaining 6 tablespoons (90 ml) water, and bring to a boil either in the microwave (use a deep microwave-safe bowl, as the mixture will have a tendency to bubble up) for 50 seconds, or in a small saucepan until it is slightly gelatinous and cloudy, about 1 minute. Set aside and let cool completely before using.

Combine the cornstarch mixture, milk, sugar, salt, flour, and yeast in the bowl of a stand mixer fitted with a dough hook. Mix on medium speed for 2 minutes.

Add the coconut butter while mixing, and continue mixing for 2 minutes. Gather the dough in the center of the bowl with a spatula, tightly cover the bowl, and let stand 45 minutes. Gather the dough in the center of the bowl again.

Tightly cover and refrigerate for 18 to 24 hours. The dough will be quite stiff.

Divide into 8 portions of 2.6 ounces (75 g) each. Place on a piece of parchment paper. Loosely cover with plastic wrap, and let stand for 1 hour.

Follow the waffle iron manufacturer's instructions, and heat the machine (to 350°F, 180°C, if your machine lets you). Coat the machine with cooking spray between each waffle. Add a portion of dough on the iron. Place it in the center of the iron, press closed for a few seconds, and cook for about 6 minutes, until golden brown and the dough on the side is cooked through. Repeat with remaining waffles. Let cool 5 minutes before eating. Dust with powdered sugar before serving. These are best served fresh.

YIELD: 8 waffles

CINNAMON RAISIN PULL-APART LOAVES

Remember to add the raisins while you prepare the brioche dough! If you want to make these all the more decadent, drizzle with the glaze from the "Celine Says" note in Cranberry Nut Butter Scones (page 140) made with vegan milk instead of orange juice.

1 recipe Brioche Waffles dough (page 136)
½ cup (80 g) soft and moist raisins
⅓ cup (73 g) packed light brown sugar
2¾ teaspoons (7 g) ground cinnamon
⅛ teaspoon ground nutmeg
Nonstick cooking spray or oil spray

Follow the instructions to make the dough in the waffle recipe, but add the raisins right after the coconut butter gets mixed in. Continue following the instructions, up to and including refrigeration.

In a small bowl, combine the sugar, cinnamon, and nutmeg. Lightly coat two 5¾ x 3-inch (14 x 8 cm) mini loaf pans with cooking spray.

Pat down the stiff dough on a piece of parchment paper or silicone baking mat, and roll it out into an 8 x 9-inch (20 x 23 cm) rectangle. If it is too stiff to work with, give it a few minutes to become more manageable. Place the filling evenly on top, and press it down with the rolling pin, rolling the dough into a 12-inch (30.5 cm) square. Cut into eight 1½ x 12-inch (3.8 x 30.5 cm) strips. Carefully place 4 strips on top of each other. Repeat with the remaining 4 strips to create a separate pile. Cut each pile of 4 strips widthwise into six 2 x 1½-inch (5 x 3.8 cm) stacks. Arrange cut edges up into a tight fit. Hold the stacks that are already in the pan up with one hand, and press them back to fit. Loosely cover with plastic wrap and let rise for approximately 1 hour and 15 minutes, until the dough barely reaches the edge of the pan.

Preheat the oven to 400°F (200°C, or gas mark 6). Line the oven rack with a piece of aluminum foil in case of spillage. Slowly remove the plastic wrap from the dough. Bake for 10 minutes and lower the oven to 350°F (180°C, or gas mark 4). Bake for another 18 minutes, or until the tops reach a deep golden brown color. Loosely cover with foil if tops darken too quickly. Carefully remove from pans, transfer onto a wire rack to cool completely.

YIELD: 2 small loaves

PEACH MELBA BAKED OATMEAL

* Gluten-Free Potential * Quick and Easy

Baked oatmeal often contains eggs and butter. We've happily gone without these in-gredients here by using homemade hazelnut butter for binding, richness, and flavor, as well as almond milk for added moisture. Of course, it's made all the better with a layer of tender, mouthwatering, fresh fruit baked at the bottom of the dish. Is it breakfast time yet?

Nonstick cooking spray or oil spray
¼ cup (80 g) agave nectar or pure maple syrup
¼ cup (64 g) Toasted Hazelnut Butter (page 220)
¾ cup (180 ml) plain Almond Milk (page 27) or other vegan milk, divided
1 teaspoon pure vanilla extract
1 teaspoon ground cinnamon
⅛ teaspoon fine sea salt
2 large, ripe yet very firm yellow peaches (11 ounces, or 312 g),
**   pitted and sliced**
1 heaping cup (135 g) fresh raspberries
1½ cups (144 g) extra-thick rolled oats or (120 g) old-fashioned rolled oats
¼ teaspoon baking powder

Preheat the oven to 375°F (190°C, or gas mark 5). Lightly coat an 8-inch (20 cm) square baking pan with cooking spray.

In a medium bowl, whisk to combine the agave, hazelnut butter, ¼ cup (60 ml) milk, vanilla, cinnamon, and salt.

Place sliced peaches evenly at the bottom of the pan, overlapping them slightly to fit them all. Top with raspberries.

Stir the oats and baking powder into the milk mixture. (If you notice this mixture is dry while stirring, drizzle the remaining ½ cup (120 ml) milk into it now, and stir to combine. If not, continue as follows.) Evenly place on top of the fruit.

(Skip the following step if you already added the remaining milk before.) Drizzle the remaining ½ cup (120 ml) milk on top of the oats, slightly tilting the pan to make sure it is distributed evenly.

Bake for 35 minutes, checking after 20 minutes. If the topping browns too quickly, add a loose piece of foil on top. Let stand 10 minutes before serving.

YIELD: 6 to 8 servings

SWEET DATE PUDLA

* Gluten-Free Potential * Quick and Easy

We've become so enamored with Indian pudla (see Scallion Kale Pudla, page 106) that we decided to break the mold and make a sweet version of the (potentially, if all the ingredients are double-checked) gluten-free, pancake-look-alike dish for breakfast time. Our favorite way to serve this treat is to top it with unsweetened roasted apple or pear slices, or with homemade unsweetened applesauce.

 1 cup (235 ml) plain Almond Milk (page 27) or other vegan milk,
   at room temperature so that the coconut oil doesn't seize
 1½ tablespoons (23 ml) lemon juice
 1 cup plus 1 tablespoon (128 g) chickpea flour or garbanzo fava bean flour
 ¼ cup (30 g) cashew or almond meal
 1 tablespoon (15 ml) melted coconut oil
 2 tablespoons (40 g) pure maple syrup, at room temperature
 1 teaspoon pure vanilla extract
 ¼ teaspoon baking soda
 ⅛ teaspoon fine sea salt
 1 teaspoon ground cinnamon
 ½ teaspoon ground ginger
 ¼ cup (40 g) chopped dates
 Nonstick cooking spray or oil spray

Place all the ingredients, except dates and cooking spray, in a medium bowl, whisking to thoroughly combine. Stir the dates into the mixture. Let stand 15 minutes.

Heat a large nonstick pan on medium-high heat. Lower heat to medium. Lightly coat the pan with cooking spray or oil spray once hot, away from the heat. Add a scant ½ cup (110 ml) of the batter to the skillet. The batter should spread itself to an approximately 6-inch (15 cm) circle. Cook for about 4 minutes, until the center bubbles and doesn't look wet. Carefully lift the edges of the pudla to make sure it is golden brown, which is another sign it is ready to flip.

Carefully flip with a spatula, and let cook for another 3 minutes, or until golden brown.

Lightly coat the pan again each time before cooking the remaining pudla. Serve immediately with favorite toppings.

YIELD: 2 to 4 servings

CRANBERRY NUT BUTTER SCONES

* Quick and Easy

These scones are just as good as their nonvegan alter egos, maybe even better. We've made them egg-free by using homemade yogurt for binding. We also packed them full of flavor and richness by using both coconut oil and hazelnut butter, which helps create that awesome texture one expects when biting into a freshly baked scone.

- 1¼ cups (150 g) whole-wheat pastry flour
- 1 teaspoon baking powder
- ¼ cup (48 g) organic light brown sugar (not packed)
- ¼ teaspoon fine sea salt
- 3 tablespoons (42 g) solid coconut oil

- 3 tablespoons (48 g) Toasted Hazelnut Butter (page 220) or any natural creamy nut or seed butter
- 1 teaspoon pure vanilla extract
- ¼ cup (30 g) dried cranberries
- ¼ to ½ cup (60 to 120 g) Homemade Yogurt (page 28) or store-bought vegan yogurt, as needed

Preheat the oven to 425°F (220°C, or gas mark 7). Line a baking sheet with parchment paper.

Place the flour, baking powder, sugar, and salt in a food processor. Pulse twice.

Add the oil and nut butter, pulsing just to combine. Add the vanilla, cranberries, and ¼ cup (60 g) of the yogurt, pulsing just to combine. The dough should stick together when pinched without being too dry or too wet. Add the remaining yogurt as needed, by pulsing to combine, 1 tablespoon (15 g) at a time. Gather the dough on the prepared sheet, and pat it together to shape into a 6-inch (15 cm) circle. Cut into 6 scones. Leave 2 inches (5 cm) of space between the scones.

Bake for 12 minutes, or until golden brown at the bottom and top edges. Place on a wire rack. The scones are best enjoyed freshly baked; that's why we've kept the yield on the modest side.

YIELD: 6 scones

 Celine Says

"Fancy a little glaze on your scones? Combine ⅓ cup (40 g) organic powdered sugar with fresh orange juice, 1 teaspoon at a time, and stir vigorously to break up all sugar clumps, until a not-too-thin, not-too-thick glaze is obtained. Drizzle over slightly or completely cooled scones."

STRAWBERRY CLAFOUTIS

* Quick and Easy

The mixture of chickpea flour and milk takes the place of eggs and their binding power in this fruity clafoutis. We think it tastes even better reheated the next day. The advantage of preparing it ahead of time is that it makes for a quick breakfast treat.

1¼ cups (295 ml) plain Almond Milk (page 27) or other vegan milk, divided
¼ cup (30 g) chickpea flour or garbanzo fava bean flour
1 tablespoon (15 ml) fresh lemon juice
¼ cup (80 g) agave nectar
¼ cup (48 g) evaporated cane juice or vegan granulated sugar
2 tablespoons (30 ml) neutral-flavored oil
1 teaspoon pure vanilla extract
Zest from 1 small lemon
1½ cups (180 g) whole-wheat pastry flour
1 tablespoon (8 g) arrowroot powder
1 teaspoon baking powder
⅛ teaspoon fine sea salt
Nonstick cooking spray or oil spray
Generous 2 cups (330 g) halved fresh strawberries, chopped
Organic powdered sugar, or more agave nectar,
  or any curd (page 144) for serving

Preheat the oven to 375°F (190°C, or gas mark 5). Place a 10- or 11-inch (25 or 28 cm) oven-safe skillet in the oven while preheating.

In a large bowl, whisk together ¼ cup (60 ml) of milk with the chickpea flour. Pour the remaining 1 cup (235 ml) on top and whisk together with the lemon juice, agave, evaporated cane juice, oil, vanilla, and lemon zest. Sift the flour, arrowroot, baking powder, and salt on top. Whisk until combined. No lumps should remain.

Remove the skillet from the oven (careful, it will be hot), and coat it with cooking spray. Fold the chopped strawberries into the batter, and pour the batter into the greased pan. Bake 28 minutes, or until golden brown, and that the edges pull away from the pan. Let cool 10 minutes before carefully removing from the skillet, then another 30 minutes before serving. Sift sugar on top of each portion upon serving, or drizzle with agave or curd. Store covered leftovers in the refrigerator, and reheated in a 350°F (180°C, or gas mark 4) oven for 20 minutes, until heated through.

YIELD: 8 servings

FLOUR-FREE HAZELNUT COOKIES

* Gluten-Free Potential   * No Added Oil   * Quick and Easy

Arrowroot powder and vegan yogurt are what keeps these delicious cookies on the straight and narrow. Arrowroot powder is the element that combines with the yogurt to ensure proper binding, while the yogurt pulls double duty and takes care of bringing moisture to the goods, too. As is the case with all our baking recipes, we highly recommend weighing the ingredients for the most accurate measurements.

1 heaping cup (150 g) shelled whole hazelnuts
3½ tablespoons (42 g) turbinado sugar (or Sugar in the Raw)
2 tablespoons (16 g) arrowroot powder
½ teaspoon baking powder
Pinch fine sea salt
½ teaspoon pure hazelnut extract
½ teaspoon pure vanilla extract
4 teaspoons (20 g) Homemade Yogurt (page 28) or store-bought
vegan yogurt, more if needed

Preheat the oven to 350°F (180°C, or gas mark 4). Have a large baking sheet lined with parchment paper or a silicone baking mat handy.

Place the hazelnuts, sugar, arrowroot, baking powder, and salt in a food processor. Process until ground a little less fine than store-bought nut meal. Add the extracts and yogurt. Pulse to thoroughly combine. Pulse in extra yogurt, 1 teaspoon at a time, if the dough is dry. Grab 1 packed tablespoon (20 g) of dough per cookie, and place on the prepared mat. Do not flatten the dough, just leave it as it comes out of the tablespoon, flat side down. Repeat with remaining dough, and bake 10 to 12 minutes. The cookies won't become golden brown on top and won't spread, but they should be slightly golden at the bottom and look set. Transfer to a wire rack, and enjoy warm or cooled. The flavor will be maximized when the cookies are cooled. Store leftovers in a cookie tin at room temperature for up to 4 days.

YIELD: 12 cookies

PASSION FRUIT CURD

* Gluten-Free Potential

Regular curd is usually made with egg yolks to create a thick and intensely fruity spread. You'll see that it's got nothing on ours—thickened with a little cornstarch, made richer with coconut butter, and perfectly tart thanks to the passion fruit and lemon juice combo. You'll find it in recipes such as Curd Thumbprints (page 147) and Passion Fruit Curd and Cream Pops (page 60). We also love to simply add it to yogurt (page 28) with a handful of granola (page 38).

> ¾ cup (180 ml) unsweetened passion fruit juice
> 6 tablespoons to ½ cup (120 to 160 g) agave nectar, to taste
> ¼ cup (60 g) Coconut Butter (page 25) (measured at room temperature)
> 2 tablespoons (30 ml) fresh lemon juice
> Pinch fine sea salt
> 1 tablespoon (8 g) cornstarch (preferably organic)
> 1 tablespoon (15 ml) water

In a blender, combine the juice, 6 tablespoons (120 g) agave, Coconut Butter, lemon juice, and salt. Taste the mixture to see if you want to add the remaining 2 tablespoons (40 g) of agave. If bits of coconut from the coconut butter remain after blending and it bothers you, strain the mixture in a fine-mesh sieve. Transfer to a medium, heavy-bottomed saucepan. Combine the cornstarch with the water in a small bowl, until completely dissolved. Pour this mixture into the passion fruit preparation. Whisk to combine. Heat on medium-high heat, and cook until it starts to thicken, 8 to 10 minutes, whisking constantly. Transfer into jars, and put the lids on once the curd has cooled. Store in the refrigerator for up to 2 weeks.

YIELD: 1⅓ cups (370 g)

Celine Says

"To make Raspberry or Strawberry Curd: Thaw 12 ounces (340 g) of frozen raspberries or strawberries, strain through a fine-mesh sieve; you will get a slightly generous ¾ cup (180 ml) thick juice. The rest of the recipe remains the same except that we only use ¼ cup (80 g) agave nectar, so adjust to taste.

To make Orange or Pineapple Curd: Replace the passion fruit juice with fresh orange or pineapple juice. Adjust agave nectar to taste. Instructions remain the same."

CURD THUMBPRINTS

* Gluten-Free Potential   * No Added Oil   * Quick and Easy   * Soy-Free

How can flour-free cookies hold themselves together so well, you ask? It's the starch-and-water combo magic! See "Celine Says" in the Passion Fruit Curd recipe, (page 144), to make it raspberry-flavored. You can also use only one of the curd flavors, in which case you'll need 2 tablespoons (36 g) of the chosen flavor.

1 cup (140 g) raw cashews
5 tablespoons (60 g) turbinado sugar (or Sugar in the Raw)
Pinch fine sea salt
3 tablespoons (36 g) potato starch or (24 g) cornstarch (preferably organic)
½ teaspoon pure vanilla extract
2 tablespoons (30 ml) water, as needed
1 tablespoon (18 g) Passion Fruit Curd (page 144)
1 tablespoon (18 g) Raspberry Curd (page 144)

Preheat the oven to 350°F (180°C, or gas mark 4). Line a large cookie sheet with parchment paper or a silicone baking mat.

Place the cashews, sugar, salt, and potato starch in a food processor. Pulse until the cashews are ground, but not too finely. Add the vanilla and water, 1 tablespoon (15 ml) at first and then droplets at a time, until the mixture sticks together easily when pinched, without being too wet. Don't be too heavy-handed with the water, or the cookies will spread while they bake.

Use 1 packed tablespoon (24 g) of dough per cookie, and place on the prepared sheet, reforming the dough into the shape of the inside of a tablespoon if needed, with the flat side down. Use the back of a teaspoon measure to indent the center of the mound, and fill six indents with a ½ teaspoon (or however much will fit without overflowing) of Passion Fruit Curd, and the remaining six with a ½ teaspoon of raspberry curd. Bake for 10 minutes, until set. Remove from oven and leave on the sheet for another 10 minutes. Transfer to a wire rack, and let cool completely before serving. Leftovers can be stored in a cookie tin at room temperature or in the refrigerator for up to 2 days.

YIELD: 12 cookies

TROPICAL OATMEAL COOKIES

* Quick and Easy * Soy-Free

Wee little, power-packed, chia seeds are a great substitute for eggs when combined with water. They expand and create a goopy mixture (what is more technically called a mucilage) that's similar to the texture of an egg. You can observe their mad binding skills in action in these scrumptious, tropical-flavored cookies. A little trick to chop sticky dried fruit such as mango and banana: Use clean kitchen scissors to cut the fruit for a less frustrating "chopping" experience.

> **6 tablespoons (72 g) evaporated cane juice or vegan granulated sugar**
> **6 tablespoons (72 g) light brown sugar (not packed)**
> **3 tablespoons (45 ml) liquid coconut oil**
> **1 tablespoon (10 g) chia seeds (regular or white)**
> **3 tablespoons (45 ml) lukewarm water, divided, more if needed**
> **1 teaspoon pure vanilla extract**
> **1 cup (96 g) extra-thick rolled oats or old-fashioned rolled oats**
> **¾ cup (90 g) whole-wheat pastry flour**
> **¼ cup (35 g) chopped dried (soft) mango**
> **¼ cup (20 g) unsweetened shredded coconut**
> **3 tablespoons (20 g) chopped dried (soft, not chips) banana**
> **½ teaspoon fine sea salt**
> **¼ teaspoon baking powder**

Preheat the oven to 350°F (180°C, or gas mark 4). Line two cookie sheets with parchment paper or silicone baking mats.

In a large bowl, whisk to combine the evaporated cane juice, sugar, oil, chia seeds, 2 tablespoons (30 ml) lukewarm water, and vanilla. Add the oats, flour, mango, coconut, banana, salt, and baking powder. Start to stir, and add the remaining 1 tablespoon (15 ml) of lukewarm water while doing so. Stir until fully combined. If the dough doesn't hold together, add extra water, 1 tablespoon (15 ml) at a time as needed.

Use 1 packed, slightly heaping tablespoon (22 g) of dough per cookie. Place on the prepared sheets, and flatten slightly as the cookies won't spread much while baking.

Bake for 12 to 14 minutes, until golden brown around the bottom edges. Remove the sheets from the oven and leave the cookies on the baking sheets for another 10 minutes before transferring to a cooling rack. Store in a cookie tin at room temperature for up to 2 days.

YIELD: 20 cookies

STRAWBERRY LEMONADE CUPCAKES

Like a sweet sip of lemonade on a summer's day, the magic here is in the way the cupcakes puff up in the oven, then sink in the middle as they cool, leaving the perfect receptacle for a nice dollop of sweet strawberry jam.

FOR THE CUPCAKES:

1 cup (235 ml) soy, coconut, or Almond Milk (page 27)

¼ cup (60 ml) lemon juice

⅓ cup (80 ml) neutral-flavored oil

1¼ cups (250 g) evaporated cane juice or vegan granulated sugar

1 tablespoon (15 ml) pure vanilla extract

1 teaspoon pure lemon extract

2¼ cups (281 g) all-purpose flour

3 tablespoons (24 g) cornstarch (preferably organic)

1½ teaspoons baking powder

¾ teaspoon baking soda

½ teaspoon salt

¾ cup (270 g) real fruit strawberry jam or jelly

FOR THE FROSTING:

1 cup (240 g) Chia Seed Cream Cheese (page 76)

½ cup (180 g) real fruit strawberry jam or jelly

+/– 5 cups (600 g) powdered sugar

To make the cupcakes: Preheat the oven to 350°F (180°C, or gas mark 4). Have ready a standard cupcake pan lined with cupcake papers.

In a medium-size mixing bowl, whisk together the milk, lemon juice, oil, evaporated cane juice, vanilla, and lemon extract. In a separate bowl, mix together flour, cornstarch, baking powder, baking soda, and salt. Carefully, mix the dry into the wet until well combined taking care not to overmix.

Fill cupcake papers three-quarters full and bake for 20 to 22 minutes, or until golden and a toothpick inserted into the center comes out clean. Remove from oven, and allow to cool for 5 minutes, before removing from the tin and allowing to cool completely on a cooling rack.

Once completely cool, spoon 1 tablespoon (20 g) of the strawberry jam into the indentation on the top of the cupcake.

To make the frosting: Add the cream cheese and jam to the bowl of your mixer and cream together. Carefully add the powdered sugar, ½ cup (60 g) at a time, until you reach your desired consistency. For a spreadable frosting, you will need less sugar. For a pipe-able frosting you want to pile high, you will need more. Keep frosting refrigerated until ready to use.

YIELD: 12 cupcakes

CONFETTI CUPCAKES WITH SPRINKLES

Better for you than the ones out of the box, with just as much fun!

FOR THE RAINBOW SPRINKLES:

- ½ cup (60 g) powdered sugar
- 3 ounces (85 g) raw cocoa butter, melted
- Assorted natural vegan food colors, such as India Tree

FOR THE CUPCAKES:

- 1 tablespoon (15 ml) apple cider vinegar
- 1 cup (235 ml) vegan soy, coconut, or Almond Milk (page 27)
- 1½ cups (188 g) all-purpose flour
- 1 teaspoon baking powder
- 1 teaspoon baking soda
- ½ teaspoon salt
- 1 cup (200 g) evaporated cane juice or vegan granulated sugar
- ¼ cup (60 ml) neutral-flavored oil
- ¼ cup (60 ml) water
- 1 tablespoon (15 ml) lemon juice
- 1 tablespoon (15 ml) vanilla extract
- ½ recipe of Rainbow Sprinkles
- 1 recipe frosting from the Strawberry Lemonade Cupcakes (page 150), made without the strawberry jam

To make the sprinkles: Mix the powdered sugar into the melted cocoa butter and divide equally into enough small bowls to match the amount of colors you want to use. (Individual-size ramekins work perfectly for this.) Add food colors to each dish and mix until desired vibrancy is achieved. Place in the freezer to harden. Once hardened, carefully remove the colored white chocolate from the dishes and chop into tiny chunks.

To make the cupcakes: Preheat the oven to 350°F (180°C, or gas mark 4). Line a standard cupcake tin with papers.

In a small bowl, add the vinegar to the milk and set aside. It will curdle and become like buttermilk. In a medium mixing bowl, mix together flour, baking powder, baking soda, and salt. In a separate bowl, mix together evaporated cane juice, oil, water, lemon juice, and vanilla. Add the curdled milk mixture and stir to combine.

Carefully add the dry to the wet and mix to combine, taking care not to overmix. Fill each cupcake paper three-quarters full. Add half of the sprinkles all over the top of the cupcake batter. (Note that if you opt to use store-bought sprinkles instead of making your own, you can fold them into the batter.)

Bake 18 to 20 minutes, until golden and a toothpick entered into the center comes out clean. Remove from oven and cool for 5 minutes before removing from the pan and transferring to a wire rack to cool completely.

Frost cupcakes as desired, and top with remaining sprinkles.

YIELD: 12 cupcakes

CHOCOLATE ALMOND SOUFFLÉS

* Gluten-Free Potential * No Added Oil

Soufflés are generally made with eggs and cream. This here soufflé is made with tofu and nuts. Once cooked, you can serve this not-too-sweet dessert in the dish, or invert it onto a plate. Either way, it is fun to top it with something . . . powdered sugar, ice cream, berries, chocolate, or fruit compote. Any number of toppings are a great addition to this recipe.

Nonstick cooking spray
12 ounces (340 g) soft silken tofu
¾ cup (90 g) almond meal
½ cup (60 g) powdered sugar
¼ cup (20 g) unsweetened cocoa powder
2 tablespoons (16 g) arrowroot powder
2 teaspoons pure vanilla extract
1 teaspoon pure almond extract

Preheat the oven to 350°F (180°C, or gas mark 4).

Spray 4 individual oven-safe ramekins with cooking spray. Place all the ingredients into a blender, and purée until very smooth. Pour an equal amount of mixture in each ramekin. Place the ramekins on a baking sheet, just in case it cooks over in the oven.

Bake for 45 minutes. Remove from oven. Serve in the dish, or invert onto plate. Top with desired toppings.

YIELD: 4 servings

Joni Says

"Not a fan of almond? No problem—replace the almonds with ground cashews or macadamia nuts, or Brazil nuts, or walnuts, or pecans . . . you get the idea—and replace the almond extract with the flavor of your choice."

SALTED PEANUT BUTTER POTS DE CRÈME

* Gluten-Free Potential   * No Added Oil

Traditional pots de crème are made as a baked custard and often have a chocolate component. These are a nice change of pace. Rich with peanut flavor, and the salt that gives it that nice sophisticated finish. Top with a dollop of Whipped Coconut Cream (page 64) or a drizzle of Chocolate Syrup (page 65) if desired.

Nonstick cooking spray
12 ounces (340 g) soft silken tofu
¾ cup (192 g) creamy peanut butter
½ cup (60 g) powdered sugar
¼ cup (80 g) agave nectar
2 tablespoons (16 g) arrowroot powder
2 teaspoons (10 ml) pure vanilla extract
½ teaspoon fine sea salt
1 tablespoon (18 g) coarse sea salt, for finishing

Preheat the oven to 350°F (180°C, or gas mark 4).

Lightly coat 4 individual oven-safe ramekins with cooking spray. Place all the ingredients, except coarse sea salt, into a blender, and purée until very smooth. Pour an equal amount of mixture in each ramekin. Place ramekins on a baking sheet, just in case it cooks over in the oven.

Bake for 45 minutes. Remove from oven. Sprinkle tops with coarse sea salt.

Cool for at least 1 hour in the refrigerator before serving.

YIELD: 4 servings

SECTION THREE

How to Best Substitute for Protein

WHEN *THE COMPLETE GUIDE TO VEGAN FOOD SUBSTITUTIONS* came out, the market was already fairly ripe with cruelty-free substitutes for meat. Can you believe that the quantity and quality of these substitutes have grown exponentially since?

IF THE LACK OF TIME TO MAKE EVERYTHING FROM SCRATCH is what has kept you from going vegan up until now, you're in luck. We have gluten-free chickenless strips, fishless fillets, and a limitless variety of veggie burgers that have far surpassed their cardboardlike predecessors. There seems to be a convenient, convincing, vegan version of just about every protein available. Even vegan shrimp and vegan smoked salmon are available for purchase at well-stocked health food or vegan markets.

Now, more than ever, there are so many tasty and convenient vegan options— both store-bought and homemade (such as the ones in the coming pages). You'll see that it's easy to drop chicken, beef, seafood, and bacon from your diet, and replace them with delicious substitutes and alternatives.

And if you are concerned about getting enough protein while following a vegan lifestyle, you can take comfort in the fact that most of us consume far more protein than we actually need. In order to help people calculate their own individual daily protein intake needs, the World Health Organization (WHO) recommends using the following formula:

(Your ideal weight in pounds) X 0.36 = daily protein intake in grams

Or

(Your ideal weight in kilograms) X 0.8 = daily protein intake in grams

With events such as Meatless Monday, there is ever-increasing public awareness that meat is neither environmentally-friendly, nor the healthiest protein source. Add to that the growing awareness of the undeniable reality of the barbarism taking place behind the doors of slaughterhouses. It is slowly becoming widespread knowledge that it's actually quite simple and deprivation-free to meet one's protein needs when consuming a healthy, varied, and balanced diet of plant-based, vegan foods, such as those listed in the chart. We highly recommend reading more on the subject of vegan nutrition in books such as *Vegan for Life* by Jack Norris, R.D. and Virginia Messina, M.P.H., R.D. (Da Capo Publishing, 2011), *Forks over Knives* by Gene Stone (The Experiment, 2011), and *Going Vegan* by Gerrie Adams and Joni Marie Newman (Fair Winds Press, 2014.)

In addition to the paradigm shift in the vegan world to a less processed way of eating, the meat-eating sector has started in with some rhetoric of their own. Local, grass-fed, pasture-raised, free-range, and humane are all buzzwords that are designed specifically to make one feel better (less guilty) about what they are eating. The truth is, whether the cow or pig was raised on a large farm with plenty of space to roam free, the end result is the same. And no matter how your phrase it, the words "humane" and "slaughter" simply do not belong in the same sentence.

There really is no reason for us to go into all of the gory details here, just watch *Meet Your Meat*, and you will see everything you need in order to give up meat for good.

Whether you want to make a quick substitute using store-bought products, or you plan on making your substitutes from scratch, the following chart will help you decide what sub will work best in the to-be-veganized recipe. **The boldface entries reference from-scratch recipes in this book.**

WHEN THE ORIGINAL RECIPE CALLS FOR . . .	REPLACE WITH . . .
CHICKEN **1 cup (235 ml) chicken broth**	• **1 cup (235 ml) water mixed with 1 teaspoon All-Purpose Chicken-Flavored Broth Powder (page 167)** • 1 cup (235 ml) chicken-flavored vegetable broth, such as Better than Bouillon No Chicken Base • **1 cup (235 ml) water mixed with 1 teaspoon to 1 tablespoon (3 to 8 g) Mushroom Broth Powder (page 218), quantity to taste depending on use** • 1 cup (235 ml) plain vegetable broth
Chicken breasts	• **All-Purpose Cluck-Free Cutlets (page 168)** • Seitan • Store-bought chicken–style breasts, such as Gardein or Match Foods

WHEN THE ORIGINAL RECIPE CALLS FOR . . .	REPLACE WITH . . .
Chicken strips or nuggets	• **All-Purpose Cluck-Free Cutlets (page 168), cut into strips or made into nuggets** • Seitan • Store-bought chicken–style strips or nuggets, such as Gardein or Beyond Meat
Ground chicken (or turkey)	• **All-Purpose Cluck-Free Cutlets (page 168), ground** • Organic textured vegetable protein, reconstituted in chicken-flavored broth
Sliced deli meats	• **Sliced homemade vegan sausages (page 177 and 178), for sandwiches** • Store-bought vegan deli meat slices, such as Tofurky or Yves
BEEF **1 cup (235 ml) beef broth**	• 1 tablespoon (15 ml) vegan steak sauce and 1 tablespoon (15 ml) soy sauce or tamari mixed with 1 scant cup (205 ml) plain vegetable broth to equal 1 cup (235 ml) beef broth • 1 cup (235 ml) store-bought beef-flavored vegetable broth, such as Better than Bouillon No Beef Base • **1 cup (235 ml) water mixed with 1 teaspoon to 1 tablespoon (3 to 8 g) Mushroom Broth Powder (page 218), quantity to taste depending on use** • 1 cup (235 ml) plain vegetable broth
Ground beef	• Store-bought ground beef substitute, such as Lightlife Gimme Lean or Beyond Meat Beefless Crumbles • 1 cup (96 g) organic textured vegetable protein, reconstituted with 1 scant cup (220 ml) beef-flavored broth yields about the same as 1 pound (454 g) ground beef in volume, not weight
Steaks or burgers	• **All-Purpose Cluck-Free Cutlets (page 168)** • Seitan • Portobello mushrooms, marinated and grilled • Store-bought veggie burgers, such as Gardein, Wildwood, or Morningstar
Beef strips	• Portobello mushrooms, marinated and grilled, cut into strips • Seitan • Store-bought beef-style strips or nuggets, such as Gardein
Hot dogs	• Homemade seitan hot dogs • Store-bought vegan hot dogs, such as Tofurky or Tofupups

How to Best Substitute for Protein   157

WHEN THE ORIGINAL RECIPE CALLS FOR . . .	REPLACE WITH . . .
SEAFOOD **Fish fillets**	• Store-bought vegan fish fillets, such as Gardein or Sophie's Kitchen
Lump crab	• Store-bought imitation crab, such as Match Foods
Flaked tuna, tuna salad	• **Sunflower Artichoke Salad (page 198)** • Smashed chickpeas, combined with traditional tuna dressing made with vegan ingredients • Store-bought mock tuna, such as Meatless Select Fishless Tuna or VeganToona
Shrimp	• **Panko Fried Artichokes (page 200)** • Store-bought vegan shrimp, such as Sophie's Kitchen
Scallops	• **Bacon-Seared King Oyster Scallops with Crispy Shallots (page 201)** • Store-bought vegan scallops, such as Sophie's Kitchen
Smoked salmon	• **Sweet Potato and Avocado Sushi (page 196)** • Store-bought vegan smoked salmon, such as Sophie's Kitchen
BACON **Bacon bits**	• **Coconut Bacon (page 209)** • **Bacon Bits (page 210)** • Store-bought coconut bacon, such as Phoney Baloney's • Store-bought imitation bacon bits, such as Bacuns
Bacon strips	• **Soy Bacon (page 208)** • **Seitan Slab o' Bacon (page 212)** • Store-bought vegan bacon, such as Tofurky Smoky Maple Bacon Tempeh, Lightlife Smoky Tempeh Strips, or Lightlife Smart Bacon
Bacon grease	• **Bacon Grease (page 211)** • Store-bought bacon grease, such as Magic Vegan Bacon Grease

WHEN THE ORIGINAL RECIPE CALLS FOR . . .	REPLACE WITH . . .
NO MIMICKING MEAT	Meet optimal daily protein intake by eating a healthy, varied and balanced diet over a 24-hour period, making sure to include protein-rich, minimally-processed, plant-based foods such as: • Cooked-to-perfection beans and legumes (black beans, chickpeas, edamame, kidney beans, lentils, and split peas), enjoyed for example in the form of patties or balls (pages 126 and 224) • Flavorful, al dente whole grains (amaranth, buckwheat, farro, freekeh, and quinoa), enjoyed for example in pilafs or salads (pages 237 and 230) • Plain or lightly salted, raw or dry roasted nuts and seeds, and their butters (almonds, cashews, chia seeds, hemp seeds, sesame seeds, and peanuts) • Grilled, baked, or pan-fried tempeh or tofu slices or cubes (cooked to a pleasurable crispiness) • Raw or steamed, fresh or frozen vegetables (such as broccoli, Brussels sprouts, carrots, cauliflower, and kale)

CHAPTER 5
Chicken and Beef Substitutions

SURE, YOU COULD GO AHEAD AND BUY CRUELTY-FREE chicken and beef items from the store, but where's the fun in that? Making your own substitutes from scratch will take just a little more time and effort than choosing store-bought versions does. The undeniable advantage is that you have complete control over everything they contain, and you can even adapt our recipes (or anyone else's) to your own liking and needs, down to the levels of fat and salt.

This chapter is about to show you how to make irresistible chicken and beef stand-ins from various tasty vegan and protein-rich food sources, such as seitan, tofu, tempeh, beans, and even vegetables. And don't let yourself be deterred by the still fairly common accusation that tofu is bland and quite unappealing when left unprepared. As far as we know, chicken meat is no beauty queen either until it benefits from some heavy seasoning and a bit of cooking!

Practice Makes for Perfect Substitutions

The best way to demonstrate how easy it is to transform a nonvegan recipe into a cruelty-free wonder is to showcase how it's done. Let's go through a sample recipe step by step! Once you know the basics, it's easy to put into practice on any recipe.

< *Ras El Hanout Tofu Sticks, page 176*

CLASSY CHICKEN SALAD WITH DATES & WALNUTS

This recipe is an excerpt from *Back to Butter*, by Molly Chester and Sandy Schrecengost (Fair Winds Press, 2014). We will substitute vegan ingredients for the chicken, bacon, and mayonnaise, and rewrite the directions accordingly.

3 cups (420 g) medium diced precooked chicken

6 ounces (170 g) bacon, roughly chopped, cooked until crisp, and drained

½ cup (90 g) finely diced medjool dates

¼ cup (25 g) thinly sliced scallion, both white and green parts

⅓ cup (30 g) finely sliced celery, cut on the diagonal

1 cup (150 g) seedless red grapes, halved

1 cup (225 g) mayonnaise

1 teaspoon sea salt

½ cup (50 g) toasted walnut halves, roughly chopped

Place the chicken, bacon, dates, scallion, celery, and grapes in a medium-size glass mixing bowl. Stir to combine. Pour the mayonnaise on top and sprinkle with the sea salt. Toss to combine, making sure to coat all the ingredients well. Refrigerate until chilled, adding the walnuts just prior to serving, but after the salad is chilled.

YIELD: 4 to 6 servings

CLASSY CHICKEN SALAD WITH DATES & WALNUTS

Veganized!

We can never say no to vegan versions of chicken salad. We chose to substitute fiber-rich chickpeas for the chicken here, or use chicken-style seitan cutlets as another alternative. If you want to add some flavor to your chickpeas, you can prepare them as in Dill-y Chickpeas (page 226), replacing the oil with just enough prepared vegetable broth to easily combine all the ingredients, about 2 teaspoons or more.

For a lower-fat version to the simple substitution of vegan mayonnaise, replace up to half of the vegan mayonnaise with unsweetened, plain, vegan yogurt, store-bought or homemade (page 28), to taste.

For a soy-free way to dress the salad, you can also completely replace the mayonnaise with our Sour Cream Dressing ("Celine Says," page 30), adding it as needed. (Note that the salad itself won't be soy-free.)

This book offers a few substitutes for bacon, and we chose to use Coconut Bacon here, as it takes very little time to prepare and yields outstanding results. We're adding it at the last minute to avoid sogginess.

3 cups (492 g) cooked chickpeas or 4 All-Purpose Cluck-Free Cutlets (12 ounces, or 340 g) (page 168), diced]— **chicken substitute**

½ cup (90 g) finely diced medjool dates

¼ cup (25 g) thinly sliced scallion, both white and green parts

⅓ cup (30 g) finely sliced celery, cut on the diagonal

1 cup (150 g) seedless red grapes, halved

½ to 1 cup (113 to 225 g) vegan mayonnaise, store-bought or homemade (page 118), as needed]— **mayonnaise substitute**

½ recipe Coconut Bacon (page 209), to taste]— **bacon substitute**

½ cup (50 g) toasted walnut halves, roughly chopped

Salt, to taste and optional

Place the chickpeas or diced cutlets **(this is your chicken substitute)**, dates, scallion, celery, and grapes in a medium-size glass mixing bowl. Stir to combine. Add just enough (start with ½ cup, or 113 g) vegan mayonnaise **(this is your mayonnaise substitute)** to coat all the ingredients well. Toss to combine. Refrigerate until chilled, adding the Coconut Bacon **(this is your bacon substitute)** and walnuts just prior to serving, but after the salad is chilled. Adjust seasoning to taste and add extra mayonnaise if needed, to moisten the salad.

YIELD: 4 to 6 servings

BREAKFAST SAUSAGE PATTIES

* Nut-Free

These little fellers are awesome as a side dish for breakfast alongside tofu scrambled eggs (pages 114) or a chickpea scramble (page 112).

1½ cups (216 g) vital wheat gluten flour
½ cup (60 g) whole-wheat pastry flour (or whole-wheat flour)
¼ cup (30 g) nutritional yeast
1½ teaspoons ground black pepper
1½ teaspoons onion powder
1 teaspoon paprika
½ teaspoon dried sage
¾ cup (180 ml) water
¼ cup (60 ml) tamari or soy sauce
3 tablespoons (45 ml) neutral-flavored oil
3 tablespoons (51 g) organic ketchup
2 tablespoons (30 ml) pure maple syrup
1 teaspoon minced garlic
1 medium green apple, cored and very finely diced
1 teaspoon liquid smoke
Oil, as needed, for frying

Add the flours, nutritional yeast, pepper, onion powder, paprika, and sage to a mixing bowl and combine. In a separate bowl, mix together water, tamari, oil, ketchup, syrup, garlic, diced apple, and liquid smoke.

Add wet to dry and knead until a uniform and slightly elastic dough is formed. Divide into 6 equal portions for burger-size patties or 12 for mini patties. Form into balls, cover and let rest for 30 minutes to allow gluten to develop.

Flatten the balls into patties about ¼-inch (6 mm) thick. If the apple pieces are falling out, that's okay, just press them into the surface of your patties once flattened. You might lose a few in the cooking process, but they will still add flavor in the pan.

Preheat oil in a nonstick pan or cast iron skillet with a lid, over medium heat. Add patties to the pan and cook, covered, for 7 to 8 minutes, flip and cook for an additional 7 to 8 minutes, or until browned and firm.

For a lower-fat alternative, you can bake the sausage instead of frying. Preheat the oven to 350°F (180°C, or gas mark 4). Arrange patties in a single layer on a baking sheet lined with parchment or a nonstick baking mat. Cover lightly with foil, and bake for 20 minutes, carefully uncover and flip and bake for an additional 20 minutes, or until browned and firm.

YIELD: 6 burger-size patties, or 12 mini ones

ITALIAN-STYLE SAUSAGE CRUMBLES

* Quick and Easy

These crumbles work wonderfully as a topping for pizza, stirred into pasta sauce, mixed into a tofu scramble, or anywhere a ground Italian sausage is needed.

1 cup (144 g) vital wheat gluten flour
1 tablespoon (1 g) dried parsley
1 tablespoon (12 g) sugar
1 teaspoon (2 g) dried fennel seed
1 teaspoon dried basil
½ teaspoon black pepper
½ teaspoon dried oregano
¼ teaspoon red chili flakes
2 tablespoons (30 ml) olive oil
½ cup (80 g) minced white onion
2 tablespoons (17 g) minced garlic
½ cup (120 ml) vegetable broth
1 tablespoon (15 ml) tamari
½ teaspoon liquid smoke

In a small mixing bowl, mix together vital wheat gluten flour, parsley, sugar, fennel, basil, black pepper, oregano, and chili flakes. Set aside.

Add oil to a nonstick pan or cast iron skillet and heat over medium-high heat. Add the onions and sauté until translucent and fragrant, 3 to 5 minutes. Add garlic and continue to sauté until lightly browned, 2 to 3 more minutes. Add the vegetable broth, tamari, and liquid smoke, and stir. Bring to a boil.

Reduce heat to medium and add the gluten mixture. Stir to mix with liquid. It will ball up into dry clumps, but keep working it. It will begin to break apart and start to resemble ground sausage. If your mixture is absolutely too dry and won't come together, go ahead and add a bit of water, 1 tablespoon (15 ml) at a time.

Continue to cook, tossing constantly for 5 minutes, or until crumbles are browned and firm.

YIELD: Just under 1 pound, about 2 cups (450 g)

SMOKY STRAWBERRY BBQ SAUCE

* Gluten-Free Potential * Nut-Free * Soy-Free

Strawberry barbecue sauce? Absolutely. It's sweet and sassy and it's got a bit of smoky heat from the chipotle. You can use it as you would any BBQ sauce, but it is a great sauce to use in the BBQ Kale Parfait (page 184) and the BBQ Jackfruit Pizza (page 186).

2 tablespoons (30 ml) vegetable oil
½ cup (80 g) diced yellow onion
½ cup (80 g) diced red onion
2 tablespoons (17 g) minced garlic
1 pound (454 g) fresh strawberries, stems removed and cut into quarters
¼ teaspoon salt
¼ teaspoon black pepper
1 can (15 ounces, or 425 g) diced tomatoes in juice
8 ounces (227 g) tomato sauce
½ cup (110 g) tightly packed brown sugar
¼ to ½ teaspoon chipotle powder, more or less to taste
¼ teaspoon red chili flakes, more or less to taste

In a pot, heat oil over medium-high heat. Add the yellow and red onions and sauté for 3 minutes. Add garlic and sauté an additional 3 minutes, or until fragrant and translucent.

Add the strawberries, salt, and pepper. Continue to cook for an additional 5 minutes, stirring often. Stir in the diced tomatoes, tomato sauce, brown sugar, chipotle powder, and chili flakes. Bring to a boil, reduce to a simmer and simmer uncovered for 30 minutes, returning to stir a few times.

Remove from heat. Using an immersion blender (or carefully transfer to a tabletop blender) blend smooth, if desired. Store in an airtight container in the refrigerator for up to 2 weeks.

YIELD: 3 cups (705 ml)

ALL-PURPOSE CHICKEN-FLAVORED BROTH POWDER

* Gluten-Free Potential   * No Added Oil   * No Added Sugar   * Nut-Free
* Quick and Easy   * Soy-Free

Don't get us wrong. We love some Better than Bouillon No Chicken Base, but it's so satisfying to make a meal from scratch—all the way down to the broth.

¾ cup (90 g) nutritional yeast
¼ cup (4 g) dried parsley
¼ cup (32 g) onion powder
1 tablespon plus 2 teaspoons (14 g) garlic powder
1 tablespoon plus 2 teaspoons (30 g) salt
1 tablespoon (6.5 g) celery seed
2 teaspoons (1 g) dried oregano
2 teaspoons (1 g) dried thyme
1 teaspoon black pepper
1 teaspoon turmeric
1 teaspoon dried rosemary, optional

Add all the ingredients to a very dry blender, spice grinder, or coffee grinder and grind into a very fine powder. Store in an airtight container.

To use, mix 1 teaspoon of powder mixed with 1 cup (235 ml) water. Add additional salt to taste.

YIELD: 1¾ cups (420 g)

ALL-PURPOSE CLUCK-FREE CUTLETS

* No Added Oil   * No Added Sugar   * Nut-Free   * Soy-Free

Gardein, Beyond Meat, Morningstar . . . the list of companies making mock chicken goes on and on. Some soy-free. Some gluten-free. But you know what? They cost a bunch, and not everyone has access to those types of products. (Hello, North Long Beach, why do you not have any good vegan options at the local market?) So we came up with a generic, all-purpose, chicken-style recipe that can be used in all sorts of recipes. You can fry it, chop it, dice it, slice it, grill it, sauté it, add it to soup . . . do anything you want with it.

   1½ cups (216 g) vital wheat gluten flour
   ½ cup (60 g) chickpea flour
   ¼ cup (30 g) nutritional yeast
   1 tablespoon (1 g) dried parsley
   2 teaspoons (6 g) onion powder
   1 teaspoon garlic powder
   1 teaspoon dried oregano
   ½ teaspoon salt
   ¼ teaspoon ground celery seed
   11½ cups (2.7 L) vegan chicken-flavored broth,
      store-bought or homemade (page 167), divided

In a medium-size mixing bowl, mix together all the ingredients except broth. Add 1½ cups (355 ml) of the broth and knead until a wet and elastic dough is formed.

Allow to sit for 15 minutes to allow the gluten to develop. Divide into 8 equal portions and flatten each portion into a cutlet shape. Allow to rest an additional 10 minutes. While resting, place remaining 10 cups (2.35 L) of broth in a pot.

Carefully add each cutlet into the pot, and bring to a boil. Reduce to a gentle simmer, and simmer for one hour. Returning occasionally to give a stir. Remove from heat. To keep moist, store in an airtight container, covered in broth, in the refrigerator, until ready to use.

The cutlets are only partially cooked, and will need to be finished off before consuming. To use, cook according to desired recipe.

YIELD: 8 cutlets

FIESTA CHOPPED CHICKEN SALAD

* Nut-Free

Feel free to substitute any of your favorite proteins, either store-bought or homemade, in place of the cutlets. A simple, chopped tofu, some tempeh, or even black beans would make a tasty substitute.

FOR THE ROASTED FIESTA VEGETABLES:

2 ears corn on the cob, husks removed

1 red bell pepper, cut into strips

1 green chile, such as Anaheim, Hatch, or pasilla, cut into strips

2 tablespoons (30 ml) olive oil

¼ teaspoon salt

¼ teaspoon black pepper

¼ teaspoon oregano

¼ teaspoon paprika

¼ teaspoon dried epazote, optional

FOR THE DRESSING:

¾ cup (168 g) vegan mayo, store-bought or homemade (page 118)

2 tablespoons (30 ml) lime juice

2 tablespoons (15 g) nutritional yeast

½ teaspoon minced garlic

¼ teaspoon red chili flakes, more or less to taste

¼ teaspoon cumin

¼ teaspoon chipotle powder, more or less to taste

FOR THE SALAD:

1 to 2 tablespoons (15 to 30 ml) neutral-flavored oil

4 pieces All-Purpose Cluck-Free Cutlets (page 168), chopped into small pieces

Salt and pepper, to taste

8 ounces (227 g) chopped greens such as romaine, kale, chard, spinach, or arugula

2 Roma tomatoes, seeded and chopped

1 cup (160 g) diced red onion

¼ cup (4 g) chopped cilantro

¼ cup (25 g) scallion

¼ cup (g) pepitas (pumpkin seeds)

To make the roasted fiesta vegetables: Preheat the oven to 400°F (200°C, or gas mark 6). Line a baking sheet with foil. Arrange the corn and peppers in a single layer and drizzle with olive oil. Sprinkle salt, pepper, oregano, paprika, and epazote (if using) all over the vegetables and roast for 30 minutes. Remove from oven and allow to cool.

To make the dressing: Whisk all the ingredients together and set aside. For a lower-fat dressing replace up to half of the mayo with vegetable broth.

To make the salad: Heat 1 to 2 tablespoons (15 to 30 ml) oil in a frying pan over medium-high heat. (Or vegetable broth if you are avoiding added oil.) Add Cluck-Free Cutlets pieces to the pan and sauté until lightly browned and firm. Add salt and pepper to taste. Set aside to cool as you assemble the rest of the salad. Add chopped greens, tomato, red onion, cilantro, scallions, and pumpkin seeds to a large bowl. Chop and add the cooled roasted fiesta vegetables, along with the cooled cutlets. Add the dressing and toss to mix. Serve immediately.

YIELD: 4 main-dish servings

ORANGE SEITAN

* Nut-Free

Why order take-out when you can make-in? Using rice flour instead of wheat flour gives these little nuggets an extra light and crispy crust.

Neutral-flavored oil for frying
½ cup (80 g) rice flour
4 pieces All-Purpose Cluck-Free Cutlets (page 168), cut into bite-size cubes
½ cup (120 ml) water
½ cup (120 ml) orange juice
2 tablespoons (30 ml) lemon juice
2 tablespoons (30 ml) rice vinegar
1 tablespoon plus 1½ teaspoons (23 ml) tamari
¼ cup (55 g) tightly packed brown sugar
½ teaspoon ground ginger
¼ to ½ teaspoon red chili flakes, more or less to taste
2 tablespoons (16 g) cornstarch (preferably organic)
¼ cup (60 ml) water
2 tablespoons (12 g) orange zest

Have ready a plate lined with paper towels.

Heat enough oil to equal ½-inch (1.3 cm) deep in a frying pan to 350°F (180°C). Add rice flour to a resealable plastic bag. Add the cutlet cubes and shake to coat.

Add the coated cutlet cubes to the hot oil and fry until golden and crispy. About 2 minutes per side. Remove from the oil and place on paper towel–lined plate to absorb excess oil.

In a separate pan, mix together water, orange juice, lemon juice, vinegar, tamari, brown sugar, ginger, and red chili flakes. Bring to a boil. Reduce to a simmer.

In a small measure, mix together cornstarch and water to make a slurry. Carefully stir in the slurry and continue to cook until thickened and glossy, stirring constantly, about 3 minutes.

Add the fried seitan pieces and toss to coat. Continue to cook until the seitan is heated all the way through. Garnish with orange zest. Serve immediately.

YIELD: 2 main-dish or 4 side-dish servings

CHILI CORN WAFFLES

These savory waffles make for the perfect stand-in for cornbread, and they make the perfect base for a hearty cheesy chili. Chili purists need not apply.

FOR THE THREE BEAN CHEESY CHILI:

- 1 cup (8 ounces, or 227 g) tomato sauce
- ½ cup (130 g) prepared pinto beans, rinsed and drained
- ½ cup (125 g) prepared black beans, rinsed and drained
- ½ cup (130 g) prepared kidney beans, rinsed and drained
- 1 cup (235 ml) vegetable broth or water
- 1 cup (160 g) finely diced onion
- 1 tablespoon (8 g) garlic powder
- 1 tablespoon (8 g) onion powder
- 1 tablespoon (8 g) chili powder
- 1 teaspoon cumin
- 1 jalapeño pepper, diced
- 1 cup (240 g) plain Sour Cream (page 30)
- 1 tablespoon (18 g) white miso
- ¼ cup (30 g) nutritional yeast

FOR THE SAVORY CORN WAFFLES:

- 1 cup (235 ml) unsweetened almond or soymilk
- 2 tablespoons (30 ml) lemon juice
- ¼ cup (60 ml) warm water
- 2 tablespoons (13 g) ground flaxseed
- 2 tablespoons (30 ml) vegetable oil
- 1 cup (125 g) all-purpose flour
- ¾ cup (110 g) yellow cornmeal
- 2 teaspoons baking powder
- 1 teaspoon freeze-dried chives, or 1 tablespoon (1 g) fresh
- ½ teaspoon sea salt
- ½ teaspoon paprika
- ½ teaspoon garlic powder
- ¼ teaspoon freshly ground black pepper
- 1 cup (154 g) yellow corn kernels

To make the chili: Into a pot, combine the tomato sauce, beans, vegetable broth, onion, garlic powder, onion powder, chili powder, cumin, and jalapeño peppers. Bring to a boil. Reduce to a simmer, cover, and simmer for 20 minutes. Reduce heat to low, and stir in sour cream, miso, and nutritional yeast. Keep warm until ready to serve

To make the waffles: Preheat your waffle iron. Mix together the milk and lemon juice and set aside to curdle and thicken. In a small bowl, whisk together the warm water and ground flaxseed. Add the vegetable oil and stir to combine. In a separate mixing bowl, mix together the flour, cornmeal, baking powder, chives, salt, paprika, garlic powder, and pepper. Add the curdled milk to the flaxseed mixture. Add the wet mixture to the dry and stir to combine; do not overmix. Fold in the corn kernels. Your batter will be thick (not pourable) and you will need to spoon the batter onto a well-oiled waffle iron. Add the mixture to your waffle iron and cook according to manufacturer's instructions. Ladle chili onto each waffle and serve immediately.

YIELD: 6 servings

CHICKPEA TERIYAKI CROQUETTES

* Quick and Easy

Forget traditional chicken teriyaki. It's got nothing on our tender chickpea croquettes that are held together with flour and breadcrumbs. If you like a lot of sauce, double its quantity and follow doneness cues.

¾ teaspoon potato starch or cornstarch (preferably organic)

5 tablespoons (75 ml) water, divided

2 tablespoons (24 g) evaporated cane juice or vegan granulated sugar (use half for less sweet)

2 tablespoons (30 ml) cooking sake

2 tablespoons (30 ml) tamari

Nonstick cooking spray or oil spray

1 can (15 ounces, or 425 g) chickpeas, drained and rinsed

1 tablespoon (16 g) tahini or creamy natural peanut butter

1 teaspoon toasted sesame oil

2 teaspoons (10 ml) fresh lemon juice

1 teaspoon sriracha, optional

1 large clove garlic, minced

2 tablespoons (20 g) minced shallot

2 tablespoons (2 g) minced fresh cilantro or (8 g) parsley

¼ teaspoon fine sea salt, to taste

1½ tablespoons (11 g) whole-wheat pastry flour

1½ tablespoons (8 g) panko breadcrumbs

¼ teaspoon baking soda

Add starch to the bottom of a small bowl. Dissolve with 1 teaspoon water. Combine with 2 tablespoons plus 2 teaspoons (40 ml) water, sugar, sake, and tamari in a small saucepan. Cook on medium-high heat, whisking frequently, until syrupy and slightly thickened, about 6 minutes. Set aside.

Preheat the oven to 400°F (200°C, or gas mark 6). Lightly coat 16 holes out of a 24-hole mini muffin tin with cooking spray.

Place chickpeas in a food processor. Pulse to break chickpeas: You're not looking for a paste, but there should be no whole chickpeas left.

In a large bowl, whisk to combine 2 tablespoons (30 ml) water, the tahini, oil, lemon juice, and sriracha. Add chickpeas, garlic, shallot, cilantro, and salt. Fold to combine. Add flour, breadcrumbs, and baking soda. Fold to combine.

Gather 1 slightly heaping, packed tablespoon (25 g) of mixture, shape into a ball and place in the tin. Repeat with remaining mixture. Lightly coat with cooking spray.

Bake for 15 minutes, carefully flip, and lightly coat with cooking spray. Bake for 10 to 15 minutes, or until golden brown. Remove from oven, let stand 10 minutes before serving with sauce.

YIELD: 16 croquettes, ⅓ cup (80 ml) sauce

CAULIFLOWER TACO CRUMBLES

* Gluten-Free Potential * No Added Sugar * Nut-Free
* Quick and Easy * Soy-Free

Our favorite way to serve this fiber-rich, soy-free meat substitute is as follows: Toast a vegan flour tortilla until light golden and crisp, top it with mashed avocado or with a thin layer of Spicy Chia Cashew Sauce (page 78, applied before toasting the tortilla), shredded lettuce, diced tomatoes, favorite salsa, and this ground "meat." It hits the spot every time! It'll also work in regular tacos, burritos, and anywhere ground meat would be used. You might think that cauliflower contains no protein, but it turns out that while it doesn't offer as much as, say, vital wheat gluten, it's doing alright with 2 g of protein for every 100 g (3.5 ounces).

12 ounces (340 g) fresh, small cauliflower florets

2 teaspoons (5 g) mild to medium chili powder

2 teaspoons (5 g) nutritional yeast

2 teaspoons (4 g) oat flour

1 teaspoon onion powder

1 teaspoon ground cumin

½ teaspoon dried oregano

½ teaspoon fine sea salt, to taste

½ teaspoon garlic powder

½ teaspoon smoked paprika

1/16 to 1/8 teaspoon cayenne pepper, to taste

1 tablespoon (15 ml) olive oil

Spin dry the cauliflower florets to avoid extra moisture. Preheat the oven to 425°F (220°C, or gas mark 7). Line a baking sheet with parchment paper.

(What follows might need to be divided and done in two batches depending on the size of the food processor, but will fit in a 7-cup, or 1.65 L, machine.) Add the chili powder, nutritional yeast, oat flour, onion powder, cumin, oregano, salt, garlic powder, paprika, cayenne pepper, florets, and oil to a food processor. Pulse a few times until it resembles ground meat.

Place evenly on the prepared sheet, and bake for 6 to 10 minutes, until the cauliflower is al dente without being neither too raw, nor too soft. Remove from oven, and let cool slightly before using. The cauliflower is at its best slightly warm, or at room temperature.

YIELD: 2 cups (295 g)

Celine Says

"Cut the florets fairly small before adding them to the food processor so that you don't have to pulse for too long and risk making the crumbles too powdery."

CASHEW BUTTER, PEPPER JELLY, AND TEMPEH SANDWICHES

This is inspired 100 percent by a definitely-not-vegan recipe from the Bayona restaurant in New Orleans!

2 teaspoons (10 ml) grapeseed oil

6 ounces (170 g) scallions, trimmed, cut lengthwise, then into 2-inch (5 cm) pieces

2 tablespoons (30 ml) apple cider vinegar

Salt, to taste

Nonstick cooking spray or oil spray

¼ cup (60 ml) tamari

¼ cup (60 ml) vegetable broth

2 tablespoons (15 g) nutritional yeast

1 tablespoon (15 ml) regular molasses

1 to 2 tablespoons (15 to 30 ml) sriracha, to taste

1 tablespoon (15 ml) olive oil

1 teaspoon ground cumin

1 teaspoon mild chili powder

1 teaspoon liquid smoke

1 teaspoon onion powder

1 pound (2 packages, or 454 g) tempeh, each block cut in half widthwise, then lengthwise, then vertically to make 8 small patties (16 in all)

6 tablespoons (96 g) roasted cashew butter or peanut butter

12 slices of vegan whole-grain sourdough bread

6 tablespoons (120 g) vegan hot pepper jelly

Heat the oil in a skillet. Add the onions and sauté until just tender. Transfer to a medium bowl, add vinegar and salt, and stir to combine. Cover and set aside for 1 hour.

Lightly coat a 9 x 13-inch (23 x 33 cm) baking pan with cooking spray. Add tamari through onion powder to the pan, whisking to combine. Soak the tempeh in the marinade and chill for 1 hour.

Preheat the oven to 400°F (200°C, or gas mark 6). Bake the tempeh in the marinade for 8 minutes. Turn the slices over, and bake for 8 minutes, or until the liquid has been mostly absorbed but is still saucy. Make sure the marinade doesn't burn at the edges of the pan.

To assemble, spread 1 tablespoon (16 g) of cashew butter each on 6 slices of bread. Spread 1 tablespoon (20 g) of hot pepper jelly each on 6 other slices of bread. Add 3 slices of tempeh on 1 slice of cashew-buttered bread. Top with a handful of marinated onions. Top with 1 slice of hot-pepper-jellied bread. Toast in the oven until crispy, and serve immediately.

YIELD: 6 sandwiches

RAS EL HANOUT TOFU STICKS

* No Added Oil

After years of being intrigued by ras el hanout (a rich, Moroccan spice blend), we put it to the test in what turned out to be irresistible, crispy tofu sticks. Purchase ras el hanout online, or at well-stocked or international markets.

> ¼ cup (60 g) Homemade Yogurt (page 28) or store-bought unsweetened plain vegan yogurt
>
> 2 tablespoons (30 ml) fresh lemon juice
>
> 1 to 2 tablespoons (15 to 30 ml) vegetable broth
>
> 2 tablespoons (16 g) ras el hanout, plus 1 teaspoon for coating
>
> 1 tablespoon (8 g) onion powder, plus 1 teaspoon for coating
>
> 4 teaspoons (26 g) agave nectar, divided
>
> 1 teaspoon garlic powder
>
> Generous ½ teaspoon fine sea salt, plus ¼ teaspoon for coating
>
> 1 pound (454 g) super firm tofu, cut into ½-inch (1.3 cm) sticks
>
> 20 vegan buttery crackers (2.1 ounces, or 60 g), such as Late July, finely crushed
>
> 6 tablespoons (90 ml) plain Homemade Creamer (page 26) or extra vegan yogurt

In an 8-inch (20 cm) square baking dish, whisk the yogurt, lemon juice, 1 tablespoon (15 ml) broth, ras el hanout, onion powder, 2 teaspoons (13 g) agave, garlic powder, and generous ½ teaspoon salt to combine. The marinade will be thick, but if it is so thick it could break the sticks, add 1 extra tablespoon (15 ml) broth to thin out. Dip the sticks in the marinade, making sure every side gets coated, including the tips. Cover and store in the refrigerator for 2 hours.

Preheat the oven to 375°F (190°C, or gas mark 5). Line a large baking sheet with parchment paper or silicone baking mat.

In a shallow bowl, combine the crackers, 1 teaspoon ras el hanout, 1 teaspoon onion powder, and ¼ teaspoon salt. Using one hand for the wet and the other for the dry, dip each tofu stick into the cracker mixture, shaking the excess. Transfer to the prepared sheet. Repeat with remaining sticks. Keep the remaining marinade! Bake for 20 minutes. Flip to the other side, and bake for another 15 to 20 minutes, or until golden brown and firm. Remove from oven, and let stand 10 minutes before serving. In the meantime, make the sauce by whisking the remaining marinade, creamer, and remaining 2 teaspoons (13 g) agave, and serve.

YIELD: About 20 sticks, ½ cup (120 ml) dipping sauce

SAUSAGES À LA PROVENÇALE

* No Added Sugar   * Nut-Free   * Soy-Free

These sausages are good to eat by the slice, but they're also great in Mediterranean–style sandwiches, or chopped and browned to serve with ratatouille or any vegetable-rich salad.

1 cup (235 ml) water, more if needed
1 tablespoon (8 g) Mushroom Broth Powder (page 218)
½ cup (82 g) cooked chickpeas
6 large garlic-stuffed or plain green olives (2 ounces, or 56 g)
3 tablespoons (23 g) nutritional yeast
2 tablespoons (30 ml) capers with brine
2 tablespoons (14 g) julienne-cut, soft, sun-dried tomato
2 tablespoons (33 g) tomato paste
1 tablespoon (15 ml) olive oil
1 tablespoon (15 g) maca powder (or extra nutritional yeast)
1 tablespoon (4 g) herbes de Provence
2 teaspoons (5 g) onion powder
2 teaspoons (6 g) garlic powder
½ teaspoon smoked or regular paprika
½ teaspoon fine sea salt
¼ teaspoon cayenne pepper
1 cup plus 2 tablespoons (160 g) vital wheat gluten, more if needed

Place all the ingredients, except vital wheat gluten, in a blender or food processor. Process until smooth. Transfer to a large bowl, and add the gluten on top. Stir with a spoon, then switch to stirring with one hand, making sure to squeeze the mixture to thoroughly combine.

Add an extra 1 tablespoon (15 ml) water or (8 g) gluten if needed to make a soft, workable dough.

Divide the mixture evenly (6 ounces, or 170 g, each) between four 12-inch (30.5 cm) pieces of foil. Form into 4 sausages of about 6.5 inches (17 cm) long. If you prefer thinner sausages, make 6 sausages (4 ounces, or 113 g, each) instead: The instructions remain the same, just use 6 pieces of foil. Roll the foil tightly around the mixture, twisting the ends to enclose the sausages.

Prepare a steamer. Steam the sausages for 1 hour 15 minutes. Remove foil (careful of the steam), and let cool on a wire rack.

The sausages taste best when they spend a night in the refrigerator before serving. Store tightly wrapped in the refrigerator for up to 1 week, or freeze for up to 2 months.

YIELD: Four or six 6½-inch (17 cm) sausages

CHIPOTLE SAUSAGES

* No Added Sugar   * Nut-Free

Vital wheat gluten is a fantastic source of protein, with 75 g of protein for every 100 g (3.5 ounces). Steaming these spicy sausages after tightly wrapping them in foil makes for highly enjoyable results. Serve them simply sliced as is, or even chopped and browned in a pan. We also like to grill their thinner version whole, and add them to lightly toasted buns with guacamole and corn salsa for a Mexican take on hot dogs.

½ cup (82 g) cooked chickpeas
½ cup (120 ml) water, more if needed
2 tablespoons (30 ml) fresh lime juice
2 tablespoons (32 g) tahini
2 tablespoons (36 g) white miso
2 tablespoons (30 ml) adobo sauce from a can of chipotle peppers
2½ teaspoons (17 g) canned chipotle pepper
1 teaspoon Mushroom Broth Powder (page 218)
2 teaspoons (5 g) onion powder
1 teaspoon garlic powder
¼ teaspoon fine sea salt
3 tablespoons (23 g) nutritional yeast
1 tablespoon (15 g) maca powder (or extra nutritional yeast)
2 teaspoons (10 ml) olive oil
1 cup (144 g) vital wheat gluten, more if needed

Place all the ingredients, except vital wheat gluten, in a blender or food processor. Process until smooth, stopping to scrape the sides. Transfer to a large bowl, and add the gluten on top. Stir with a spoon, then switch to stirring with one hand, making sure to squeeze the mixture to thoroughly combine.

Add an extra 1 tablespoon (15 ml) water or (8 g) gluten if needed to make a soft, workable dough.

Divide the mixture evenly (4.7 ounces, or 133 g, each) between four 12-inch (30.5 cm) pieces of foil. Form into 4 sausages of about 6-inches (15 cm) long. If you prefer thinner sausages, make 6 sausages (3 ounces, or 88 g, each) instead: The instructions remain the same, just use 6 pieces of foil. Roll the foil tightly around the mixture, twisting the ends to enclose the sausages.

Prepare a steamer. Steam the sausages for 1 hour 15 minutes. Remove foil (careful of the steam), place on a wire rack, and let cool completely before use. The sausages taste best when they spend a night in the refrigerator before serving. Store tightly wrapped in the refrigerator for up to 1 week, or freeze for up to 2 months.

YIELD: Four or six 6-inch (15 cm) sausages

ASIAN-FLAVORED NUGGETS

* Nut-Free

Chock-full of protein and serious flavor, these nuggets are held together with a combination of blended chickpeas, flour, and vital wheat gluten. Serve them with extra sriracha if you see it as ketchup's spicier cousin like we do, or with the teriyaki sauce from our Chickpea Teriyaki Croquettes (page 172) if you prefer things that are a bit milder.

1 cup (164 g) cooked chickpeas
8 ounces (227 g) tempeh
¼ cup (40 g) minced red onion
2 tablespoons (32 g) tahini
1½ tablespoons (23 ml) fresh lemon juice
1½ tablespoons (23 ml) seasoned rice vinegar
1 tablespoon (15 ml) toasted sesame oil
1 tablespoon (15 ml) neutral-flavored oil
1 tablespoon (18 g) white miso
1 tablespoon (15 ml) tamari
1 tablespoon (15 ml) sriracha, plus extra for serving
1 teaspoon agave nectar
4 cloves garlic, grated or pressed
2 tablespoons (15 g) whole-wheat pastry flour
2 tablespoons (18 g) vital wheat gluten
Nonstick cooking spray or oil spray

Mash the beans in a large bowl: It's okay if just a few pieces of beans are left. Finely crumble (do not mash) the tempeh on top. Add the onion, tahini, lemon juice, vinegar, oils, miso, tamari, sriracha, agave, and garlic on top. Stir to thoroughly combine. Sprinkle the flour and gluten on top, stir again to thoroughly combine. Have a large baking sheet lined with parchment paper or a silicone baking mat handy. Grab 2 packed tablespoons (37 g) of the mixture. Place on the prepared sheet, and shape into a 3-inch (8 cm) nugget of about ½-inch (1.3 cm) thickness. Repeat with remaining mixture. You should get 18 nuggets in all. Cover the nuggets with plastic wrap, and refrigerate for 3 hours, or overnight.

Preheat the oven to 350°F (180°C, or gas mark 4). Remove the plastic wrap, and lightly coat each nugget with cooking spray. Bake 15 minutes, carefully flip the nuggets, coating the other side with spray, and bake for another 10 minutes, or until golden brown and firm. Transfer to a wire rack, and let cool 10 minutes before serving with sriracha for dipping. The nuggets are also great served at room temperature.

YIELD: 18 nuggets

LASAGNA MAC

* No Added Sugar

Less fussy than traditional layered lasagna, with all the flavor.

1 pound (454 g) elbow macaroni
2 cups (470 ml) of your favorite vegan marinara sauce
1 cup (227 g) Almond Cashew Ricotta (page 73)
1 cup (226 g) Cottage-Style Cheese (page 72)
1 recipe Italian-Style Sausage Crumbles (page 165)
½ cup (126 g) diced tomatoes

Prepare the macaroni according to package instructions in lightly salted water.

Preheat the oven to 375°F (190°C, or gas mark 5). Have ready a 9 x 13-inch (23 x 33 cm) baking dish.

Drain the pasta and return to the pot. Add all the other ingredients to the pot and stir to combine. Spread the mixture evenly into baking dish. Bake uncovered for 30 minutes.

YIELD: 8 servings

Joni Says

"For extra cheesy goodness, sprinkle liberally (after baking) with vegan Parmesan, like the Hemp Parm on page 72."

BARBECUE JACKFRUIT

* Gluten-Free Potential   * Nut-Free   * Soy-Free

Jackfruit is one of those foods that when you discover how amazingly versatile it is, you want to put it in everything. It's such a perfect substitute for meat in so many different ways. In this recipe, it does a knock-out job of replacing pulled pork or brisket in a saucy preparation that works well in sandwiches, wraps, over rice, or more specifically in the BBQ Kale Parfait (below) or the BBQ Jackfruit Pizza (page 186).

¼ cup (60 ml) vegetable oil
1 cup (160 g) diced yellow onion
1 can (10 ounces, or 283 g) young green jackfruit in brine, drained and rinsed
1 cup (235 ml) Smoky Strawberry BBQ Sauce (page 166), or your favorite vegan barbecue sauce
1 cup (235 ml) vegetable broth, store-bought or homemade (page 218)
Salt and pepper, to taste

In a pot with a tight-fitting lid, heat oil over medium-high heat. Add the onions and sauté for 2 minutes. Add the jackfruit and sauté for 5 more minutes, tossing frequently. Add the sauce and broth. Bring to a boil, reduce to a simmer, cover and simmer for 1 hour, or until most liquid has been absorbed and the jackfruit is tender and stringy. Return to stir and break up the jackfruit with your spoon, every 15 minutes. Add salt and pepper to taste.

YIELD: 2 cups (18 ounces, or 510 g)

• •

BBQ KALE PARFAIT >>

* Gluten-Free Potential   * Nut-Free

Joni was inspired by an nonvegan version of the same dish made by her friend and colleague, Chef Dennis Horton. This parfait is perfect for packing up for easy lunches throughout the week, a picnic in the park, or a party to minimize dish duty.

4 mason jars (16-ounces, or 470 ml, each), or other glass serving dish
2 cups (4 ounces, or 113 g) chopped dino lacinto kale, tightly packed
2 cups (390 g) cooked brown rice
1 recipe Barbecue Jackfruit (above)
1 recipe Creamy Cilantro Coleslaw (page 114)

Add ½ cup (28 g) chopped kale to the bottom of each jar. Add ½ cup (40 g) brown rice over the kale. The heat of the rice lightly cooks the kale to make it tender. Add ½ cup (98 g) Barbecue Jackfruit over the rice. Finally, top it off with ½ cup (85 g) coleslaw. Serve immediately, or seal and store in the refrigerator for up to 5 days.

YIELD: 4 parfaits

BBQ JACKFRUIT PIZZA

* Nut-Free

Seriously guys, this one is the one that might make your omni friends say, "This is vegan?" And you can proudly say, "Yes," even though this pizza has tofu *and* jackfruit—two *weird* vegan ingredients that are gussied up with tons of flavor.

FOR THE EASY TOFU FETA:

½ block (6 ounces, or 170 g) extra-firm tofu, drained and pressed
1 tablespoon (15 ml) olive oil
1 tablespoon (15 ml) lemon juice
1 teaspoon dried basil, or 1 tablespoon (2.5 g) finely chopped fresh basil
Salt and pepper, to taste

FOR THE PIZZA:

1 pound (454 g) vegan pizza dough, store-bought or homemade (page 187)
1 cup (235 ml) Smoky Strawberry BBQ Sauce (page 166), or your favorite BBQ sauce, divided
1 recipe Barbecue Jackfruit (page 184)
1 small red onion, sliced into rings
2 tablespoons (30 ml) olive oil
¼ cup (4 g) chopped fresh cilantro

To make the feta: Crumble the tofu into a small bowl until it resembles feta. Add all the other ingredients and mix together with your hands. Keep covered and refrigerated until ready to use. This tastes even better after sitting overnight in the refrigerator to really let the flavors develop.

To make the pizza: Preheat the oven to 450°F (230°C, or gas mark 8). Have ready a lightly floured baking sheet. Roll the pizza dough into a 12 x 10-inch (30 x 25 cm) rectangle.

Evenly apply ¾ cup (180 ml) of the barbecue sauce all over the dough. Evenly apply jackfruit all over the pizza, then sprinkle evenly with tofu feta. Top with onion rings. Drizzle the remaining ¼ cup (60 ml) barbecue sauce all over the top. Brush the edges crust with olive oil. Bake for 16 minutes, or until the pizza is golden brown.

Remove from oven and garnish with chopped cilantro.

Slice into 8 pieces and serve immediately.

YIELD: 1¼ cups (300 g) Easy Tofu Feta, 8 servings pizza

FANTASTICA PIZZA AND STROMBOLI DOUGH

* Nut-Free * Soy-Free

Whether you are craving a crispy, fully loaded pizza pie or a Stromboli, this recipe is sure to become your new go-to! The more gluten flour you add, the chewier and more tender the results. It's a matter of personal preference, so follow your own taste.

1 cup (235 ml) water, divided

1 envelope (¼ ounce, or 7 g) active dry yeast

1 teaspoon evaporated cane juice or vegan granulated sugar

2 cups (250 g) all-purpose or bread flour or (240 g) white or regular whole-wheat flour

¼ to ½ cup (36 to 72 g) vital wheat gluten flour, to taste (see headnote)

½ teaspoon salt

1 to 2 tablespoons (15 to 30 ml) extra-virgin olive oil, divided, as needed

Heat ½ cup (120 ml) of water to lukewarm. Mix together the yeast, evaporated cane juice, and warm water. Let stand 10 minutes in order to proof the yeast. The mixture will foam and indicate that the yeast is alive and ready to go.

In a mixing bowl, mix together the flours and salt. Add the yeast mixture, remaining ½ cup (120 ml) water, and 1 tablespoon (15 ml) of oil on top, and stir to combine. Add extra all-purpose flour or whole-wheat flour if the dough is too wet, more water if too dry, a little bit at a time. Your goal is a soft elastic dough ball that is easy to handle and not sticky.

Knead for about 10 minutes.

Divide into two, form each piece into a ball. Brush with a light coat of oil: This step isn't entirely necessary, but is recommended to prevent drying. Cover with plastic wrap, and let rise for 1 hour.

Preheat the oven to 450°F (230°C, or gas mark 8), or follow the guidelines of the recipe the dough is used in. It's best to preheat the pizza stone or baking sheet at the same time the oven preheats to get a well-baked, crispy pizza underside.

Punch down the dough, knead an additional 2 to 3 minutes and form into a pizza crust. Add your favorite toppings, and transfer onto the preheated pizza stone or baking sheet. Bake for about 10 minutes, or until the crust is a nice golden brown. Be sure to follow the guidelines of the recipe the dough is used in, for accurate baking cues.

YIELD: 2 pizza crusts

CHAPTER 6
Seafood Substitutions

IF HUMAN OVER-CONSUMPTION OF FISH CONTINUES at today's pace, our oceans will be completely depleted of seafood by 2050. Marine life helps keep the ocean environment stable, but marine biologists have already noticed a sharp decline in the amount of ocean life due to overfishing.

Over 50 percent of the fish used for food actually comes from farms. Fish farming has its own set of environmental and cruelty issues: Did you know that a farmed salmon or tuna can eat over twenty times its own weight in wild-caught anchovies and herring? Indeed, many fish farms raise their fish using wild-caught feeder fish, which is a very unsustainable practice. Add to that the rising levels of water pollution, and it's clear that it has never been so timely to switch to vegan fish alternatives.

Luckily, it isn't hard to bring the taste of the ocean onto your vegan plate. The freezer and shelves of well-stocked grocery stores are increasingly filled with vegan-friendly fish products. And as always, if you're more inclined to making your own alternatives or don't have access to the aforementioned products, you have plenty of great options. The following pages will demonstrate that a little seaweed and clever blends of spices combined with mushrooms, rice, sweet potato, sunflower seeds, and more will do wonders in replicating the flavor (and oftentimes, texture) of fish.

Practice Makes for Perfect Substitutions

The best way to demonstrate how easy it is to transform a nonvegan recipe into a cruelty-free wonder is to showcase how it's done. Let's go through a sample recipe step by step! Once you know the basics, it's easy to put into practice on any recipe.

< *Sweet Potato and Avocado Sushi, page 196*

SUSTAINABLE SWORDFISH AND PINEAPPLE KABOBS

Non-Veganized

This recipe is an excerpt from *Make-Ahead Meals Made Healthy*, by Michele Borboa (Fair Winds Press, 2011). We will substitute vegan ingredients for the honey and swordfish steaks, and rewrite the directions accordingly.

⅓ cup (80 ml) olive oil
½ cup (120 ml) pineapple juice
½ cup (20 g) fresh basil
3 cloves garlic
Zest and juice of 1 orange
½ teaspoon salt
¼ teaspoon freshly ground black pepper
2 tablespoons (30 ml) white wine vinegar
2 tablespoons (40 g) honey
2 pounds (908 g) swordfish steaks, cut into 24 cubes
24 large cubes fresh pineapple
8 wooden skewers, soaked in water for 30 minutes

In a food processor, combine oil, pineapple juice, basil, garlic, orange zest and juice, salt, pepper, vinegar, and honey. Transfer to a large plastic bag and add fish. Refrigerate for 2 to 3 hours.

Preheat grill to medium-high. Thread swordfish and pineapple onto skewers. Oil grill grate and grill kabobs for 3 to 4 minutes per side or until just medium-rare. Remove from grill and allow to cool completely.

YIELD: 8 skewers, or 8 servings

SUSTAINABLE SWORDFISH AND PINEAPPLE KABOBS

Veganized!

Well, if there is one thing that is sustainable, it's not eating animals from the sea! So we are replacing the swordfish with your choice of king oyster mushrooms or tofu. You will also notice that we cut the marinade in half. Because tofu and mushrooms are not as absorbant as meat or fish, the extra marinade is not necessary. If you find your marinade is more like a paste, feel free to add a little bit of water to thin it out. It will depend on the amount of juice in your orange, and how much moisture is in your basil and garlic.

- **3 tablespoons (45 ml) olive oil**
- **¼ cup (60 ml) pineapple juice**
- **¼ cup (10 g) fresh basil**
- **2 cloves garlic**
- **Zest and juice of ½ an organic orange**
- **¼ teaspoon fine sea salt**
- **⅛ teaspoon freshly ground black pepper**
- **1 tablespoon (15 ml) white wine vinegar**
- **1 tablespoon (20 g) agave nectar** —(honey substitute)
- **2 pounds (908 g) super firm tofu, or the stems from 8 king oyster mushrooms, cut into 24 cubes** —(swordfish steaks substitute)
- **24 large cubes fresh pineapple**
- **8 wooden skewers, soaked in water for 30 minutes**

In a food processor, combine oil, pineapple juice, basil, garlic, orange zest and juice, salt, pepper, vinegar, and agave **(this is your honey substitute)**. Transfer to a large plastic bag and add tofu or king oyster mushrooms **(this is your swordfish substitute)**. Refrigerate for 2 to 3 hours.

Preheat grill to medium-high. Thread tofu or mushrooms and pineapple cubes onto skewers. Oil grill grate and grill kabobs for 3 to 4 minutes per side or until golden brown. Remove from grill and allow to cool completely.

YIELD: 8 skewers, or 8 servings

HEART OF PALM RINGS

* No Added Sugar

These little golden rings of goodness make for a great substitute for fried calamari, especially when served with Dill-y Tartar Sauce for dipping. When you purchase your hearts of palm, make sure that you do not buy the salad-cut variety. Buy whole hearts of palm, so that you will be able to slice them into rings. If your hearts do not easily separate into rings, that's okay. They will still be just as tasty, they just won't look like calamari rings . . . they'll be more like calamari nuggets.

1 cup (235 ml) full-fat coconut milk
2 tablespoons (30 ml) lemon juice
1 tablespoon (15 ml) sriracha
1 can (14 ounces, or 396 g) whole hearts of palm,
 drained and rinsed, sliced into thin rings
1 cup (125 g) all-purpose flour
½ teaspoon paprika
½ teaspoon cayenne pepper
1 teaspoon garlic powder
Oil, for frying
Lemon wedges, for serving
1 recipe Dill-y Tartar Sauce (page 118), for dipping

Stir together the coconut milk, lemon juice, and sriracha sauce in a small bowl. It will thicken and become like buttermilk. Add sliced hearts of palm to the thickened coconut mixture and let soak for 20 minutes.

Add the flour, paprika, cayenne pepper, and garlic powder to a shallow dish, or resealable plastic bag.

If you have a deep fat fryer, now is a good time to use it. Otherwise fill a pot with oil to equal 1 inch (2.5 cm) and heat to 350°F (180° C). Have ready a plate or tray lined with paper towels.

Remove the rings from the coconut milk mixture and shake off excess milk. The rings should be wet, but not dripping. Add them to the flour to coat. Carefully transfer to the hot oil, a few at a time, and fry until golden and crispy. About 3 minutes. Carefully remove from the oil and transfer the lined plate to absorb excess oil.

Repeat until all rings are fried. Serve immediately with lemon wedges and Dill-y Tartar Sauce for dipping.

YIELD: 2 appetizer servings

FREEKEH FRITTERS

* No Added Sugar   * Nut-Free   * Soy-Free

Freekeh is an ancient, middle eastern grain that is actually young, green wheat. It is roasted, and then the chaff gets rubbed off. The literal translation of freekeh is "to rub." These fritters are prepared in a way that mimics crab cakes. The hijiki seaweed gives them a nice seafood-y flavor, along with the Old Bay Seasoning that is a familiar favorite for crab cake lovers everywhere. Make them extra special by serving them with Dill-y Tartar Sauce (page 118), Spicy Sauce (page 196), or your favorite aioli.

2½ cups (590 ml) water
1 cup (160 g) whole freekeh
¼ cup (12 g) hijiki seaweed
1 teaspoon salt
½ cup (60 g) whole-wheat flour
¼ cup (40 g) minced onion
1 tablespoon (7 g) Old Bay Seasoning
1 tablespoon (1 g) dried parsley
Oil for frying

Add the water, freekeh, seaweed, and salt to the bowl of your rice cooker and cook according to machine instructions. Alternatively, add the water, freekeh, seaweed, and salt to a pot and bring to a boil, reduce to a simmer and simmer for 20 to 25 minutes, or until tender.

Allow the mixture to cool enough to handle. Add the flour, onion, Old Bay, and parsley. Mix together with your hands. Form the mixture into 12 patties about 2 inches (5 cm) in diameter.

If you have a deep fat fryer, now is a good time to use it. Otherwise fill a frying pan with enough oil to equal ½-inch (1.25 cm) deep to 350°F (180° C). Have ready a plate or tray lined with paper towels.

Carefully add the patties to the hot oil and fry for 2 to 3 minutes per side, or until golden and crispy. Carefully transfer to the lined plate to absorb excess oil. Serve immediately.

For a lower-fat version, you can bake them instead of frying. Preheat the oven to 350°F (180°C, or gas mark 4). Arrange the fritters in a single layer on a baking sheet lined with parchment or a nonstick baking mat. Cover lightly with foil, and bake for 20 minutes, carefully uncover and flip and bake for an additional 20 minutes, or until browned and firm.

YIELD: 12 fritters

FLAKY FISH-Y TACOS WITH RADISH RELISH

* Gluten-Free Potential   * No Added Sugar

The fish-y component is seaweed-infused rice that is flaky and flavorful. If you like things really fishy, go ahead and double the amount of hijiki, and soak it in the rice water for up to an hour before cooking the rice.

FOR THE FLAKY FISH-Y RICE:

- **1 cup (180 g) uncooked long grain rice (such as basmati or jasmine)**
- **2 cups (470 ml) water**
- **1 tablespoon (3 g) hijiki seaweed**
- **½ teaspoon salt, to taste**
- **¼ teaspoon cumin**
- **⅛ teaspoon red chili flakes, to taste**

FOR THE RADISH RELISH:

- **1 cup (116 g) finely diced red radish**
- **1 cup (160 g) finely diced red onion**
- **1 green chile (jalapeño pepper, Anaheim, or pasilla), finely diced**
- **¼ cup (4 g) chopped cilantro**
- **1 tablespoon (9 g) minced garlic**
- **1 tablespoon (15 ml) lime juice**
- **Salt and pepper, to taste**

FOR THE TACOS:

- **6 to 12 corn tortillas (depending on the size you use)**
- **2 cups (140 g) shredded red or green cabbage (or a mix of both!)**
- **1 recipe Dill-y Tartar Sauce (page 118)**
- **1 recipe Pepita Pignola Sprinkles (page 236)**

To make the rice: Stir all the ingedients in the bowl of your rice cooker and cook according to machine instructions. If you do not have a rice cooker, add water and seaweed to a pot with a tight-fitting lid. Bring to a boil, stir in rice and spices to the boiling water, reduce to a simmer, cover and simmer for 15 to 20 minutes until fluffy and tender.

To make the relish: Combine the ingredients and keep refrigerated until ready to use.

To make the tacos: Heat the tortillas in a dry pan until browned on both sides. Transfer to a tortilla warmer. To each tortilla, add a scoop of rice, a pinch of cabbage, tartar sauce, relish, and top with the Pepita Pignola Sprinkles. Serve immediately.

YIELD: 6 to 12 tacos

 Joni Says

"Hijiki works best due to its strong sea flavor and ability to hold shape. Other seaweeds can be used (except Nori; it dissolves into a slimy mess!) Simply double the amount, tie it up in cheesecloth, place in the water when boiling, and remove before serving."

SWEET POTATO AND AVOCADO SUSHI

* Gluten-Free Potential   * Nut-Free

This clever roll mimics the look of an inside-out salmon roll, with thin slices of sweet potato standing in for the salmon. The sweet rice plays nicely with the spicy sauce, scallion, and bell pepper. Because of the cooling and prep time involved, you can make this in two nights. One night for prep, and the next day assembly.

FOR THE RICE:

1 cup (180 g) arborio rice (sushi rice)
2 cups (470 ml) water
1 tablespoon (20 g) agave nectar
1 tablespoon (15 ml) rice vinegar
½ teaspoon salt

FOR THE SWEET POTATOES:

¼ cup (60 ml) tamari (use certified gluten-free)
¼ cup (60 ml) water
2 tablespoons (30 ml) mirin
2 tablespoons (17 g) minced garlic
2 tablespoons (28 g) packed brown sugar
1 tablespoon (15 ml) sesame oil
1 large (about 1 pound, or 454 g) sweet potato

FOR THE SPICY SAUCE:

¼ cup (56 g) vegan mayo, store-bought or homemade (page 118)
1 tablespoon (15 ml) sriracha
2 teaspoons (10 ml) sesame oil

FOR THE ROLLS:

3 sheets of nori, cut in half
2 avocados
1 red bell pepper, julienne
6 stalks scallion, ends trimmed
Black sesame seeds, optional as garnish

YOU WILL ALSO NEED:

Aluminum foil
A bamboo sushi rolling mat
A gallon-size (1 L) resealable plastic bag
Plastic wrap

To make the rice: Place all the ingredients in a rice cooker and follow the instructions on your machine. If you do not have a rice cooker, bring water and salt to a boil in medium saucepan. Stir in the rice, agave, and vinegar. Return to a boil, reduce to a simmer, cover, and cook until rice is tender and has absorbed all the liquid, 16 to 18 minutes. Remove from heat and cool completely.

To make the sweet potatoes: Preheat the oven to 375°F (190°C, or gas mark 5). Have ready an 8-inch (20 cm) square baking dish.

In a small mixing bowl, whisk together all the ingredients except the sweet potato. Pour a small amount of marinade in the bottom of the baking dish. Peel the sweet potato and slice into thin slices, approximately ⅛ inch (3 mm). Dip each slice in marinade and layer in the baking dish. Pour any remaining marinade into the dish. Cover tightly with foil and bake for 30 minutes. Remove from oven, remove foil and cool completely.

To make the spicy sauce: Whisk the ingredients together until well combined. Keep refrigerated until ready to use.

To assemble the rolls: Place your bamboo mat inside a resealable bag. Place on a flat work surface with the bag opening facing away from you. Place 1 half-sheet of nori on the plastic wrap. Add a layer of cooled rice to completely cover the nori about ¼-inch (6 mm) thick. Flip over so the rice is face down on the plastic and nori side is up. Spread a thin layer of spicy sauce on the nori.

To the center of the nori sheet, layer 2 to 3 slices of cooled sweet potato, one-quarter of one avocado, sliced, about 3 julienne strips of red bell pepper, and 1 stalk of scallion. Carefully roll the sushi as tightly as possible to close and create an inside-out roll.

Open the mat and make sure roll is seam side up. Lay several pieces of sweet potato over the seam, making sure to overlap the edges. Cover the entire roll with plastic wrap, then re-roll in the bamboo mat to form the sweet potato around the roll. Leaving the roll in the plastic wrap, lay the roll sweet potato side up.

Using a very sharp knife, cut off each end of the roll and discard (or eat!). Then cut the roll in half. Then cut each half into quarters, and finally each quarter into eighths.

Carefully remove each piece from the plastic and plate. Garnish with black sesame seeds if desired.

Serve with spicy sauce for dipping.

YIELD: 6 rolls (48 pieces)

SUNFLOWER ARTICHOKE SALAD

* Gluten-Free Potential * No Added Sugar * Nut-Free
* Quick and Easy

Who needs tuna fish? This salad works perfectly on a sandwich, in a wrap, or over a bed of greens. It also makes a pretty snazzy No-Tuna BeLT (page 199).

1 cup (128 g) sunflower seeds
1 can (14 ounces, or 396 g) artichoke hearts, drained, rinsed, and finely chopped
½ cup (80 g) finely diced red onion
¼ cup (15 g) finely chopped fresh parsley
¼ cup (25 g) finely chopped scallion
2 tablespoons (23 g) diced pimientos
½ cup (112 g) vegan mayonnaise, store-bought or homemade (page 118)
1 tablespoon (15 ml) fresh lemon juice
½ teaspoon dried dill or 1½ teaspoons fresh dill
¼ teaspoon cayenne pepper, more or less to taste
Salt and pepper, to taste

Add the sunflower seeds, artichoke hearts, red onion, parsley, scallion, and pimientos to a mixing bowl.

In a separate small bowl mix together the mayo, lemon juice, dill, and cayenne pepper. Add dressing to salad and mix well. Add salt and pepper to taste.

Keep refrigerated until ready to serve.

YIELD: About 3 cups (615 g)

NO-TUNA B(E)LT

This sandwich is a fusion of a tuna melt and a BLT (hence the silly name). It makes an awesome dinner served up alongside your favorite tomato soup.

FOR THE SPREAD:

¼ cup (56 g) vegan mayonnaise, store-bought or homemade (page 118)
½ teaspoon mild Dijon mustard
½ teaspoon dried dill, or 1½ teaspoons fresh
¼ teaspoon onion powder
¼ teaspoon chipotle powder, or cayenne pepper

FOR THE SANDWICH:

¼ cup (56 g) Vegan Butter (page 24) or Bacon Grease (page 211), softened
4 slices sourdough bread
4 slices 'Merican Cheese (page 70) or any vegan cheese
1 cup (205 g) Sunflower Artichoke Salad (page 198)
2 slices of tomato
4 slices (or more) Veggie (page 207) or Soy Bacon (page 208)
2 large leaves red or green leaf lettuce

To make the spread: Whisk together the ingredients and set aside.

To make the sandwich: Spread 1 tablespoon (14 g) of butter or Bacon Grease on 1 side of each slice of bread. Then turn the bread over and spread 1 heaping tablespoon (16 g) spread on each slice of bread. Add 1 slice of cheese and 1 lettuce leaf to each slice of bread, then top 2 slices with ½ cup (103 g) of the Sunflower Artichoke Salad. On top of the salad, place 1 slice of tomato and 2 slices of Veggie Bacon. Top with remaining 2 slices of bread.

Heat a frying pan or cast iron skillet over medium heat. Place the sandwich in the hot pan and grill until golden brown, crisp, and toasty. Flip and repeat on the other side. Serve hot.

YIELD: 2 sandwiches

Joni Says

"The key to making a perfect grilled cheese or melt is steam! Use a stainless steel mixing bowl, or a pot with a handle, to cover your sandwich on a pan heated over medium heat. This traps in the steam and helps to melt your cheese before the bread burns. Use care when removing the bowl, as it can get hot! I use a spatula and a potholder to remove it."

PANKO FRIED ARTICHOKES

* No Added Sugar   * Nut-Free (If using soymilk)   * Quick and Easy
* Soy-Free (If using coconut or almond milk)

These crispy, golden-fried nuggets are the perfect snack or appetizer when you crave or miss fried shrimp. They taste great dipped in the Dill-y Tartar Sauce (page 118), the Special Sauce (page 128), Spicy Sauce (page 196), or your favorite aioli. If you can't find quartered artichoke hearts, simply buy them whole and cut them in half lengthwise as they can be more delicate and difficult to cut.

1 can (14 ounces, or 396 g) quartered artichoke hearts, drained and patted dry
½ cup (120 ml) unsweetened plain soy, almond, or coconut milk
1 tablespoon (15 ml) apple cider vinegar
½ cup (62 g) all-purpose flour
½ teaspoon onion powder
½ teaspoon garlic powder
½ teaspoon dried parsley
¼ teaspoon paprika
¼ teaspoon salt
¼ teaspoon pepper
¾ cup (60 g) panko bread crumbs
Neutral-flavored oil for frying

Set up a frying station near your stove or deep-fat fryer.

Place your drained and dried artichoke heart on a plate. In a shallow bowl, mix together milk and vinegar, it will curdle and become like buttermilk. Set aside. In a separate shallow dish, mix together the flour, onion powder, garlic powder, parsley, paprika, salt, and pepper. Place panko bread crumbs in a separate shallow dish. And, finally, line an additional plate with paper towels.

Add enough oil to the bottom of a pot or pan to equal ½-inch (1.3 cm) deep and heat to 350°F (or 180°C).

Take 1 piece of quartered artichoke (holding on to the stem end) and dip in the milk, then into the flour mixture to coat, then back into the milk, then into the panko to coat, then finally into the oil to fry.

Fry 1 to 2 minutes per side, or until golden and crispy. Transfer to the paper towel–lined plate to absorb excess oil. Repeat with remaining pieces. Serve immediately.

YIELD: 18 to 20 pieces

BACON-SEARED KING OYSTER SCALLOPS WITH CRISPY SHALLOTS

* Quick and Easy

Sometimes we cook for fun, and we think this is a really fun dish. It's whimsical, yet sophisticated—just look at the name! The coconut oil in the bacon grease gives these mushrooms a buttery flavor that really makes 'em taste like scallops.

4 fresh king oyster mushrooms
¼ cup (60 ml) vegan Bacon Grease (page 211)
1 shallot, thinly sliced
1 teaspoon minced garlic
Salt and pepper, to taste

For this recipe, you will only use the stems of the mushrooms. Save the caps to use in another dish, or simply discard. Carefully cut the mushroom stems into scallop-size pieces. Depending on the size of your mushrooms, you will get as few as 2 or as many as 5 per stem. Set aside.

Heat the Bacon Grease in a pan over medium-high heat. Add the shallot, and sauté for 2 to 3 minutes. Add the garlic and cook an additional 2 minutes.

Reduce heat to medium and add the mushroom pieces in a single layer, cut side down. Cook for 3 to 4 minutes, or until browned. Flip over and cook an additional 3 to 4 minutes. This time spoon some of the grease over the top. Season with salt and pepper.

Remove from heat and allow the mushrooms to sit in the pan for a few minutes to absorb a little more of the oil. Serve immediately.

YIELD: 2 servings

CHAPTER 7
Bacon Substitutions

IT MIGHT BE SOMEWHAT SURPRISING TO HEAR, but the second main reason given by folks who feel they just can't commit to veganism is the idea of a life without bacon. (The first reason is, less surprisingly, the fear of cheeselessness.)

We've already touched on this in the first volume of *The Complete Guide to Vegan Food Substitutions*: The appeal of bacon isn't the animal or body part it comes from. No, what most people are after when thinking bacon is the smokiness, saltiness, fattiness, and a little hint of sweet flavor. Not dead pig.

So turn the pages and dive into recipes that make use of protein sources such as tempeh, tofu, and seitan to offer everything you look for in bacon, in a cruelty-free way. We also make bacon substitutes from couldn't-be-more-plant-based vegetables and coconut flakes. Long live veggie bacon—and pigs!

Practice Makes for Perfect Substitutions

The best way to demonstrate how easy it is to transform a nonvegan recipe into a cruelty-free wonder is to showcase how it's done. Let's go through a sample recipe step by step! Once you know the basics, it's easy to put into practice on any recipe.

< *Veggie Bacon, page 207*

AUNT MIMI'S NEW POTATOES, GREEN BEANS, AND BACON WITH DILL

Non-Veganized

This recipe is an excerpt from *Back to Butter*, by Molly Chester and Sandy Schrecengost (Fair Winds Press, 2014). We will substitute vegan ingredients for the bacon and butter, and rewrite the directions accordingly.

1 pound (454 g) bacon, cut into ½-inch (1.3 cm) pieces
3 tablespoons (54 g) sea salt, divided, plus more to taste
1½ pounds (680 g) fingerling potatoes, scrubbed, bad spots removed
7 cups (about 2 pounds [908 g]) fresh green beans, trimmed and cut into 1-inch (2.5 cm) pieces
3 tablespoons (42 g) butter
3 tablespoons (45 ml) extra-virgin olive oil
3 tablespoons (12 g) chopped fresh dill
2 tablespoons (8 g) chopped fresh flat-leaf parsley
Freshly ground pepper, to taste

Fill a large-size pot with 3 quarts (2.7 L) water, cover, and bring to a boil.

While the water is heating, in a large-size sauté pan over medium-high heat, sauté the bacon until very crisp but not burned, approximately 15 minutes. With a slotted spoon, remove the cooked bacon to drain on a paper towel. Reserve 3 tablespoons (45 ml) of the bacon fat.

Once the water has reached a boil, add 2 tablespoons (36 g) of the sea salt and the potatoes. Lower heat to medium, cover with a lid, and boil for 5 minutes, then add the beans and remaining 1 tablespoon (18 g) sea salt. Raise heat to bring back to a boil, then lower heat to medium and boil for 15 minutes, or until the beans are crisp tender and the potatoes are fork tender (do not allow them to get past this).

While the vegetables are boiling, melt the butter in a small-size saucepan, then add the reserved bacon fat, olive oil, dill, and parsley. Stir to combine.

As soon as the vegetables are cooked, remove from heat and drain in a large-size colander. Return the vegetables to the hot pot, then pour the butter mixture over the hot vegetables and carefully fold to distribute. Season to taste with additional sea salt and pepper. Sprinkle with bacon and serve.

YIELD: 4 servings

AUNT MIMI'S NEW POTATOES, GREEN BEANS, AND BACON WITH DILL

Veganized!

The way we see it, this recipe is super-easy to make vegan, and as a bonus, you will still get all of the flavor with about a third of the salt and fat. And because we are lovers of vegetables, we chose to cut back on the boiling time on the green beans to leave them crisp and bright green.

1 tablespoon (18 g) sea salt, divided, plus more to taste

1½ pounds (680 g) fingerling potatoes, scrubbed, bad spots removed

7 cups (about 2 pounds [908 g]) fresh green beans, trimmed and cut into 1-inch (2.5 cm) pieces

3 tablespoons (45 ml) vegan Bacon Grease (page 211) — (bacon fat substitute)

¼ cup (60 ml) vegetable broth, the Mushroom Broth Powder (page 218) works wonderfully here — (butter and oil substitute)

3 tablespoons (12 g) chopped fresh dill

2 tablespoons (8 g) chopped fresh flat-leaf parsley

Freshly ground pepper, to taste

1 cup (70 g) Coconut Bacon (page 209), or (102 g) Bacon Bits (page 210) — (bacon substitute)

Fill a large-size pot with 3 quarts (2.7 L) water, cover, and bring to a boil.

Once the water has reached a boil, add 2 teaspoons (12 g) of the sea salt and the potatoes. Lower heat to medium, cover with a lid, and boil for 15 minutes, then add the beans and remaining 1 teaspoon sea salt. Raise heat to bring back to a boil, then lower heat to medium and boil for 5 minutes, or until the beans are crisp tender and the potatoes are fork tender (do not allow them to get past this).

While the vegetables are boiling, melt the vegan Bacon Grease **(this is your substitute for the butter and the bacon fat)** in a small-size measure (you can do this in the microwave, if desired), then add the vegetable broth **(this is your substitute for the additional fat)**, dill, and parsley. Stir to combine.

As soon as the vegetables are cooked, remove from heat and drain in a large-size colander. Return the vegetables to the hot pot, then pour the bacon grease mixture over the hot vegetables and carefully fold to distribute. Season to taste with additional sea salt and pepper. Sprinkle with Coconut Bacon or Bacon Bits **(this is your bacon substitute)** and serve.

YIELD: 4 to 8 servings

ALL-PURPOSE BACON MARINADE

* Nut-Free * Quick and Easy

You can use this marinade to turn just about any vegetable into bacon. Recipes for different versions are on the following pages, but don't be afraid to try out your own versions. It's great for anything from carrots to soy beans. What about potato bacon? Parsnip bacon? The possibilities really are endless.

¼ cup (60 ml) maple syrup
2 tablespoons (30 ml) liquid smoke
2 tablespoons (30 ml) tamari
2 tablespoons (30 ml) neutral-flavored oil
1 tablespoon (14 g) tightly packed brown sugar
2 teaspoons (10 ml) apple cider vinegar
½ teaspoon onion powder
½ teaspoon garlic powder
½ teaspoon black pepper
¼ teaspoon paprika

Mix together all the ingredients, use according to recipe instructions.

YIELD: ¾ cup (180 ml)

- -

ALL-PURPOSE BACON SEASONING

* Gluten-Free Potential * No Added Oil * Nut-Free * Quick and Easy
* Soy-Free

Use this seasoning to take your homemade bacon to the next level. This seasoning also tastes great on popcorn and salads, as it imparts a sweet and smoky flavor to anything you adorn with it.

1 tablespoon (14 g) tightly packed brown sugar
½ teaspoon smoked salt
¼ teaspoon garlic powder
¼ teaspoon onion powder
¼ teaspoon paprika
¼ teaspoon black pepper

Add all the ingredients to a spice grinder or coffee grinder, and grind into a very fine powder. Store in an airtight container.

YIELD: About 2 tablespoons (20 g)

VEGGIE BACON

* Nut-Free

Seriously, guys, just about any vegetable can be turned into bacon. Eggplants, carrots, mushrooms, even zucchini. We've talked about it before. What you're after is smoky, salty, fatty, and a little hint of sweet flavor. Not dead pig. So feast on veggie bacon!

1 recipe All-Purpose Bacon Marinade (page 206)
1 pound (454 g) sliced vegetables, cut to no more than ¼-inch (6 mm) thick slices

Add sliced vegetables to a resealable plastic bag, or a shallow dish with a lid, and add enough marinade to cover completely. Allow the vegetables to soak in marinade for at least 1 hour.

Preheat the oven to 350°F (180°C, or gas mark 4). Line a rimmed baking sheet with parchment, and arrange the marinated vegetables, including any extra marinade, in a single layer.

Bake for 1 hour, flipping halfway through. See note below. Vegetables should have absorbed the liquid and browned. They should be crisp around the edges, but soft and chewy in the centers.

Remove from oven and allow to cool completely before storing in the refrigerator until ready to use. If a crispier strip is desired, you can panfry on medium-high heat in a bit of oil, until desired crispness is reached.

YIELD: Varies depending on amount and type of vegetables used

Joni Says

"Different vegetables have different levels of water content, so cooking times will vary. For example, zucchini tends to have more water, and generally takes more time to cook."

SOY BACON

* Nut–Free

So much bacon, so little time! This is the traditional way most vegans make bacon. With thin strips of tofu or tempeh. We gave it a little extra oomph by adding the All-Purpose Bacon Seasoning to the final product.

1 block (12 to 16 ounces, or 340 to 454 g) extra or super firm tofu, drained and pressed

Or

1 block (8 ounces, or 227 g) plain soy tempeh
1 recipe All-Purpose Bacon Marinade (page 206)
2 tablespoons (20 g) All-Purpose Bacon Seasoning (page 206), more or less to taste

To make tofu bacon: Preheat the oven to 250°F (120°C, or gas mark ½). Have ready a baking sheet lined with parchment or a reusable silicone baking mat. Slice the tofu into thin slices (aim for ⅛ inch, or 3 mm). Arrange in a single layer on the baking sheet and bake for 1 hour, flipping halfway through. Remove from oven.

To make tempeh bacon: Slice the tempeh into thin slices (aim for ⅛ inch, or 3 mm). Place slices in your steamer and steam for 20 minutes. (I use a pot filled with about 2 inches [5 cm] of water, with a steamer basket inserted.)

Add the precooked tofu or tempeh to a shallow dish or resealable bag along with the marinade and allow to marinate for at least an hour and up to overnight.

Preheat the oven to 350°F (180°C, or gas mark 4). Line a rimmed baking sheet with parchment or a reusable silicon baking mat. Arrange the marinated strips in a single layer on the sheet and then pour any excess marinade over the strips.

Bake for 15 minutes, flip and bake for an additional 15 minutes. Finished product should be a rich chocolate brown in color, dry but still flexible. Remove from oven, transfer to a clean tray or plate and sprinkle with All-Purpose Bacon Seasoning.

Use immediately, or store in an airtight container in the refrigerator until ready to use. You can eat them cold, or reheat in a toaster oven, microwave, or even panfry them in a bit of oil to get 'em nice and crispy.

YIELD: 18 to 20 pieces

COCONUT BACON

Coconut is in everything these days, so why shouldn't it be made into bacon? Now, we are pretty darn confident that there are at least 10 million recipes for coconut bacon already available on the interwebs. Shoot, you can even buy premade coconut bacon from awesome, vegan companies such as Phoney Baloney's. But since this is a book of substitutions, here you go!

2 tablespoons (30 ml) olive oil
2 tablespoons (30 ml) pure maple syrup
1 tablespoon (15 ml) liquid smoke
2 tablespoons (30 ml) tamari
1 cup (60 g) unsweetened coconut flakes (not shreds)
1 recipe All-Purpose Bacon Seasoning (page 206)

Mix together olive oil, syrup, liquid smoke, and tamari. Add the coconut to marinade, toss to coat, set aside for about 15 minutes.

Preheat the oven to 400°F (200°C, or gas mark 6).

Line a baking sheet with parchment and spread the marinated coconut, along with excess marinade, in a single layer. Bake it for 5 minutes, remove from oven, toss it about, and put it back in the oven for 5 more minutes, watching carefully to avoid burning.

Remove from oven. Prop one end of the baking sheet up so that any remaining excess marinade drains away from the coconut. Let it cool completely. As it cools, it will crisp up. Once completely cooled, sprinkle liberally with the Bacon Seasoning.

Store in an airtight container in a cool dark space for up to a week. Refrigeration is not recommended, as it will make the bacon soggy.

YIELD: 1 cup (70 g)

BACON BITS (SOY-FREE AND GLUTEN-FREE VERSIONS)

* Gluten-Free Potential (If using TVP version) * Soy-Free (If using gluten version) * Nut-Free * Quick and Easy

Super quick and easy, these bits make a great topper for salads and baked potatoes. They also make a great addition to your veggie burger mixes and tofu scrambles.

1 cup (96 g) organic TVP granules (for gluten-free version)

Or

1 cup (144 g) vital wheat gluten flour (for soy-free version)
2 tablespoons (20 g) All-Purpose Bacon Seasoning (page 206)
¾ cup (180 ml) water (for gluten-free version)

Or

⅓ cup (80 ml) water (for soy-free version)
2 tablespoons (30 ml) liquid smoke
¼ cup (60 ml) neutral-flavored oil, divided
Salt, to taste

To make the gluten-free version in the microwave: Mix together the TVP and Bacon Seasoning in a microwave-safe bowl. Add water, liquid smoke, and 2 tablespoons (30 ml) of the oil and mix. Cover the dish tightly with plastic wrap and microwave on high for 5 minutes. Remove from microwave, carefully remove plastic wrap and fluff with a fork.

Alternatively, to make it on the stovetop: Mix together the TVP and Bacon Seasoning in a heat-safe bowl. Bring water to a boil and then add it, the liquid smoke, and 2 table-spoons (30 ml) of the oil to the bowl, and mix to combine. Cover tightly and allow to sit for 10 minutes to absorb the liquid. Fluff with a fork.

Heat the remaining 2 tablespoons (30 ml) of oil in a frying pan over medium-high heat. Add the bacon bits and panfry 3 to 5 minutes, or until crisp and browned. Add salt to taste.

To make the soy-free version: In a nonstick frying pan, mix together gluten and Bacon Seasoning. In a small measure, mix together water, liquid smoke, and oil. Turn to medium-high heat. Slowly mix the wet into the dry, right in the pan, and mix together with a spatula or wooden spoon. Continue to cook and stir, and break apart into crum-bles of desired size, until browned and firm. Add salt to taste.

For both versions, allow to cool completely before transferring to an airtight container and storing in the refrigerator for up to 2 weeks.

YIELD: Just over 1¼ cups (128 g)

BACON GREASE

* Quick and Easy

We don't know about you all, but when Joni was a kid, her Dad made everything in bacon grease. After he made a batch of bacon, he would pour the grease into an old coffee can, and keep it in the refrigerator, where it solidified into a solid block. When it came time to fry anything, he would forego the butter or oil, and go straight for the bacon grease. From eggs, to collard greens, to peppers and onions, everything Dad fried was in bacon grease.

Flash forward to now, Dad has diabetes (no wonder!) and Joni, her sister, and a few cousins . . . are vegan. So, no more bacon grease for them. But, wait a minute. What if there was a way to make bacon grease using plant-based ingredients that are full of heart-healthy fats, that can still impart a smoky, salty, fatty flavor into sautéed greens and tofu scrambles? That is when Joni discovered Vegan Magic Bacon Grease. Yep, vegan bacon grease already exists. You can buy it at select specialty vegan stores around the country or online. But what if you want it right now? Well, here is a simple recipe to make your own at home.

1 cup (235 ml) refined coconut oil, softened but not completely melted (This is important, because it needs to be partially solid in order to suspend the particles, otherwise the bacon bits and spices will sink to the bottom.)

1 tablespoon (15 ml) liquid smoke

1 tablespoon (10 g) All-Purpose Bacon Seasoning (page 206)

2 tablespoons (16 g) TVP Bacon Bits (page 210)

Mix all the ingredients together and store in an airtight container (such as a mason jar) in the refrigerator indefinitely.

YIELD: 1¼ cups (295 ml)

SEITAN SLAB O' BACON

* Nut–Free

Alright, friends, let's not get all huffy about how much oil is in this recipe. It's bacon! It's supposed to be fatty. Now take into consideration that you will not be eating this whole slab in one sitting. You will be slicing it into thin pieces and eating it a little bit at a time, most likely on a sandwich, or in a breakfast burrito. So it really isn't *that* much oil, if you look at it that way, right?

FOR THE FATTY WHITE PART:

1 cup (144 g) vital wheat gluten
1½ teaspoons garlic powder
1½ teaspoons onion powder
½ teaspoon salt
1 cup (235 ml) vegetable broth
¼ cup (60 ml) neutral-flavored oil

FOR THE MEATY RED PART:

1 cup (144 g) vital wheat gluten
1 recipe All-Purpose Bacon Marinade (page 206)
**A few drops all-natural red food color, or beet juice,
    optional for extra red color**

FOR THE BACON:

¼ cup (60 ml) neutral-flavored oil
1 recipe All-Purpose Bacon Seasoning (page 206)

To make the fatty white part: In a medium-size mixing bowl mix together the gluten, garlic powder, onion powder, and salt. Mix together the veggie broth and oil. Add wet to dry and stir to combine. Using your hands, knead together until a bouncy elastic dough is formed, about 5 minutes. Divide dough into 2 equal portions, set aside and allow to rest.

To make the meaty red part: Put the gluten in a medium-size mixing bowl, add All-Purpose Bacon Marinade and food color (if using) to the bowl and stir to combine. Using your hands, knead together until a bouncy elastic dough is formed, about 5 minutes. Divide dough into 2 equal portions, set aside and allow to rest for 20 minutes.

To make the bacon: Flatten each piece of dough into a rectangle about 4-inches (10 cm) wide by 6-inches (15 cm) long. It's okay of your dough shrinks back a little, It doesn't have to be perfect. When it bakes it will expand and form a near perfect loaf, so don't stress too much over it. Layer the dough white, red, white, red, and press together. Place on a flat surface, lined with foil or waxed paper, top with another piece of foil or waxed paper, and press by placing a heavy pot or book on top. Allow to rest an additional 30 minutes.

Preheat the oven to 375°F (190°C, or gas mark 5). Lay out a large piece of aluminum foil on a flat surface. Place pressed bacon dough in the center of the foil. Rub half of the oil all over the top, flip over and rub remaining oil all over the other side. Rub half of the All-Purpose Bacon Seasoning into the dough like a dry rub, flip and repeat on the other side with the remaining seasoning.

Wrap tightly in the foil. It's important to wrap it tightly, so that the dough does not expand when baking, ensuring that the seitan is dense and firm, not puffy and bready. Place seam side down in a baking dish. Bake for 1 hour, carefully flipping halfway through. Remove from oven and allow to cool enough to handle before unwrapping.

When you unwrap it, it should be blackened and firm to the touch. The blackened edge will make a wonderfully flavorful, crispy edge.

Store in the refrigerator in an airtight container, or freeze until ready to use. When ready to enjoy, slice into very thin slices. Enjoy as is, or panfry in a little more oil (or vegan Bacon Grease!) for an extra crispy slice of bacon.

YIELD: About 24 slices

CHAPTER 8
No Mimicking Meat

QUITE A FEW VEGAN FOLKS ARE OF THE MIND that if one doesn't eat meat for ethical reasons, there's absolutely no point in mimicking it at all—even when done in cruelty-free ways. Others also find that most vegan meat alternatives available on the market, or even made at home, contain far too many processed ingredients and fillers.

We can definitely understand this point of view, which is why we're including the following recipes. They are just happy being their own delicious selves, with minimal processing, and without trying to be stand-ins for anything else. The good news is so many vegan foods are naturally packed with protein that it isn't hard to find this vital nutrient. A complete protein is a food which contains all nine amino acids in the proper ratio needed for a body to function at its best. It used to be believed that a complete protein had to be consumed at every meal, be it by choosing complete protein sources such as quinoa, tofu, tempeh, or seitan, or by combining incomplete sources of protein such as whole grains and legumes together in one meal in order to form a complete protein.

Recently, this has been recognized as unnecessary. Your body will manage to build complete proteins from the healthy, well-balanced, and varied vegan diet you feed it within a 24-hour period. You don't need to combine, say, rice and beans in one single meal. Have rice for lunch, beans for supper, along with a nice variety of nutrition-packed foods throughout the day's meals and *boom*: Complete protein status is easily and happily achieved.

Practice Makes for Perfect Substitutions

The best way to demonstrate how to transform a nonvegan recipe into a cruelty-free wonder is to show how it's done. Let's go through a sample recipe, step by step! Once you know the basics, it's easy to put into practice.

< *Potacos, page 236*

COOK-OFF CHILI WITH ROASTED CORN

Non-Veganized

This recipe is an excerpt from *Back to Butter*, by Molly Chester and Sandy Schrecengost (Fair Winds Press, 2014). Normally, we would substitute vegan ingredients for the butter, ground beef, chicken liver, and cream, and rewrite the directions accordingly. In this case though, we want to highlight the fact that it isn't necessary to replace meat with vegan equivalents in order to get a sufficient—and satisfying—amount of protein in your diet.

3 tablespoons (42 g) butter
1 cup (160 g) diced red onion
3 cups (140 g) sliced cremini mushrooms, optional
1 tablespoon (10 g) minced garlic
1 cup (150 g) diced red bell pepper (about 1 large)
¼ cup (36 g) seeded and diced jalapeño pepper (about 2 medium, optional)
1 pound (454 g) ground beef
2 tablespoons (15 g) chili powder
1 tablespoon (7 g) ground cumin
⅛ teaspoon cayenne pepper
2 teaspoons (12 g) sea salt
½ teaspoon freshly cracked pepper
1 tablespoon (14 g) minced chicken liver, optional
1 can (28 ounces, or 784 g) fire-roasted crushed tomatoes
1 can (15 ounces, or 420 g) tomato sauce
3 cups (530 g) cooked kidney beans
2 cups (260 g) roasted corn (see page 68)
2 tablespoons (30 ml) cream

In a large-size pot, melt the butter over medium heat. Add the onion, mushrooms, garlic, red pepper, jalapeño pepper, and ground beef. Occasionally breaking up the meat with a wooden spoon, sauté for 10 minutes, until the beef is browned through and the mushrooms have softened and released their moisture.

Add the chili powder, cumin, cayenne, salt, pepper, and chicken liver, if using. Sauté for 1 minute so the dried spices can release their oils. Add the tomatoes, tomato sauce, and kidney beans. Cover and bring to a boil, then lower heat to a simmer. Simmer, covered, for 1 hour, stirring occasionally. Remove the lid. Stir in the roasted corn and cream. Serve.

YIELD: 6 servings

COOK-OFF CHILI WITH ROASTED CORN

Veganized!

The flavor that won't be coming from the beef is found in dried mushrooms, broth powder, and nutritional yeast instead. The dried and fresh mushrooms also add texture. Beans bring a generous amount of protein (15 g per cooked cup) to the chili.

0.88 ounce (25 g) dried shiitake mushrooms ⎤ ground beef substitute, for texture
1 cup (235 ml) vegetable broth
1 cup (160 g) diced red onion
3 cups (140 g) sliced cremini mushrooms
1 tablespoon (10 g) minced garlic
2 cups (248 g) chopped yellow squash
1 cup (150 g) diced red bell pepper
¼ cup (36 g) seeded and diced jalapeño pepper, to taste and optional
2 tablespoons (15 g) chili powder
2 tablespoons (15 g) Mushroom Broth Powder (page 218) ⎤ ground beef substitute, for depth of flavor
1 tablespoon (7 g) ground cumin
⅛ teaspoon cayenne pepper
½ teaspoon fine sea salt, to taste
½ teaspoon freshly cracked pepper
⅓ cup (40 g) nutritional yeast ⎤ ground beef substitute, for depth of flavor
1 can (28 ounces, or 784 g) fire-roasted diced tomatoes
1 can (15 ounces, or 420 g) tomato sauce
3 cups (530 g) cooked kidney beans
2 cups (260 g) roasted corn (see page 68)

Rinse the dried mushrooms, and place in a medium bowl. Add broth on top, and soak for 10 minutes. Gently squeeze broth from the mushrooms and reserve. It will be used to cook the vegetables. Chop mushrooms and set aside.

In a large-size pot, place onion, mushrooms, garlic, squash, peppers, and 2 tablespoons (30 ml) of mushroom broth, and heat over medium heat. Sauté for 6 minutes, until the mushrooms soften. Add extra mushroom broth if needed.

Add chili powder, broth powder, cumin, cayenne, salt, and pepper. Sauté for 1 minute. Add the nutritional yeast, tomatoes, tomato sauce, and beans. Cover and bring to a boil, then lower heat. Simmer for 20 to 30 minutes, until thickened, stirring occasionally. For a thinner chili, add some of the mushroom broth, to taste. Remove the lid. Stir in the roasted corn. Serve.

YIELD: 6 to 8 servings

MUSHROOM BROTH POWDER

* Gluten-Free Potential * No Added Oil * No Added Sugar
* Nut-Free * Quick and Easy * Soy-Free

We're sneaking this easy-to-make recipe right here, because it's widely used throughout the book. It adds a lot of flavor to our dishes, while being fairly low in salt compared with most store-bought vegan broth powders or cubes. It also makes for a great all-purpose seasoning if you need to add a little *oomph* to your plate and would rather not use plain salt. Just sprinkle a little of the broth powder (to taste) on top of almost any savory food you're eating, stir well, and enjoy.

1 ounce (28 g) dried mushroom of choice
1½ cups (180 g) nutritional yeast
2 tablespoons (15 g) onion powder
1 tablespoon (8 g) dried garlic powder
1 tablespoon (18 g) fine sea salt
1½ tablespoons (2 g) dried parsley
1 tablespoon (7 g) julienne-cut, soft, sun-dried tomato
1 tablespoon (7 g) smoked or regular paprika
1 tablespoon (3 g) dried oregano leaves
(not powder, use only 1 teaspoon if powder)
1 teaspoon dried basil
1 teaspoon dried thyme
Ground rainbow peppercorn, quantity to taste
1 teaspoon red pepper flakes, optional

Place the mushrooms in a food processor. Process until ground as finely as possible, but it's okay if a few small pieces are left. Add the remaining ingredients, and process until thoroughly combined. Store the broth powder in an airtight container at room temperature for up to 1 month. To prepare as 1 cup (235 ml) of broth, add 1 teaspoon (for lighter broth) or up to 1 tablespoon (for strongly-flavored broth) (3 to 9 g) of the mix per 1 cup (235 ml) of water, depending on personal taste and use.

YIELD: 1¾ cups (245 g)

Celine Says

"If you're concerned about grit in the dried mushrooms as cleanliness varies with the brand, consider dehydrating your own gently cleaned mushrooms for this use. Search online for 'dehydrating mushrooms,' and you'll find plenty of useful tips."

TOASTED HAZELNUT BUTTER AND CHOCOLATE HAZELNUT BUTTER

* Gluten-Free Potential   * No Added Oil   * Quick and Easy   * Soy-Free

We love to spread natural peanut butter on our breakfast toast instead of vegan butter for a small protein boost, but occasionally we crave a change of pace. While hazelnut butter can cost a pretty penny when purchased ready-made, you can save a few bucks by making your own. Be sure not to use soymilk if you want to keep the recipe soy-free.

FOR TOASTED HAZELNUT BUTTER:

1 cup (135 g) skinned whole hazelnuts

FOR CHOCOLATE HAZELNUT BUTTER:

1 recipe toasted hazelnut butter

¼ cup (80 g) pure maple syrup or agave nectar, divided, more if needed

3½ tablespoons (18 g) unsweetened cocoa powder

1 teaspoon pure vanilla extract

½ teaspoon pure hazelnut extract, optional

⅛ teaspoon fine sea salt

¼ cup (60 ml) plain Almond Milk (page 27) or other vegan milk, more if needed

To make toasted hazelnut butter: Preheat the oven to 375°F (190°C, or gas mark 5). Place the hazelnuts on a small rimmed baking sheet, and bake for 6 to 8 minutes, or until golden brown: Keep a close eye on the hazelnuts so that they don't burn, and stir if needed. Remove from oven, and transfer to a food processor. Process until a nut butter forms. Processing time will take between 10 and 15 minutes, depending on the machine. Stop the machine occasionally to scrape the sides with a rubber spatula. If the motor of the machine starts to overheat, power off to let it cool before continuing. Store in an airtight jar in the refrigerator for up to 2 weeks.

To make chocolate hazelnut butter: Before transferring the nut butter to a jar, add 3½ tablespoons (53 ml) syrup or nectar, the cocoa powder, extracts, and salt on top of it in the food processor. Process until combined. Stop the machine occasionally to scrape the sides with a rubber spatula. Have a taste, and add the remaining 1½ teaspoons syrup or nectar, or more to taste, for a sweeter outcome. Add ¼ cup (60 ml) of milk, and more if needed, 1 tablespoon (15 ml) at a time, to get a spreadable consistency. Store in an airtight jar in the refrigerator for up to 2 weeks.

YIELD: Heaping ½ cup (142 g) of hazelnut butter, or 1 heaping cup (270 g) chocolate hazelnut butter

SAVORY BREAKFAST SALAD

* No Added Oil   * No Added Sugar   * Quick and Easy   * Soy-Free

Walnuts are known to be rich in protein with 18 g per cup (120 g), so we've whipped up the perfect dressing to drizzle over veggies for a nutritious and invigorating breakfast. The sassiness of the dressing was kept a little on the low side considering the time of day. If you eat this at a different mealtime, consider replacing some of the water with an equal extra amount of either vinegar or lemon juice, or both, to taste. Extra garlic would be good, too!

FOR THE WALNUT DRESSING:

- 3 tablespoons (9 g) minced fresh chives
- ¾ teaspoon Mushroom Broth Powder (page 218)
- ½ cup plus 2 tablespoons (150 ml) water
- 1 clove garlic, grated or pressed
- ¼ cup plus 1 tablespoon (40 g) toasted walnut halves
- 1 tablespoon (15 ml) white balsamic vinegar
- 1 tablespoon (15 ml) fresh lemon juice
- ¾ teaspoon mild Dijon mustard
- Salt and pepper, to taste

FOR THE SALAD:

- 2 cups (weight will vary, between 300 and 400 g) cooked whole grain (e.g., rye berries, spelt berries, or barley)
- 5 ounces (142 g) fresh baby greens or spinach
- 2 large oranges of choice, peeled, pith removed, chopped
- 1 to 2 pitted, peeled, and chopped avocados, to taste
- Chopped scallion, optional

To make the dressing: Combine all the ingredients in a small blender, or use an immersion blender. Blend until perfectly smooth. Adjust seasoning to taste. Store in the refrigerator for at least 2 hours, or overnight, before use. Stir again before use.

To make the salad: Place ½ cup (75 to 100 g) cooked grain, a packed handful (35 g) of greens, half a chopped orange, and a quarter or one-half chopped avocado in an individual bowl that's large enough to toss the salad. Toss with desired amount of dressing (2 to 3 tablespoons, or 30 to 45 ml), and serve immediately with chopped scallions on top, if using. Repeat with remaining 3 servings. If there are dressing leftovers, store them in a jar in the refrigerator for up to 4 days.

YIELD: 4 servings, ¾ cup (180 ml) dressing

CHIPOTLE MISO HUMMUS

* Gluten-Free Potential   * No Added Oil   * No Added Sugar
* Nut-Free   * Quick and Easy

The quintessential vegan food—made spicy! Hummus, the beloved bean-based dip, is at its best when using home-cooked chickpeas instead of canned, if you can spare the time and effort. For the smoothest results (and if you *really* have time to kill), you can also peel the cooked chickpeas. You probably don't need us to tell you how to use it, but just in case: Serve it with raw vegetable spears, baked pita chips, vegan crackers, or use as a sandwich spread.

1½ cups (246 g) cooked chickpeas
1 to 2 large cloves garlic, grated or pressed, to taste
3 tablespoons (48 g) tahini
1 tablespoon (18 g) white miso
2 teaspoons (10 ml) adobo sauce from a can of chipotle peppers
2 to 3 tablespoons (30 to 45 ml) fresh lemon juice, to taste
Scant ⅓ cup (28 g) coarsely chopped scallion
½ to 1½ teaspoons canned chipotle pepper, to taste
¼ teaspoon fine salt, to taste
2 to 3 tablespoons (30 to 45 ml) filtered water, as needed

Place all the ingredients, except chipotle pepper, salt, and water in a food processor, and process until mostly smooth. Stop to scrape the sides with a rubber spatula once or twice. Add chipotle pepper and salt, to taste. Process until smooth. For a thinner hummus, add water as needed, 1 tablespoon (15 ml) at a time. Store in an airtight container in the refrigerator for 1 hour before use. Leftovers will keep for up to 3 days.

YIELD: 1½ cups (420 g)

Celine Says

"Adjust the amount of chipotle pepper according to taste: If you don't like spicy, start with ½ teaspoon to be on the safe side.

Go easy on the salt at first, too, because it will depend on the miso you use.

Play with the amount of adobo sauce after making it at least once as written."

MOROCCAN LENTIL BALLS

* No Added Sugar

Take things up another notch by serving our protein-rich lentil balls with Simple Yogurt Dip (page 31).

1 cup (192 g) dry green lentils, cooked to al dente (about 26 minutes), drained

¼ cup (40 g) minced shallot

2 tablespoons (30 ml) fresh lemon juice

1 tablespoon (16 g) cashew butter or tahini

1 tablespoon (15 ml) toasted sesame oil

1 tablespoon (15 ml) white balsamic vinegar

2 teaspoons to 1 tablespoon (10 to 15 g) harissa paste, to taste

2 teaspoons (5 g) nutritional yeast

4 cloves garlic, grated or pressed

1 teaspoon dried cilantro or parsley, or 1 tablespoon (1 g) fresh cilantro or (4 g) fresh parsley

1 teaspoon ground cumin

1 teaspoon ground coriander

½ teaspoon fine sea salt

2 tablespoons (15 g) whole-wheat pastry flour

2 tablespoons (16 g) potato starch or cornstarch (preferably organic)

¼ teaspoon baking soda

Nonstick cooking spray or oil spray

Place the cooked lentils in a food processor, and pulse about 10 times to break down the lentils slightly: They must not be completely puréed, but most must not be left whole either.

Preheat the oven to 400°F (200°C, or gas mark 6). Lightly coat a 24-hole mini muffin tin with cooking spray.

In a large bowl, combine the shallot, lemon juice, cashew butter, oil, vinegar, harissa paste, nutritional yeast, garlic, cilantro, cumin, coriander, and salt. Add the broken down lentils on top, and stir to combine. Sprinkle the flour, starch, and baking soda on top, and stir with one hand until thoroughly combined.

Gather 1 packed, slightly heaping tablespoon (23 g) of mixture per ball, gently shape into a ball and place in the mini muffin tin. Repeat with remaining mixture. You should get 24 lentil balls in all. Bake for 12 minutes, carefully flip each ball, and lightly coat with spray. Bake for another 8 minutes, or until golden brown. Remove from oven, let stand 10 minutes before serving.

YIELD: 24 lentil balls

DILL-Y CHICKPEAS

* Gluten-Free Potential * No Added Sugar * Nut-Free
* Quick and Easy * Soy-Free

These simple beans make a great salad topper, such as in the Mexican Cobb Salad (page 122). They are also good on their own as an easy, no-cook side dish.

1 can (15 ounces, or 425 g) chickpeas, rinsed and drained
2 tablespoons (30 ml) olive oil
1 teaspoon mild Dijon mustard
1 teaspoon minced garlic
½ teaspoon dried dill, or 1½ teaspoons fresh
¼ teaspoon salt, to taste

Mix all the ingredients together. Keep refrigerated until ready to serve. The longer they marinate the better. These taste even better the next day.

YIELD: Just over 1½ cups (460 g)

Joni Says

"Turn these beans into an awesome sandwich by smashing them up with a dollop of vegan mayonnaise, store-bought or homemade (page 118), and a bit of the hard-boiled egglike crumbles from the Mexican Cobb Salad (page 122). Pile it all onto a slice of bread lined with a few leaves of lettuce, and top it off with a few slices of Veggie Bacon (page 207)."

SASSY HOT SAUCE CHICKPEA STICKS

* Gluten-Free Potential   * No Added Sugar

Forget potato fries! Crispy outside, tender inside . . . these look-alikes make for a spicy snack that's far more protein-packed than your average French fry.

2 cups (470 ml) water

2 teaspoons (5 g) Mushroom Broth Powder (page 218)

1½ to 2 tablespoons (23 to 30 ml) hot sauce (use lower amount with Tabasco brand, higher if Frank's)

2 tablespoons (15 g) nutritional yeast

2 teaspoons (10 ml) vegan Worcestershire sauce

½ teaspoon celery salt

½ teaspoon onion powder

½ teaspoon garlic powder

¼ teaspoon fine sea salt

1 cup (120 g) chickpea flour or garbanzo fava bean flour

2 tablespoons (15 g) corn flour (not cornmeal or cornstarch, preferably organic)

Nonstick cooking spray or oil spray

1 recipe Ranch-y Dipping Sauce (page 31) or Sour Cream Dressing (See "Celine Says," page 30), for serving

Place all the ingredients, except cooking spray and dipping sauce, in a blender, and blend until smooth. Transfer to a large saucepan, and cook on medium heat, whisking constantly, until the mixture starts to thicken. Reduce heat to medium-low, continue whisking almost constantly, and cook for another 6 minutes, or (and this is important) until the mixture is so thick that when you slash a line through its center with the whisk all the way to the bottom of the pan, the mixture doesn't slide back to cover the bottom of the pan. Be sure to adjust the temperature to avoid scorching.

Remove from heat, and spread evenly in an 8-inch (20 cm) square baking pan coated with cooking spray, using an angled spatula. Do not cover the pan, and once it's cool enough, cover it and place it in the refrigerator for at least 2 hours, or overnight.

Remove the chilled mixture from the pan, and cut in ½-inch (1.3 cm) strips, then cut once in the middle widthwise. You should get 32 sticks of approximately 4 x ½ inches (10 x 1.3 cm).

Preheat the oven to 425°F (220°C, or gas mark 7). Line a baking sheet with parchment paper or a silicone baking mat. Space the sticks evenly on the prepared sheet, and lightly coat with cooking spray.

Bake for 15 minutes, flip the sticks, and bake for another 15 minutes, or until golden brown and crispy. Let stand for 5 minutes before serving. Serve with dipping sauce.

YIELD: About 32 sticks

BARLEY BEAN PATTIES

* No Added Sugar

Have we mentioned already how much we adore chickpeas? If they weren't so stubbornly perfect, we'd probably be more quiet about it. We use chickpeas here not only for their high protein and fiber content, but also to help the bread crumbs bind the patties.

FOR THE PATTIES:

1 can (15 ounces, or 425 g) chickpeas, drained and rinsed

3 tablespoons (30 g) chopped shallot

½ teaspoon ground cumin

½ teaspoon ground coriander

Scant ½ teaspoon fine sea salt

Scant ½ cup (105 g) Cilantro Sauce (page 83)

2 large cloves garlic, grated or pressed

2 teaspoons (5 g) nutritional yeast

2 teaspoons (10 ml) toasted sesame oil

2 teaspoons (10 ml) fresh lemon juice

½ cup (25 g) panko bread crumbs

1 cup (170 g) cooked pearled barley

Nonstick cooking spray or oil spray

FOR THE SAUCE:

Scant ¼ cup (50 g) Savory Cashew Sauce (page 34)

Scant ¼ cup (50 g) plain vegan yogurt, store-bought or homemade (page 28)

1 tablespoon (15 g) Cilantro Sauce (page 83)

To make the patties: Add the chickpeas, shallot, cumin, coriander, salt, Cilantro Sauce, garlic, nutritional yeast, oil, and lemon juice to a food processor. Pulse to break chickpeas. Place half of mixture in a large bowl. Add panko to the food processor, and process until a paste forms. Transfer this and the barley to the large bowl and combine. If the mixture is dry and not cohesive, add water or broth, 1 tablespoon (15 ml) at a time. Divide into 8 equal portions of 2.6 ounces (76 g). Shape into 3-inch (7.6 cm) patties, and place on a baking sheet lined with parchment paper. Store in the refrigerator for at least 2 hours, up to overnight.

To make the sauce: Combine all ingredients in a small bowl, cover, and refrigerate until ready to serve.

Heat a large skillet on medium-high heat. Move the skillet away from the stove, and lightly coat with cooking spray. Cook patties in batches until golden brown, about 4 minutes per side. Adjust heat if needed. Serve immediately with the sauce.

YIELD: 8 patties, ½ cup (120 g) sauce

SUMMERY SPELT SALAD

* No Added Oil * No Added Sugar * Nut-Free * Quick and Easy

This oil-free salad is bursting with great flavor and texture and is also a good source of protein and fiber.

1 cup (180 g) dry spelt berries, rinsed and drained
3 cups (705 ml) water
1 tablespoon (8 g) Mushroom Broth Powder (page 218)
Scant ½ cup (70 g) minced shallot
3 medium bell peppers, trimmed and diced (any color)
1¼ teaspoons ground cumin
1¼ teaspoons ground coriander
Scant 1 teaspoon smoked or regular paprika
½ teaspoon turmeric
½ teaspoon fine sea salt, to taste
3 tablespoons (45 ml) fresh lemon juice, divided
1 cup (164 g) cooked chickpeas
½ cup (120 g) plain vegan yogurt, store-bought or homemade (page 28)
2 tablespoons (32 g) tahini
1 to 2 cloves garlic, grated or pressed, to taste
⅓ to ½ cup (53 to 80 g) raisins or 2 chopped avocados
Fresh mint or parsley leaves, minced, for serving

Place the spelt berries, water, and broth powder in a rice cooker, and cook according to manufacturer's instructions, until al dente, about 1 hour. (Alternatively, follow the instructions on the package of spelt to cook on a stovetop.) Let cool before use.

Place the shallot, bell peppers, cumin, coriander, paprika, turmeric, salt, and 2 table-spoons (30 ml) lemon juice in a large skillet. Cook on medium-high heat until the peppers start to soften, stirring occasionally, about 4 minutes. Add the chickpeas, stir and cook another 2 minutes.

In the meantime, combine the yogurt, the remaining 1 tablespoon (15 ml) of lemon juice, tahini, and garlic in a large bowl. Add the cooled cooked spelt on top, along with the bell pepper mixture. If using raisins, add them now and fold to thoroughly combine. Adjust seasoning if needed. Store in an airtight container in the refrigerator for 1 hour before serving, topped with minced fresh herbs. If using avocado instead of raisins, add just before serving. Leftovers (without the avocado) will keep for up to 4 days.

YIELD: 6 to 8 servings

MOROCCAN COUSCOUS SALAD

* Nut-Free

This refreshing, protein-rich salad is perfect during the summer months.

Nonstick cooking spray or oil spray

1 can (15 ounces, or 425 g) chickpeas, drained and rinsed

1 teaspoon toasted sesame oil

1 teaspoon tamari

1 teaspoon agave nectar

1 teaspoon pure lemon juice, more if needed

¼ to ½ teaspoon harissa paste, to taste

½ cup (120 ml) water

1 tablespoon (15 ml) fresh orange juice, more if needed

1½ teaspoons Mushroom Broth Powder (page 218)

½ cup (88 g) dry whole-wheat regular couscous

1 large organic orange

2 cups (80 g) minced fresh kale

¼ cup (40 g) yellow raisins

¼ cup (20 g) minced scallion

1 large clove garlic, grated or pressed, to taste

1 tablespoon (2 g) minced fresh mint, to taste

¼ teaspoon ground cumin

6½ tablespoons (98 g) plain vegan yogurt, store-bought or homemade (page 28)

Salt and pepper, to taste

Preheat the oven to 300°F (150°C, or gas mark 2). Lightly coat a small rimmed baking pan with cooking spray. In a medium bowl, combine chickpeas, oil, tamari, agave, lemon juice, and harissa paste. Transfer to the pan, and bake for 20 minutes. Stir, and bake for another 20 minutes, until the chickpeas are golden brown. Set aside to cool.

Bring water, orange juice, and broth powder to a boil in a small saucepan. Remove from heat. Add the couscous and stir, cover, and let stand for 5 minutes. Fluff with a fork. Set aside to cool.

Place chickpeas and couscous in a large bowl. Zest orange on top. Peel it, and use one hand to squeeze out the juice and scrape out the flesh in pieces over the bowl. Add remaining ingredients, and stir to thoroughly combine. Add additional orange juice, as needed. Store covered in the refrigerator for 2 hours before serving. Adjust seasoning and squeeze extra lemon or orange juice on each serving, to taste.

YIELD: 4 side-dish servings

 Celine Says

"Store-bought vegan yogurt is thicker than homemade. If using store-bought, you might have to add extra orange juice, 1 tablespoon (15 ml) at a time, in order to get a sufficiently saucy salad."

MEXICAN POLENTA BAKE

* Gluten-Free Potential   * No Added Sugar

If you still believe that veganism equals deprivation, you must try this complete Mexican bake. It offers everything a good casserole should: cheesiness (cashew sauce), creaminess (polenta and cashew sauce), and protein (Hello, Mister Beans!). It's got it all.

FOR THE TOMATO SAUCE:

2 teaspoons (10 ml) olive oil
¼ cup (40 g) minced shallot
4 cloves garlic, minced
4 ounces (113 g) tomato paste
1 tablespoon (8 g) mild to medium chili powder
1 teaspoon ground cumin
½ teaspoon smoked paprika
½ teaspoon fine sea salt, to taste
2 cups (470 ml) water

FOR THE BAKE:

1 tub (1 pound, or 454 g) of vegan plain cooked polenta,
**   cut into ¼-inch (6 mm) slices (18 slices in all)**
1¾ cups (287 g) thawed corn
1 can (15 ounces, or 425 g) black beans, drained and rinsed
Nonstick cooking spray or oil spray
1 cup (260 g) Spicy Chia Cashew Sauce (page 78)

To make the tomato sauce: Heat the oil on medium heat in a medium pot. Add the shallot and garlic, and cook until fragrant while stirring occasionally, about 2 minutes. Add the tomato paste, chili powder, cumin, paprika, and salt. Sauté for 4 minutes, stirring frequently. Slowly whisk in the water, and simmer until thickened, about 30 minutes, whisking frequently. Remove from heat and set aside.

To make the bake: Preheat the oven to 350°F (180°C, or gas mark 4). Line a baking sheet with parchment paper or a silicone baking mat. Place the polenta slices on the prepared sheet, and bake for 15 minutes. Set aside.

Lightly coat an 8-inch (20 cm) square baking pan with cooking spray. Place 9 of the polenta slices at the bottom of the pan. Fold the corn and black beans into the pot of tomato sauce, until combined. Evenly place the mixture on top of the polenta slices. Top with the remaining 9 slices of polenta. Evenly spread the cashew sauce on top of the dish. Bake for 30 minutes, until the topping is set and light golden brown. Let stand 15 minutes before serving.

YIELD: 8 servings

ASOPAO DE FRIJOLES

* No Added Oil * No Added Sugar * Nut-Free * Soy-Free

We clearly took a few liberties with this Puerto Rican stew that is most commonly made with chicken and rice!

¾ cup (135 to 165 g) dry whole grain of choice

3 tablespoons (24 g) Mushroom Broth Powder (page 218)

1 teaspoon dried oregano leaves

1 teaspoon chili powder

1 teaspoon ground cumin

1 teaspoon onion powder

½ teaspoon fine sea salt, to taste

½ teaspoon garlic powder

½ teaspoon smoked or regular paprika

¼ teaspoon red pepper flakes

¼ teaspoon ground black pepper

3¼ cups (484 g) diced bell pepper (any color, about 3 peppers)

1 cup (160 g) diced red or yellow onion

4 cloves garlic, minced

1 generous tablespoon (24 g) tomato paste

1 can (14.5 ounces, or 411 g) diced fire-roasted tomatoes

3 cups (705 ml) water

1 dried bay leaf

1½ cups (258 g) cooked black beans

2 teaspoons (6 g) drained capers, minced

6 large pimento-stuffed green olives, chopped

¼ cup (4 g) chopped fresh cilantro

2 fresh avocados, pitted, peeled, and sliced

Precook the grain of choice just so that only 20 minutes of cooking time remain. Drain, and set aside.

Combine broth powder through black pepper in a small bowl. Add spice mix, bell peppers, onion, garlic, and tomato paste to a large pot. Stir to combine. On medium-high heat, cook and stir occasionally until vegetables soften, about 3 minutes. If the veggies stick to the pot, add water as needed, 1 tablespoon (15 ml) at a time. Add tomatoes, water, precooked grain, and bay leaf, and bring to a boil. Lower heat, cover with lid, and simmer 10 minutes, stirring occasionally. Add beans, capers, and olives. Simmer covered for 10 minutes, until the grain is tender. Remove bay leaf, and serve with cilantro and avocado.

YIELD: 6 servings

POTACOS

* Gluten-Free Potential   * No Added Oil Option   * Soy-Free

Taco purists, please don't be offended. Take one bite, and be converted.

FOR THE SALSA FRESCA:

1 green chile, seeded and diced
1 cup (160 g) diced red onion
1 cup (252) diced tomatoes
⅓ cup (5 g) chopped cilantro
1 tablespoon (9 g) minced garlic
1 tablespoon (15 ml) lime juice
1 tablespoon (15 ml) olive oil, optional
Salt and pepper, to taste

FOR THE PEPITA PIGNOLA SPRINKLES:

2 tablespoons (16 g) pepitas (pumpkin seeds)
2 tablespoons (15 g) pignolas
1 tablespoon (8 g) nutritional yeast
¼ teaspoon cumin
¼ teaspoon oregano
¼ teaspoon chipotle powder or cayenne pepper
¼ teaspoon smoked salt

FOR THE POTACOS:

4 medium russet potatoes, cut in half lengthwise
½ teaspoon salt, divided
1 teaspoon sugar
2 teaspoons (3 g) chili powder
1 teaspoon garlic powder
1 teaspoon onion powder
1 teaspoon cumin
1 teaspoon paprika
¼ to ½ teaspoon chipotle powder or cayenne pepper, to taste
2 tablespoons (30 ml) olive oil, optional
1 cup (70 g) shredded cabbage
1 avocado, pitted, peeled, and sliced

To make the salsa fresca: Combine the ingredients and refrigerate until ready to serve.

To make the pepita pignola sprinkles: Add all the ingredients to a spice grinder (or coffee grinder) and grind until a coarse mixture is formed. Preheat a dry pan over medium heat. Add spice mix and toast for 1 to 2 minutes, until toasty and fragrant. Remove from heat and set aside until ready to use.

To make the potacos: Preheat the oven to 400°F (200°C, or gas mark 6). Place the potatoes, cut side up, on a baking sheet and sprinkle with ¼ teaspoon of salt. Bake 1 hour, or until fork tender. Remove from heat. Cool enough to handle. Carefully scoop out the flesh of the potatoes, leaving about ¼ inch (6 mm) of the flesh inside the skin to make a Potaco shell, and place in a mixing bowl. Add the remaining salt, all of the spices, and the olive oil to the scooped-out flesh and mix to combine. Pile the taco-flavored potato mixture back into the shells. Top with cabbage, salsa fresca, avocado, and then with Pepita Pignola Sprinkles. Serve warm or at room temperature.

YIELD: 8 potacos

ORANGE MISO OAT AND KALE PILAF

* Gluten-Free Potential

Crunchy pecans and chewy oat groats pair up nicely in this fragrant dish and bring a fair amount of protein to your vegan table.

1½ teaspoons agave nectar

1 teaspoon neutral-flavored oil

½ teaspoon smoked paprika

½ teaspoon onion powder

¼ teaspoon ground cumin

⅛ teaspoon fine sea salt

⅛ teaspoon cayenne pepper, to taste

½ cup (50 g) pecan halves

1 teaspoon grapeseed oil or olive oil

1 cup (184 g) dry oat groats, rinsed and drained

¼ cup (40 g) minced shallot

2⅓ cups (550 ml) vegetable broth, divided

Scant 4 cups (150 g) minced fresh kale leaves

1 tablespoon (18 g) white miso

1 tablespoon (15 ml) warm water

Zest from 1 organic orange

2 tablespoons (30 ml) fresh orange juice

1½ teaspoons seasoned rice vinegar

1 teaspoon toasted sesame oil

1 small clove garlic, grated or pressed

Preheat the oven to 325°F (170°C, or gas mark 3). Combine the agave, oil, and spices in a medium bowl. Add the pecans and stir to coat. Place in an even layer on a parchment paper–lined baking sheet, and bake for 6 minutes. Stir and bake for another 4 minutes, until toasty and dry-looking, being careful not to let the nuts burn. Remove from oven and let cool. Chop coarsely, and set aside.

Heat the oil in a large skillet on medium heat. Toast the groats and shallot, stirring frequently, until the shallot softens, about 3 minutes.

Add 2 cups (470 ml) of broth, bring to a boil, and lower heat. Cover with a lid, and simmer 30 minutes, stirring occasionally. Add some or all of the remaining ⅓ cup (80 ml) of broth if needed. Add the kale, stirring to combine, cover, and simmer 10 minutes. Whisk to combine the miso and water in a small bowl. Add zest, juice, vinegar, oil, and garlic, whisking to combine. Remove the lid from the skillet: The liquid should be absorbed, and the groats tender. Fold the sauce into the groats, and serve with pecans.

YIELD: 4 side-dish servings

SECTION FOUR

Have Kitchen Success, Will Travel

CHAPTER 9
The New-and-Improved Complete Chart of Vegan Food Substitutions

Please note that the boldface entries reference from-scratch recipes in this book.

SECTION 1: DAIRY

WHEN THE ORIGINAL RECIPE CALLS FOR . . .	REPLACE WITH . . .
¼ cup (56 g) butter	• **¼ cup (56 g) Mattie's Regular Vegan Butter (page 24)** • **¼ cup (60 g) Coconut Butter (page 25) (for spreading on bread, and some other applications, see page 25)** • ¼ cup (56 g) store-bought non-hydrogenated vegan butter, such as Earth Balance
1 cup (235 ml) buttermilk	• Place 2 teaspoons (10 ml) fresh lemon juice or apple cider vinegar at the bottom of a bowl. Top with 1 cup (235 ml) unsweetened, plain vegan milk of choice, then stir. Let stand 5 minutes to curdle.
1 cup (235 ml) heavy cream or creamer	• **1 cup (235 ml) plain Homemade Creamer (page 26)** • 1 cup (235 ml) canned full-fat and unsweetened coconut milk or cream • 1 cup (235 ml) store-bought plain soy creamer, such as Silk or Wildwood • 1 cup (235 ml) store-bought plain coconut creamer, such as So Delicious • 1 cup (235 ml) almond creamer, such as Califia Farms or So Delicious
2 scoops ice cream (various flavors)	• **2 scoops Cherry Cheesecake Chocolate Chunk Ice Cream (page 61) or Lemon Cream and Strawberry Swirl Ice Cream (page 62)** • 2 scoops store-bought soy, rice, almond, cashew, or coconut ice cream, such as So Delicious

WHEN THE ORIGINAL RECIPE CALLS FOR . . .	REPLACE WITH . . .
1 cup (235 ml) milk (e.g., cow, goat, or sheep)	• **1 cup (235 ml) plain Almond Milk (page 27)** • 1 cup (235 ml) unsweetened plain soy, almond, almond-coconut, rice, or hemp milk • 1 cup (235 ml) unsweetened plain canned or refrigerated coconut milk
½ cup (120 g) sour cream	• **½ cup (120 g) Sour Cream (page 30)** • ½ cup (120 g) store-bought vegan sour cream, such as Tofutti, or Follow Your Heart
½ cup (30 g) whipped cream	• **½ cup (30 g) Whipped Coconut Cream (page 64)** • ½ cup (30 g) store-bought vegan whipped soy or rice cream from a box, such as Soyatoo! (We cannot recommend the cans, as these rarely work properly.)
½ cup (120 g) yogurt (e.g., cow, goat, or sheep)	• **½ cup (120 g) Homemade Yogurt (page 28)** • ½ cup (120 g) store-bought vegan soy yogurt, such as WholeSoy • ½ cup (120 g) store-bought vegan coconut or almond yogurt, such as So Delicious (also available in Greek-style) • ½ cup (120 g) blended soft silken tofu, such as Mori-Nu, mixed with ½ teaspoon fresh lemon juice (only in baking applications, not for eating as is)
CHEESE **½ cup (57 g) cheese (e.g., shredded jack, Cheddar, or mozzarella)**	• ½ cup (57 g) store-bought vegan shredded cheese, such as Daiya, Follow Your Heart, or Go Veggie Vegan
1 slice of cheese (for sandwiches)	• **1 slice 'Merican Cheese Slices (page 70)** • 1 slice of store-bought vegan cheese slices, such as Daiya, Tofutti, Vegusto, Go Veggie Vegan, or Chao
½ cup (120 g) cream cheese	• **½ cup (120 g) Cashew and Yogurt Spread (page 33)** • **½ cup (120 g) Cashew Coconut Spread (page 32)** • **½ cup (114 g) Chia Seed Cream Cheese (page 76)** • ½ cup (120 g) store-bought vegan cream cheese, such as Tofutti, Follow Your Heart, Wayfare, or Daiya
½ cup (85 g) cotija or queso fresco	• **½ cup (85 g) Cotija-Style Tofu Crumbles (page 73)**

WHEN THE ORIGINAL RECIPE CALLS FOR . . .	REPLACE WITH . . .
½ cup (75 g) feta crumbles	• ½ cup (120 g) Easy Tofu Feta (page 186)
½ cup (50 g) Parmesan cheese, grated for added flavor (not as a binder)	• ½ cup (56 g) Hemp Parm (page 72) • ½ cup (50 g) store-bought vegan Parmesan, such as Go Veggie, Parmela, or Parma
½ cup (123 g) ricotta cheese	• ½ cup (113 g) Almond Cashew Ricotta (page 73) • ½ cup (123 g) store-bought vegan ricotta, such as Tofutti or Kite Hill
Artisan cheeses, to serve with crackers or wine	• Store-bought artisan vegan cheeses, such as Miyoko's Kitchen, Kite Hill, Treeline, Vromage, or Parmela

SECTION 2: EGGS

WHEN THE ORIGINAL RECIPE CALLS FOR . . .	REPLACE WITH . . .
IN SAVORY DISHES **1 egg**	• 1 flax egg: 1 tablespoon (7 g) freshly ground golden flaxseeds combined with 3 tablespoons (45 ml) water, whisked and left to stand for a few minutes, until thickened and viscous. *Purpose: binding agent, leavening agent if combined with ¼ teaspoon baking powder. Works best in: veggie burgers, meatloaf, meatballs, fritters, and patties. Less expensive than chia seeds; slightly nuttier outcome.* • 1 chia egg: 1 tablespoon (10 g) white chia seeds, ground to a meal in coffee grinder, combined with 3 tablespoons (45 ml) water, whisked and left to stand for a few minutes, until thickened and viscous. *Purpose: binding agent, thickening agent. Works best in: veggie burgers, meatloaf, meatballs, fritters, and patties, as well as dressings and sauces. Note that the seeds don't need to be ground for binding purposes, but they become less visible—an advantage in certain dishes.* • 3 tablespoons (48 g) natural creamy or crunchy peanut butter, or other nut or seed butter (such as tahini, cashew, or almond), or **Cashew Coconut Spread (page 32)**, or **Cashew and Yogurt Spread (page 33)**. *Purpose: binding agent; moisturizing agent. Works best in: veggie burgers, meatloaf, meatballs, fritters, and patties.*

WHEN THE ORIGINAL RECIPE CALLS FOR . . .	REPLACE WITH . . .
1 egg (continued)	• ¼ cup (60 g) blended soft silken tofu. *Purpose: binding agent, moisturizing agent. Works best in: dressings, sauces, and to give body and lift to veggie burgers, matzo balls, and potato pancakes. Note that this option can create heavier results, so adding ¼ to ½ teaspoon of baking powder [the quantity depends on how leavened the recipe needs to be] can be indicated if using as a leavening agent. Use caution: An excess of leavening can alter both consistency and flavor.*
• ¼ cup (60 g) unsweetened plain vegan yogurt, store-bought or **homemade (page 28)**. *Purpose: binding agent, moisturizing agent. Works best in: dressings, sauces, and to give body and lift to veggie burgers, matzo balls, and potato pancakes. Note that this option can create heavier results, so adding ¼ to ½ teaspoon of baking powder [the quantity depends on how leavened the recipe needs to be] can be indicated if using as a leavening agent. Use caution: An excess of leavening can alter both consistency and flavor.*
• 2 tablespoons (16 g) cornstarch, preferably organic (or potato starch or arrowroot powder) whisked with 2 tablespoons (30 ml) water. *Purpose: binding agent. Works best in: veggie burgers, meatloaf, meatballs, and potato pancakes.*
• ¼ cup (60 g) puréed or mashed cooked vegetable (such as beans, sweet potato, regular potato). *Purpose: binding agent, moisturizing agent. Works best in: veggie burgers, meatloaf, meatballs, fritters, and patties. Note that this option can create heavier results, so adding ¼ to ½ teaspoon of baking powder (the quantity depends on how leavened the recipe needs to be) can be indicated if using as a leavening agent. Use caution: An excess of leavening can alter both consistency and flavor.*
Egg Yolks	• **Hard-Boiled Egglike Crumbles (page 122)**
• **Egg yolk from Shakshouka recipe (page 116)**
• Commercial egg yolk replacer, such as The Vegg or Beyond Eggs
Egg Whites	• **Egg white from Shakshouka recipe (page 116)**
• Plain tofu, cubed for egg-salad type use (page 122)

WHEN THE ORIGINAL RECIPE CALLS FOR . . .	REPLACE WITH . . .
Scrambled eggs	• **Bánh Mi Scramble (page 124)** • **Chickpea Scramble (page 112)** • **Plain Scrambled Eggs (page 114)** • Commercial scrambled egg replacer, such as Beyond Eggs
Frittata or Quiche	• **Chives and Scallion Soy-Free'ttatas (page 108)** • **Hash Brown–Quiche Bites (page 110)**
French toast	• **Savory *Pain Perdu* (page 104)** • **Tapenade French Toast Sandwiches (page 130)**
Egg-in-a-Hole	• **Egg-in-a-Hole (page 111)**
Omelet	• **Tofu Omelet (page 102)** • **Scallion Kale Pudla (page 106)**
Mayonnaise	• **Silky Tofu Mayo (page 118)** • Store-bought vegan mayonnaise, such as Vegenaise or Just Mayo
IN BAKING AND SWEETS **1 egg**	• 1 flax egg: 1 tablespoon (7 g) freshly ground golden flaxseeds combined with 3 tablespoons (45 ml) water, whisked and left to stand for a few minutes, until thickened and viscous. *Purpose: binding agent, leavening agent if combined with ¼ teaspoon baking powder. Works best in: most baked goods, such as cookies, cakes, muffins, waffles, pancakes, and yeast breads; less expensive than chia seeds, slightly nuttier in outcome.* • 1 chia egg: 1 tablespoon (10 g) white chia seeds, ground to a meal in coffee grinder, combined with 3 tablespoons (45 ml) water, whisked and left to stand for a few minutes, until thickened and viscous. *Purpose: binding agent, leavening agent if combined with ¼ teaspoon baking powder. Works best in: most baked goods, such as cookies, cakes, muffins, waffles, pancakes, and yeast breads. Note that the seeds don't need to be ground for binding purposes, but they become less visible—an advantage in certain baked goods.* • 3 tablespoons (48 g) natural creamy or crunchy peanut butter, or other nut or seed butter (such as tahini, cashew, or almond) *Purpose: binding agent, moisturizing agent. Works best in: cookies and muffins.*

WHEN THE ORIGINAL RECIPE CALLS FOR . . .	REPLACE WITH . . .
1 egg *(continued)*	• ¼ cup (60 g) unsweetened plain vegan yogurt, store-bought or **homemade (page 28)**. *Purpose: binding agent, moisturizing agent. Works best in: cookies, cakes, muffins, waffles, pancakes, and yeast breads. Note that this option can create heavier results, so adding ¼ to ½ teaspoon of baking powder [the quantity depends on how leavened the recipe needs to be] can be indicated if using as a leavening agent. Use caution: An excess of leavening can alter both consistency and flavor.* • ¼ cup (60 g) thoroughly blended soft or firm silken tofu. *Purpose: binding agent, moisturizing agent. Works best in: cookies, cakes, muffins, waffles, pancakes, and yeast breads. Note that this option can create heavier results, so adding ¼ to ½ teaspoon of baking powder (the quantity depends on how leavened the recipe needs to be) can be indicated if using as a leavening agent. Use caution: An excess of leavening can alter both consistency and flavor.* • 2 tablespoons (16 g) cornstarch, preferably organic (or potato starch or arrowroot powder) whisked with 2 tablespoons (30 ml) water. *Purpose: binding agent. Works best in: cookies, cakes, muffins, waffles, and pancakes.* • ¼ cup (60 g) unsweetened applesauce or other puréed or mashed fruit (such as banana, pumpkin, or avocado.) *Purpose: binding agent, moisturizing agent. Works best in: most baked goods, such as soft cookies, cakes, muffins, waffles, pancakes, and anywhere the potential added flavor and color won't be an issue. Applesauce can make for cake-y cookies, so for chewy cookie results, this substitute isn't recommended. Note that this option can create heavier results, so adding ¼ to ½ teaspoon of baking powder (the quantity depends on how leavened the recipe needs to be) can be indicated if using as a leavening agent. Use caution: An excess of leavening can alter both consistency and flavor.*

WHEN THE ORIGINAL RECIPE CALLS FOR . . .	REPLACE WITH . . .
(continued)	• ¼ cup (60 ml) water plus 1½ teaspoons cornstarch, preferably organic. Dissolve cornstarch in 2 teaspoons (10 ml) of the water, whisk the rest of the water into this slurry, and cook until gelatinous and cloudy, about 30 seconds to 1 minute, see instructions on pages 134 and 136. *Purpose: gives excellent structure without adding flavor, binding agent, leavening agent. Works best in: fluffy baked goods such as brioche, cakes, and muffins. (To boost lift, adding ¼ to ½ teaspoon of baking powder [the quantity depends on how leavened the recipe needs to be] can be indicated if using as a leavening agent. Use caution: An excess of leavening can alter both consistency and flavor.)* • 1 teaspoon psyllium seed husk (look for *whole psyllium husks*, not the powder, and not the whole seed; available at health food stores) combined with 3 tablespoons (45 ml) water, left to stand 3 minutes. Use promptly as it continues to thicken if left to stand. *Purpose: binding agent. Works best in: cookies, crackers, and waffles.* • ¼ cup (30 g) chickpea flour combined with ¼ cup (60 ml) water or vegan milk of choice. *Purpose: binding agent, moisturizing agent. Works best in: cookies, clafoutis (page 142), and cakes. Do not taste the preparation before baking or cooking, because chickpea flour doesn't taste good raw.* • 1½ teaspoons Ener-G or Bob's Red Mill egg replacer powder whisked with 2 tablespoons (30 ml) warm water, until frothy. *Purpose: binding agent, leavening agent. Works best in: cookies, but can make for chalky baked goods. Not our first choice, but works in a bind.* • 1 tablespoon (7 g) Neat Egg mix mixed into 2 tablespoons (30 ml) water. *Purpose: binding agent. Works best in: cookies, pancakes.*
1 egg yolk	• Commercial egg yolk replacer, such as The Vegg or Beyond Eggs. Note that not all of these products claim to replace the functional properties of eggs in baking applications. Always check the brand before purchase and use, for up-to-date information.

WHEN THE ORIGINAL RECIPE CALLS FOR . . .	REPLACE WITH . . .
1 egg white	• ¼ teaspoon xanthan gum whisked with ¼ cup (60 ml) water, let stand 5 minutes, whip until frothy. *Purpose: binding agent, leavening agent. Works best in: cookies, cakes, and muffins. This works well for 1 to 2 egg whites, but it isn't recommended to use to veganize an egg white–heavy recipe (such as macarons) and expect good results.* • 1½ teaspoons Ener-G or Bob's Red Mill egg replacer powder whisked with 2 tablespoons (30 ml) warm water, until frothy. *Purpose: binding agent, leavening agent. Works best in: cookies, but can make for chalky baked goods. Not our first choice, but works in a bind.* • ¼ cup (60 ml) water plus 1½ teaspoons cornstarch, preferably organic. Dissolve cornstarch in 2 teaspoons (10 ml) of the water, whisk the rest of the water into this slurry, and cook until gelatinous and cloudy, about 30 seconds to 1 minute, see instructions on pages 134 and 136. *Purpose: gives excellent structure without adding flavor, binding agent, leavening agent. Works best in: fluffy baked goods such as brioche, cakes, and muffins. (To boost lift, adding ¼ to ½ teaspoon of baking powder [the quantity depends on how leavened the recipe needs to be] can be indicated if using as a leavening agent. Use caution: An excess of leavening can alter both consistency and flavor.)*

SECTION 3: PROTEIN

WHEN THE ORIGINAL RECIPE CALLS FOR . . .	REPLACE WITH . . .
CHICKEN **1 cup (235 ml) chicken broth**	• **1 cup (235 ml) water mixed with 1 teaspoon All-Purpose Chicken-Flavored Broth Powder (page 167)** • 1 cup (235 ml) chicken-flavored vegetable broth, such as Better than Bouillon No Chicken Base • **1 cup (235 ml) water mixed with 1 teaspoon to 1 tablespoon (3 to 8 g) Mushroom Broth Powder (page 218), quantity to taste depending on use** • 1 cup (235 ml) plain vegetable broth

WHEN THE ORIGINAL RECIPE CALLS FOR . . .	REPLACE WITH . . .
Chicken breasts	• **All-Purpose Cluck-Free Cutlets (page 168)** • Seitan • Store-bought chicken–style breasts, such as Gardein or Match Foods
Chicken strips or nuggets	• **All-Purpose Cluck-Free Cutlets (page 168), cut into strips or made into nuggets** • Seitan • Store-bought chicken–style strips or nuggets, such as Gardein or Beyond Meat
Ground chicken (or turkey)	• **All-Purpose Cluck-Free Cutlets (page 168), ground** • Organic textured vegetable protein, reconstituted in chicken-flavored broth
Sliced deli meats	• **Sliced homemade vegan sausages (page 177 and 178), for sandwiches** • Store-bought vegan deli meat slices, such as Tofurky or Yves
BEEF 1 cup (235 ml) beef broth	• 1 tablespoon (15 ml) vegan steak sauce and 1 tablespoon (15 ml) soy sauce or tamari mixed with 1 scant cup (205 ml) plain vegetable broth to equal 1 cup (235 ml) beef broth • 1 cup (235 ml) store-bought beef-flavored vegetable broth, such as Better than Bouillon No Beef Base • **1 cup (235 ml) water mixed with 1 teaspoon to 1 tablespoon (3 to 8 g) Mushroom Broth Powder (page 218), quantity to taste depending on use** • 1 cup (235 ml) plain vegetable broth
Ground beef	• Store-bought ground beef substitute, such as Lightlife Gimme Lean or Beyond Meat Beefless Crumbles • 1 cup (96 g) organic textured vegetable protein, reconstituted with 1 scant cup (220 ml) beef-flavored broth yields about the same as 1 pound (454 g) ground beef in volume, not weight
Steaks or burgers	• **All-Purpose Cluck-Free Cutlets (page 168)** • Seitan • Portobello mushrooms, marinated and grilled • Store-bought veggie burgers, such as Gardein, Wildwood, or Morningstar

WHEN THE ORIGINAL RECIPE CALLS FOR . . .	REPLACE WITH . . .
Beef strips	• Portobello mushrooms, marinated and grilled, cut into strips • Seitan • Store-bought beef-style strips or nuggets, such as Gardein
Hot dogs	• Homemade seitan hot dogs • Store-bought vegan hot dogs, such as Tofurky or Tofupups
SEAFOOD Fish fillets	• Store-bought vegan fish fillets, such as Gardein or Sophie's Kitchen
Lump crab	• Store-bought imitation crab, such as Match Foods
Flaked tuna, tuna salad	• **Sunflower Artichoke Salad (page 198)** • Smashed chickpeas, combined with traditional tuna dressing made with vegan ingredients • Store-bought mock tuna, such as Meatless Select Fishless Tuna or VeganToona
Shrimp	• **Panko Fried Artichokes (page 200)** • Store-bought vegan shrimp, such as Sophie's Kitchen
Scallops	• **Bacon-Seared King Oyster Scallops with Crispy Shallots (page 201)** • Store-bought vegan scallops, such as Sophie's Kitchen
Smoked salmon	• **Sweet Potato and Avocado Sushi (page 196)** • Store-bought vegan smoked salmon, such as Sophie's Kitchen
BACON Bacon bits	• **Coconut Bacon (page 209)** • **Bacon Bits (page 210)** • Store-bought coconut bacon, such as Phoney Baloney's • Store-bought imitation bacon bits, such as Bacuns
Bacon strips	• **Soy Bacon (page 208)** • **Seitan Slab o' Bacon (page 212)** • Store-bought vegan bacon, such as Tofurky Smoky Maple Bacon Tempeh, Lightlife Smoky Tempeh Strips, or Lightlife Smart Bacon
Bacon grease	• **Bacon Grease (page 211)** • Store-bought bacon grease, such as Magic Vegan Bacon Grease

WHEN THE ORIGINAL RECIPE CALLS FOR . . .	REPLACE WITH . . .
NO MIMICKING MEAT	Meet optimal daily protein intake by eating a healthy, varied, and balanced diet over a 24-hour period, making sure to include protein-rich, minimally processed, plant-based foods such as: • Cooked-to-perfection beans and legumes (black beans, chickpeas, edamame, kidney beans, lentils, and split peas), enjoyed for example in the form of patties or balls (pages 126 and 224) • Flavorful, al dente whole grains (amaranth, buckwheat, farro, freekeh, and quinoa), enjoyed for example in pilafs or salads (pages 237 and 230) • Plain or lightly salted, raw or dry roasted nuts and seeds, and their butters (almonds, cashews, chia seeds, hemp seeds, sesame seeds, and peanuts) • Grilled, baked, or pan-fried tempeh or tofu slices or cubes (cooked to a pleasurable crispiness) • Raw or steamed, fresh or frozen vegetables (such as broccoli, Brussels sprouts, carrots, cauliflower, and kale)

Acknowledgments

Thank you, thank you to: Amanda Waddell, Betsy Gammons, Heather Godin, Jenna Patton, Katie Fawkes, and Becky Gissel for their hard work and patience while working on this book and all the previous ones.

Many thank-yous to our fantastic testers for sharing their valuable time and always-helpful feedback: Courtney Blair, Kelly and Mac Cavalier, Michelle Cavigliano, Shannon Davis, Anna Holt and sons, Doe Mora, Monique and Michel Narbel-Gimzia, Jenna Patton, Constanze Reichardt, Liz Wyman, Rochelle Krogar-West, and Jody Weiner.

Joni would like to give a super high five to Celine for not only being awesome, but for being the sane one who keeps me grounded, on schedule (mostly), and inspired. Since the beginning, you have always been an inspiration, and you continue to be to this day.

Celine gives many whole-hearted *mercis et gros bisous* to Mamou and Papou, and thank-yous to Chaz and Joni. And of course, so much love to the very reason behind all this: the animals.

About the Authors

Joni Marie Newman is the author of *The Best Veggie Burgers on the Planet*, *Vegan Food Gifts*, *Fusion Food in the Vegan Kitchen*, and coauthor of *500 Vegan Recipes*, *The Complete Guide to Vegan Food Substitutions*, *Hearty Vegan Meals for Monster Appetites*, and *Going Vegan*. She blogs at JusttheFood.com and likes to try to spread the vegan love 140 characters at a time on Twitter @JoniMarieNewman. Feel free to contact her any time at joni@justthefood.com.

Celine Steen is the coauthor of *500 Vegan Recipes*, *The Complete Guide to Vegan Food Substitutions*, *Hearty Vegan Meals for Monster Appetites*, *Vegan Sandwiches Save the Day!*, *Whole Grain Vegan Baking*, *Vegan Finger Foods*, and *The Great Vegan Protein Book*. If you need extra help veganizing specific recipes, or have any question at all, you can contact her at celine@havecakewilltravel.com.

Index